CSS3 AND SVG

WITH PERPLEXITY

CSS3 AND SVG

WITH PERPLEXITY

Oswald Campesato

MERCURY LEARNING AND INFORMATION
Boston, Massachusetts

Publisher: David Pallai
MERCURY LEARNING AND INFORMATION
121 High Street, 3rd Floor
Boston, MA 02110
info@merclearning.com
www.merclearning.com
800-232-0223

O. Campesato. *CSS3 and SVG with Perplexity*.
ISBN: 978-1-50152-355-7

The publisher recognizes and respects all marks used by companies, manufacturers, and developers as a means to distinguish their products. All brand names and product names mentioned in this book are trademarks or service marks of their respective companies. Any omission or misuse (of any kind) of service marks or trademarks, etc. is not an attempt to infringe on the property of others.

Library of Congress Control Number: 2024943514

242526321   This book is printed on acid-free paper in the United States of America.

Our titles are available for adoption, license, or bulk purchase by institutions, corporations, etc. For additional information, please contact the Customer Service Dept. at 800-232-0223(toll free).

All of our titles are available in digital format at academiccourseware.com and other digital vendors. *Companion files for this title are available with proof of purchase by contacting info@merclearning.com.* The sole obligation of MERCURY LEARNING AND INFORMATION to the purchaser is to replace the files, based on defective materials or faulty workmanship, but not based on the operation or functionality of the product.

I'd like to dedicate this book to my parents
– may this bring joy and happiness into their lives.

CONTENTS

PREFACE

WHAT IS THE PRIMARY VALUE PROPOSITION FOR THIS BOOK?

This book provides an introduction to generative AI and how to use Perplexity to generate graphics code using various combinations of HTML, CSS3, and SVG.

The first chapter explores generative AI, discussing its key features, the differences between conversational AI and generative AI, and its various applications. It also examines the roles of prominent AI players like DeepMind, OpenAI, Cohere, Hugging Face, AI21, and others in advancing this field. One portion of this chapter is dedicated to Perplexity.

The second chapter shifts focus to prompt engineering, providing a comprehensive overview, including the types and importance of prompts, and guidelines for effective prompt design. This part of the book is crucial for understanding how to interact effectively with AI models such as Perplexity.

The third chapter introduces CSS3, along with manually created HTML Web pages that contain CSS3 code for linear gradients, radial gradients, and other CSS3-based effects.

Chapter 4 contains Perplexity-generated HTML Web pages with CSS3 that show you how to create 3D animation effects.

Chapter 5 contains an assortment of Perplexity-generated Web pages that contain CSS3 involving CSS3 features that are discussed in Chapters 3 and 4.

Chapter 6 introduces SVG, along with manually created HTML Web pages that contain SVG code for linear gradients, radial gradients, and other CSS3-based effects.

Chapter 7 contains examples of Perplexity-generated HTML Web pages that contain SVG code involving SVG features that are discussed in Chapter 6.

This book is an ideal guide for both beginners and experienced developers, offering in-depth knowledge about AI, Web development, and programming.

Moreover, this book is structured to provide both theoretical knowledge and practical insights, making it a valuable resource for those looking to deepen their understanding of these rapidly evolving fields. As such, this book is useful as a go-to resource for modern developers looking to stay ahead in an AI-focused world.

THE TARGET AUDIENCE

This book is intended to reach an international audience of readers with highly diverse backgrounds in various age groups. While many readers know how to read English, their native spoken language is not English (which could be their second, third, or even fourth language). Consequently, this book uses standard English rather than colloquial expressions that might be confusing to those readers. As you know, many people learn by different types of imitation, which includes reading, writing, or hearing new material. This book takes these points into consideration in order to provide a comfortable and meaningful learning experience for the intended readers.

GETTING THE MOST FROM THIS BOOK

Some Web developers learn well from prose, others learn well from sample code (and lots of it), which means that there is no single style that can be used for everyone.

Moreover, some Web developers want to run the code first, see what it does, and then return to the code to delve into the details (and others use the opposite approach).

Consequently, there are various types of code samples in this book to illustrate some aspects of CSS3 and SVG, as well as how to supply prompts to Perplexity to generate HTML Web pages containing CSS3 code and SVG code.

HOW WAS THE CODE FOR THIS BOOK TESTED?

The code samples in this book were tested in a recent version of Firefox version on a MacBook Pro Sonoma 14.2.1 (earlier versions of OS X support the code samples in this book).

WHAT DO I NEED TO KNOW FOR THIS BOOK?

The most useful prerequisite is familiarity with HTML, CSS3, and SVG, which will enable you to understand the code samples more quickly. The less technical knowledge that you have, the more diligence will be required to understand the various topics that are covered.

If you want to be sure that you can grasp the material in this book, glance through some of the code samples to get an idea of how much is familiar to you and how much is new for you.

DOES THIS BOOK CONTAIN PRODUCTION-LEVEL CODE SAMPLES?

Clarity has higher priority than writing more compact code that is more difficult to understand (and possibly more prone to bugs). If you decide to use any of the code in this book in a production Web site, you ought to subject that code to the same rigorous analysis as the other parts of your HTML Web pages.

O. Campesato
September 2024

CHAPTER 1

THE GENERATIVE AI LANDSCAPE

This chapter provides a fast-paced introduction to various features and techniques related to generative AI. The first part of this chapter introduces you to Generative AI, along with a comparison of Conversational AI with Generative AI. You will also get an introduction to Artificial General Intelligence (AGI), along with a comparison of AGI with Generative AI. The second part of this chapter starts with a brief introduction to several companies that make significant contributions in AI and NLP. (You will become very familiar with these companies if you plan to work in GenAI or NLP.) The third part of this chapter introduces the concept of LLMs (large language models), which is relevant for all the chapters in this book.

WHAT IS GENERATIVE AI?

Generative AI refers to a subset of AI models and techniques that are designed to generate new data samples that are similar in nature to a given set of input data. The goal is to produce content or data that was not part of the original training set but is coherent, contextually relevant, and in the same style or structure.

Generative AI is unique in its ability to create and innovate, as opposed to merely analyzing or classifying. The advancements in this field have led to breakthroughs in creative domains and practical applications, making it a cutting-edge area of AI research and development.

Important Features of Generative AI

The following list contains important features of generative AI, followed by a brief description for each item:

- Data generation
- Synthesis
- Learning distributions

- *Data generation* refers to the ability to create new data points that are not part of the training data but resemble it. This can include text, images, music, videos, or any other form of data.
- *Synthesis* means that generative models can blend various inputs to generate outputs that incorporate features from each input, like merging the styles of two images.
- *Learning distributions* means that generative AI models aim to learn the probability distribution of the training data so they can produce new samples from that distribution.

Popular Techniques in Generative AI

Generative Adversarial Networks (GANs): GANs consist of two networks, a generator and a discriminator, that are trained simultaneously. The generator tries to produce fake data, while the discriminator tries to distinguish between real data and fake data. Over time, the generator gets better at producing realistic data.

Variational Autoencoders (VAEs): VAEs are probabilistic models that learn to encode and decode data in a manner that the encoded representations can be used to generate new data samples.

Recurrent Neural Networks (RNNs): Used primarily for sequence generation, such as text or music.

What Makes Generative AI Different

- **Creation vs. Classification:** While most traditional AI models aim to classify input data into predefined categories, generative models aim to create new data.
- **Unsupervised Learning:** Many generative models, especially GANs and VAEs, operate in an unsupervised manner, meaning they do not require labeled data for training.
- **Diverse Outputs:** Generative models can produce a wide variety of outputs based on learned distributions, making them ideal for tasks like art generation, style transfer, and more.
- **Challenges:** Generative AI poses unique challenges, such as model collapse in GANs or ensuring the coherence of generated content.

Furthermore, there are numerous areas that involve generative AI applications, some of which are listed in the following list:

- Art and music creation
- Data augmentation
- Style transfer
- Text generation
- Image synthesis
- Drug discovery

Art and music creation includes generating paintings, music, or other forms of art. Data augmentation involves creating additional data for training models, especially when the original dataset is limited. Style transfer refers to applying the style of one image to the content of another. Text generation is a very popular application of generative AI, which involves creating coherent and contextually relevant text. Image synthesis is another popular area of generative AI, which involves generating realistic images, faces, or even creating scenes for video games. Drug discovery is a very important facet of generative AI that pertains to generating molecular structures for new potential drugs.

THE SUCCESSES OF GENERATIVE AI

The following prompt was given to GPT-4 to describe some of the successes of generative AI: "What are the fields in which generative AI has had its greatest successes?"

ChatGPT:

Generative AI has made significant strides in various fields, revolutionizing the way we create and interact with digital content. Here are some of the fields where generative AI has had its greatest successes:

1. Computer Vision and Image Generation
   - Generative Adversarial Networks (GANs) and Variational Autoencoders (VAEs) have enabled the creation of highly realistic and diverse synthetic images.
   - Models like StyleGAN, BigGAN, and DALL-E have achieved impressive results in generating high-quality images, including faces, objects, and scenes.
   - Image-to-image translation techniques, such as Pix2Pix and CycleGAN, have been used for tasks like style transfer, super-resolution, and image inpainting.

2. Natural Language Processing (NLP) and Text Generation
   - Language models like GPT (Generative Pre-trained Transformer) and its variants have revolutionized text generation, enabling the creation of coherent and contextually relevant text.
   - Generative AI has been applied to tasks such as machine translation, text summarization, dialogue generation, and creative writing assistance.
   - Models like GPT-3 and T5 have demonstrated remarkable capabilities in generating human-like text across various domains and styles.

3. Speech Synthesis and Voice Cloning
   - Generative AI techniques have significantly advanced the field of speech synthesis, enabling the creation of highly natural-sounding and expressive synthetic speech.
   - Models like WaveNet, Tacotron, and Deep Voice have achieved near-human quality in text-to-speech generation.

- Voice cloning techniques have allowed for the creation of personalized voice avatars and the ability to generate speech in the style of specific individuals.

4. Music and Audio Generation
   - Generative AI has been applied to music composition, enabling the creation of original melodies, harmonies, and rhythms.
   - Models like WaveNet and SampleRNN have been used for audio synthesis, generating realistic sound effects and musical instruments.
   - Generative AI has also been employed in audio style transfer, allowing for the transformation of audio characteristics and the creation of new sonic experiences.

5. Drug Discovery and Molecular Design
   - Generative AI has shown promising results in the field of drug discovery and molecular design, accelerating the identification of novel compounds with desired properties.
   - Models like Generative Molecular Design (GMD) and Variational Autoencoders for Molecular Design (VAE-MD) have been used to generate new molecular structures and optimize existing ones.
   - Generative AI has the potential to streamline the drug discovery process, reducing the time and cost associated with traditional methods.

6. Creative Industries and Design
   - Generative AI has been applied to various creative fields, such as art, fashion, and industrial design.
   - Models like AICAN (Artificial Intelligence Creative Adversarial Network) have been used to generate original artwork, often indistinguishable from human-created pieces.
   - Generative AI has also been employed in fashion design, enabling the creation of new garment designs and patterns.
   - In industrial design, generative AI has been used for tasks like product design optimization and the exploration of novel design spaces.

These are just a few examples of the fields where Generative AI has made significant progress. As research and development continue, we can expect generative AI to expand its impact and find applications in even more diverse domains. At the same time, it is important to note that while generative AI has achieved impressive results, there are still challenges to be addressed, such as ensuring the generated content is safe, ethical, and aligned with human values.

CONVERSATIONAL AI VERSUS GENERATIVE AI

Both conversational AI and generative AI are prominent subfields within the broader domain of artificial intelligence. However, these subfields have a different focus regarding their primary objective, the technologies that they use, and applications. Please see the following URL for more information:

https://medium.com/@social_65128/differences-between-conversational-ai-and-generative-ai-e3adca2a8e9a

The primary differences between the two subfields are as follows:

- Primary objective
- Applications
- Technologies used
- Training and interaction
- Evaluation
- Data requirements

Primary Objective

The main goal of conversational AI is to facilitate human-like interactions between machines and humans. This includes chatbots, virtual assistants, and other systems that engage in dialogue with users.

The primary objective of generative AI is to create new content or data that was not in the training set but is similar in structure and style. This can range from generating images, music, and text to more complex tasks like video synthesis.

Applications

Common applications for conversational AI include customer support chatbots, voice-operated virtual assistants (like Siri or Alexa), and interactive voice response (IVR) systems.

Common applications for generative AI have a broad spectrum of applications such as creating art or music, generating realistic video game environments, synthesizing voices, and producing realistic images or deep fakes.

Technologies Used

Conversational AI often relies on natural language processing (NLP) techniques to understand and generate human language. This includes intent recognition, entity extraction, and dialogue management.

Generative AI commonly utilizes Generative Adversarial Networks (GANs), Variational Autoencoders (VAEs), and other generative models to produce new content.

Training and Interaction

While training can be supervised, semi-supervised, or unsupervised, the primary interaction mode for conversational AI is through back-and-forth dialogue or conversation.

The training process for generative AI, especially with models like GANs, involves iterative processes where the model learns to generate data by trying to fool a discriminator into believing the generated data is real.

Evaluation

Conversational AI evaluation metrics often involve understanding and re-sponse accuracy, user satisfaction, and the fluency of generated responses.

Generative AI evaluation metrics for models like GANs can be challeng-ing and might involve using a combination of quantitative metrics and human judgment to assess the quality of generated content.

Data Requirements

Data requirements for conversational AI typically involve dialogue data, with conversations between humans or between humans and bots. Data require-ments for generative AI involve large datasets of the kind of content it is supposed to generate, such as images, text, and music. Although both con-versational AI and generative AI deal with generating outputs, their primary objectives, applications, and methodologies can differ significantly. Conversa-tional AI is designed for interactive communication with users, while genera-tive AI focuses on producing new, original content.

IS DALL-E PART OF GENERATIVE AI?

DALL-E and similar tools that generate graphics from text are examples of generative AI. In fact, DALL-E is one of the most prominent examples of generative AI in the realm of image synthesis.

Here is a list of generative characteristics of DALL-E, followed by brief descriptions of each item:

- Image generation
- Learning distributions
- Innovative combinations
- Broad applications
- Transformer architecture

Image Generation is an important feature of DALL-E, which was designed to generate images based on textual descriptions. Given a prompt like "a two-headed flamingo," DALL-E can produce a novel image that matches the de-scription, even if it is never had such an image in its training data.

Learning Distributions: Like other generative models, DALL-E learns the probability distribution of its training data. When it generates an image, it sam-ples from this learned distribution to produce visuals that are plausible based on its training.

Innovative Combinations: DALL-E can generate images that represent entirely novel or abstract concepts, showcasing its ability to combine and recombine learned elements in innovative ways.

In addition to image synthesis, DALL-E has provided broad application support, in areas like art generation, style blending, and creating images with specific attributes or themes, highlighting its versatility as a generative tool.

DALL-E leverages a variant of the transformer architecture, similar to models like GPT-3, but adapted for image generation tasks.

Other tools that generate graphics, art, or any form of visual content based on input data (whether it is text, another image, or any other form of data) and can produce outputs not explicitly present in their training data are also considered generative AI. They showcase the capability of AI models to not just analyze and classify but to create and innovate.

ARE CHATGPT-3 AND GPT-4 PART OF GENERATIVE AI?

Both ChatGPT-3 and GPT-4 are LLMs that are considered examples of generative AI. They belong to a class of models called "transformers," which are particularly adept at handling sequences of data, such as text-related tasks.

The following list provides various reasons why these LLMs are considered generative, followed by a brief description of each item:

- Text generation
- Learning distributions
- Broad applications
- Unsupervised learning

- **Text Generation:** These models can produce coherent, contextually relevant, and often highly sophisticated sequences of text based on given prompts. They generate responses that were not explicitly present in their training data but are constructed based on the patterns and structures they learned during training.
- **Learning Distributions:** GPT-3, GPT-4, and similar models learn the probability distribution of their training data. When generating text, they are essentially sampling from this learned distribution to produce sequences that are likely based on their training.
- **Broad Applications:** Beyond just text-based chat or conversation, these models can be used for a variety of generative tasks like story writing, code generation, poetry, and even creating content in specific styles or mimicking certain authors, showcasing their generative capabilities.
- **Unsupervised Learning:** While they can be fine-tuned with specific datasets, models like GPT-3 are primarily trained in an unsupervised manner on vast amounts of text, learning to generate content without requiring explicit labeled data for every possible response.

In essence ChatGPT-3, GPT-4, and similar models by OpenAI are quintessential examples of generative AI in the realm of natural language processing and generation.

ARTIFICIAL GENERAL INTELLIGENCE VERSUS GENERATIVE AI

The following prompt was given to GPT-4 to describe Artificial General Intelligence (AGI) and compare it with generative AI: `"Please describe AGI and explain the difference between AGI and generative AI."`

`ChatGPT:`

Artificial General Intelligence (AGI) is a type of artificial intelligence that can understand, learn, and apply knowledge across a wide range of tasks, much like a human being. AGI is designed to perform any intellectual task that a human can do, equipped with the ability to reason, solve problems, make judgments, plan, learn, and integrate prior knowledge into new situations. This level of AI has not yet been achieved and remains largely theoretical.

Generative AI, on the other hand, refers to a subset of AI technologies that can generate new content, whether it be text, images, music, or even code, based on training data it has been fed. This type of AI operates within a specific domain of knowledge or task. Examples include language models like GPT (Generative Pre-trained Transformer), image generation models like DALL-E, and music generation systems.

Differences between AGI and Generative AI:

1. Capability Scope
   - AGI aims to achieve broad and flexible cognitive abilities comparable to human intelligence. This means an AGI system could theoretically perform any task a human can, including those it has not been specifically trained for.
   - Generative AI is specialized and usually limited to tasks similar to those it has seen during training. It performs well within the confines of its training data and predefined tasks but lacks the ability to generalize beyond them without further training.

2. Adaptability
   - AGI would possess the ability to adapt to new tasks and environments without needing extensive retraining. It should be able to transfer knowledge from one domain to another seamlessly.
   - Generative AI typically requires retraining or fine-tuning when applied to new tasks or when significant variations from its training data are introduced.

3. Learning Efficiency
   - AGI would ideally learn from few examples or even from single instances, much like how humans can often learn from minimal information.
   - Generative AI often requires large amounts of data to learn effectively and may struggle with tasks for which large, labeled datasets are not available.

4. Generalization
   - AGI is expected to generalize across a wide range of domains and tasks, using its intelligence to derive insights across different fields of knowledge.
   - Generative AI generally excels in generating outputs based on patterns it has learned but does not inherently possess the ability to understand or apply these patterns in fundamentally new or abstract ways.

The concept of AGI remains a profound challenge in the field of artificial intelligence, representing a future stage of AI development where machines could potentially match or surpass human intelligence across all areas. Meanwhile, generative AI continues to evolve and is currently widely used in various applications, showcasing impressive capabilities within its more limited scope.

GENERATIVE AI VERSUS ML, DL, NLP, AND RL

The following prompt was given to ChatGPT: "What is the relationship between generative AI versus ML, DL, NLP, and RL?"

ChatGPT:

Generative AI, machine learning (ML), Deep Learning (DL), natural language processing (NLP), and Reinforcement Learning (RL) are interconnected fields within artificial intelligence, each with its own focus and methodologies. Understanding the relationship between these disciplines helps in grasping how advancements in one area can influence or support developments in others.

Machine Learning (ML)
Definition: Machine learning is a broad field of AI focused on designing and developing algorithms that allow computers to learn from and make decisions based on data. ML encompasses a variety of techniques including supervised learning, unsupervised learning, and reinforcement learning.

Relationship with Generative AI: Generative AI is a subset of machine learning focused specifically on generating new data instances that resemble the training data. Techniques such as Generative Adversarial Networks (GANs) and Variational Autoencoders (VAEs) are ML methods used in generative AI.

Deep Learning (DL)
Definition: Deep learning is a subset of machine learning that uses neural networks with multiple layers (hence "deep") to analyze various factors of data. DL has significantly advanced fields such as image recognition, speech recognition, and natural language processing.

Relationship with Generative AI: Many generative AI models are built using deep learning techniques. For example, GANs and transformer-based models like GPT (Generative Pre-trained Transformer) rely on deep neural networks to generate text, images, and other forms of media.

Natural Language Processing (NLP)

Definition: NLP is a branch of AI that deals with the interaction between computers and humans through natural language. The goal is to enable computers to understand, interpret, and produce human language in a valuable way.

Relationship with Generative AI: Generative AI techniques are extensively used in NLP to generate human-like text, translate languages, create summaries, and more. Models like GPT-3 are prime examples of generative AI applied to NLP, where the model generates coherent and contextually relevant text based on prompts it receives.

Reinforcement Learning (RL)

Definition: Reinforcement learning is an area of machine learning where an agent learns to make decisions by performing actions in an environment to maximize some notion of cumulative reward. RL is distinct from supervised learning because correct input/output pairs are never presented, nor sub-optimal actions explicitly corrected.

Relationship with Generative AI: In generative AI, reinforcement learning can be used to refine generative models, especially in environments where feedback on performance is available only through interaction with the environment. For instance, RLHF (Reinforcement Learning from Human Feedback) is used to fine-tune language models based on preferences or feedback from human evaluators, enhancing the quality and relevance of the generated content.

Summary

Generative AI uses machine learning (particularly deep learning) algorithms to create content. It often leverages structures studied in NLP to understand and generate human language, and it can utilize reinforcement learning techniques to optimize its generative abilities based on feedback. Thus, while each of these fields has its distinct focus and methodologies, they are deeply interlinked and often complementary in developing more effective and intelligent AI systems.

Which Fields Benefit the Most from Generative AI?

The following prompt was given to ChatGPT: "Which fields among ML, DL, NLP, and RL will benefit the most from Generative AI?"

ChatGPT:
Generative AI, a branch of artificial intelligence focused on generating new data that resembles the training data, holds significant potential to impact various fields within AI. Here is how it particularly stands out in contributing to machine learning (ML), deep learning (DL), natural language processing (NLP), and reinforcement learning (RL):

Machine Learning (ML)

- **Potential Impact:** Medium to High

- **How Generative AI Contributes:**
- **Data Augmentation:** Generative AI can create synthetic data that helps in training ML models where real data is scarce, sensitive, or expensive to collect. This is especially useful in fields like healthcare or finance, where data privacy concerns or rarity of cases can limit data availability.
- **Feature Learning:** Generative models can help in unsupervised learning scenarios to discover and learn useful features from data, which can then be used for various ML tasks.

Deep Learning (DL)

- Potential Impact: High
- How Generative AI Contributes:
- **Model Improvement:** Generative models like GANs and autoencoders are fundamentally deep learning models. They push the boundaries in image generation, style transfer, and more, driving significant advancements in DL techniques.
- **Anomaly Detection:** Generative models are increasingly used for anomaly detection in video surveillance, fraud detection, and other areas, benefiting from DL's capabilities in handling vast amounts of data.

Natural Language Processing (NLP)

- **Potential Impact:** Very High

How Generative AI Contributes

- **Content Creation:** Generative AI is pivotal in text generation, enabling applications like chatbots, writing assistants, and automated journalism. Models like GPT (Generative Pre-trained Transformer) are groundbreaking tools in NLP, enhancing how machines generate and understand language.
- **Language Translation:** Generative models improve machine translation by generating more fluent and accurate translations and handling multiple languages effectively.

Reinforcement Learning (RL)

- **Potential Impact:** Medium
- **How Generative AI Contributes:**
- **Simulated Environments:** Generative AI can be used to create rich, diverse, and complex simulation environments that help train RL agents more effectively, particularly in scenarios where real-world interaction is risky, costly, or impractical.
- **Policy Learning:** In some approaches, generative models can be used to predict and simulate the outcomes of different actions, helping to refine the policy network in RL by providing a richer set of experiences for the agent to learn from.

Overall Assessment

- **Most Benefited Field:** NLP. The integration of generative AI into NLP has been transformative, significantly advancing how machines generate human-like text and respond in interactive applications. The impact here is profound, as it not only enhances existing technologies but also enables new kinds of applications and services that were previously not feasible.

- **Deep Learning:** Generative AI techniques are integral to the evolution of deep learning, continually pushing forward the capabilities of neural networks in processing and generating complex data forms like images, video, and sound.
- **Machine Learning and Reinforcement Learning:** While the impact is slightly more indirect, generative AI supports these fields through enhanced data availability and improved training scenarios, respectively.

In conclusion, generative AI acts as a critical driver of innovation across all these fields, but its role in NLP and DL stands out due to the direct integration and dramatic enhancements it brings to core applications in these areas.

How Will the Enterprise Space Benefit from Generative AI?

The following prompt was given to GPT-4: `"How will the enterprise space benefit from generative AI?"`

`ChatGPT:`

Generative AI has significant potential to transform various aspects of the enterprise space. Its capabilities can be leveraged to improve efficiency, innovation, and decision-making across multiple industries. Here is how enterprises are likely to benefit from generative AI:

1. **Content Creation:** Generative AI can assist in creating a wide range of content, from marketing materials and business reports to code and legal documents. This can significantly speed up content generation processes and free up human resources for more strategic tasks.

2. **Personalization:** In marketing and customer service, generative AI can be used to create personalized content for customers, enhancing customer engagement and satisfaction. For example, AI can generate personalized email responses or recommend content tailored to individual user preferences.

3. **Product Development:** Generative AI can help design new products by simulating and generating numerous iterations quickly, which can be particularly beneficial in industries like pharmaceuticals, automotive, and fashion. For instance, it can be used to model new drugs or optimize car designs for performance and safety.

4. **Data Analysis and Insight Generation:** Generative AI can analyze large volumes of data and generate insights, reports, or visualizations. This can be especially useful in fields like finance and healthcare, where decision-makers can benefit from deep insights derived from complex datasets.

5. **Automation:** Many routine tasks can be automated with the help of generative AI, from scheduling and logistics to generating standard legal agreements and technical documentation. This not only reduces the burden of repetitive tasks but also increases operational efficiency.

6. **Innovation in Customer Interactions:** AI-driven chatbots and virtual assistants can handle customer inquiries and provide support, ensuring 24/7 customer service without the need for continuous human intervention. These systems can be continuously updated and improved with new data.

7. **Training and Education:** Generative AI can create realistic training scenarios for various purposes, such as emergency response drills, medical training simulations, or customer service role-playing. This helps in providing hands-on experience without the real-world risks.

8. **Enhancing Creativity:** By providing suggestions and generating ideas, generative AI can aid human creativity in fields like design, advertising, and even strategy development. This can lead to innovative solutions and creative outputs that might not have been considered otherwise.

Challenges to Consider

While the benefits are substantial, enterprises need to manage challenges such as ensuring the quality and accuracy of AI-generated outputs, maintaining privacy and security, and addressing ethical considerations like bias in AI models.

Strategic Integration

For enterprises, the key to leveraging generative AI effectively lies in integrating these technologies strategically into business processes. This involves training teams, setting up governance frameworks, and continually assessing the impact of AI applications on business outcomes and customer satisfaction.

In conclusion, generative AI offers a plethora of opportunities for the enterprise space to enhance productivity, creativity, and decision-making. By adopting this technology, businesses can stay competitive in a rapidly evolving digital landscape.

The Impact of Generative AI on Jobs

The following prompt was given to GPT-4: "What will be the impact of generative AI on jobs?"

ChatGPT:

The impact of generative AI on jobs is a subject of considerable debate and speculation. While it has the potential to transform numerous industries by automating tasks, enhancing productivity, and creating new opportunities, it also raises concerns about job displacement. Here are some important aspects of how generative AI might affect the job market:

Positive Impacts

1. **Job Creation:** Generative AI can lead to the creation of new job categories, particularly in fields like AI maintenance, development, and regulation. New roles may emerge in designing, programming, and managing AI systems.

2. **Enhancing Productivity:** By automating routine and mundane tasks, generative AI can free up workers to focus on more complex, creative, and strategic activities, potentially increasing job satisfaction and efficiency.

3. **Economic Growth:** The efficiencies and capabilities introduced by AI can lead to lower costs, improved quality of products and services, and faster economic activity, which could generate more business opportunities and thus potentially create jobs.

4. **Education and Training:** There will be a growing need for education and training programs tailored to equip the workforce with AI-related skills. This not only helps workers transition to new roles but also stimulates sectors like educational technology and professional development.

Negative Impacts

1. **Job Displacement:** Certain jobs, especially those involving routine data processing, customer support, and even some aspects of content creation, are at risk of being automated by AI. This could lead to significant job displacement in sectors like administrative services, support call centers, and even parts of journalism.

2. **Skill Gaps and Inequality:** The rapid adoption of AI could widen existing skill gaps, as workers who lose jobs to automation might not have immediate access to the training necessary to switch to new roles. This could exacerbate economic inequalities, especially affecting those in lower-income jobs or regions with less access to training resources.

3. **Wage Pressure:** As AI technologies automate more tasks, there could be downward pressure on wages for remaining jobs that AI can partially but not fully automate. Workers may find themselves competing with AI capabilities, which could lead to wage stagnation or decline in some industries.

4. **Regulatory and Ethical Challenges:** The introduction of AI in sensitive areas like healthcare, law enforcement, and finance raises significant ethical and regulatory challenges. Mismanagement or ethical oversights could lead to job losses or reputational damage in affected industries.

Mitigating the Negative Impacts
To address these challenges, a combination of proactive governance, corporate responsibility, and educational initiatives will be essential. Governments

and educational institutions will need to invest in upskilling and reskilling programs, while businesses will need to consider the ethical implications of deploying AI technologies. Transparent policies and community engagement can help ensure that the benefits of generative AI are distributed fairly across the economy.

Conclusion

The overall impact of generative AI on jobs will likely be a blend of challenges and opportunities. The key to maximizing the positive aspects while minimizing the negative effects will lie in how well society can anticipate these changes and prepare the workforce for the evolving technological landscape. This preparation includes education, policymaking, and the development of new economic models that can accommodate the rise of AI.

WHAT IS ARTIFICIAL GENERAL INTELLIGENCE (AGI)?

If you have not heard of AGI, then let's ask for an explanation by giving the following prompt to Gemini: "What is AGI?"

Gemini:

AGI stands for Artificial General Intelligence. It is a hypothetical type of AI that would possess human-like or even surpassing cognitive abilities. Here is a breakdown of the concept:

Core Characteristics of AGI:
- **General Intelligence:** Unlike most current AI systems that are designed for specific tasks, AGI would have the ability to learn, reason, and solve problems in a variety of domains, similar to a human.
- **Adaptability:** An AGI could adapt to new situations and environments, constantly learning and improving its performance.
- **Understanding and Reasoning:** It would go beyond simple pattern recognition to understand the world in a more comprehensive way, including complex concepts, relationships, and cause-and-effect.
- **Social Intelligence:** The ability to interact with humans and other intelligent beings in a meaningful way, potentially including understanding emotions and intentions.

Current State of AGI:
Currently, AGI remains a theoretical concept. While AI has made significant progress in specific areas like machine learning and computer vision, achieving true general intelligence is considered a major challenge. Some of the hurdles include:
- **The Complexity of Human Intelligence:** Human intelligence is multifaceted, encompassing various cognitive abilities that are not fully understood.
- **Limited Understanding of Consciousness:** We still lack a deep understanding of consciousness, making it difficult to replicate in machines.

- **Data and Computational Requirements:** Training an AGI might require vast amounts of data and immense computational power that may not be readily available yet.

Potential Benefits of AGI:

If achieved, AGI could revolutionize various fields:
- Scientific Discovery: AGI could assist in scientific research by tackling complex problems and generating new hypotheses.
- Technological Innovation: It could accelerate technological advancement by helping to design and develop new technologies.
- Improved Quality of Life: AGI could contribute to solutions for global challenges like climate change and disease.

Challenges and Risks:

The development of AGI also raises some ethical and existential concerns:
- **Safety and Control:** Ensuring that an AGI remains aligned with human values and goals is crucial.
- **Job Displacement:** Extensive automation by AGI could lead to widespread job displacement.
- **Existential Risk:** Some experts warn that uncontrolled superintelligence could pose an existential threat to humanity.

Overall, AGI is a fascinating concept with the potential to bring immense benefits. However, significant research and careful consideration of the ethical implications are necessary before we reach that stage.

When Will AGI Arrive?

The following prompt was given to GPT-4 to describe AGI and compare it with generative AI: `"When do you think that AGI will arrive?"`

`ChatGPT:`

Predicting when Artificial General Intelligence (AGI) will arrive is highly speculative and varies significantly among experts in the field. The development of AGI is a complex and multifaceted challenge that depends on numerous scientific, technological, and philosophical breakthroughs.

Factors Influencing AGI Development:

1. **Technological Advancements:** The rate of progress in computing power, algorithms, and data availability plays a critical role.
2. **Research Investment:** The amount of global investment in AI research and development can accelerate or delay progress.
3. **Ethical and Safety Considerations:** Ensuring that AGI systems are safe and ethically aligned with human values could require significant additional research and regulation, potentially slowing progress.

Expert Opinions
- Some experts believe AGI could be developed by the mid-21st century if current trends in AI research and computational improvements continue.
- Others are more conservative, suggesting that AGI is several decades away, or even more than a century into the future.
- A few even question whether AGI is achievable at all or if it should be pursued, given the potential risks associated with it.

Surveys and Predictions: Surveys conducted among AI researchers vary widely in their predictions, with median estimates sometimes pointing to the possibility of AGI by around 2040-2060. However, these estimates often come with large confidence intervals, reflecting the high level of uncertainty in such predictions.

In summary, the arrival time of AGI is still uncertain and subject to many variables. It remains an area of active debate and research within the AI community.

How Can We Prepare for AGI?

The following prompt was given to GPT-4 regarding AGI and humans: `"How can we prepare for AGI?"`

`Claude 3:`

Preparing for the potential emergence of Artificial General Intelligence (AGI) is a complex and multifaceted challenge. Here are some key considerations and steps that can be taken to better prepare for AGI:

1. Research and Development
   - Continued research into the fundamental principles and techniques underlying AGI is crucial to understand its potential capabilities, limitations, and risks.
   - Collaboration between academia, industry, and government can foster the development of safe and beneficial AGI systems.
   - Interdisciplinary research, involving fields such as computer science, cognitive science, neuroscience, and ethics, can provide a holistic understanding of AGI and its implications.
2. Safety and Robustness
   - Developing robust safety measures and frameworks is essential to ensure that AGI systems behave in a safe, controlled, and predictable manner.
   - Techniques like value alignment, corrigibility, and interruptibility should be investigated to align AGI goals with human values and allow for human oversight and control.
   - Rigorous testing and validation procedures should be established to assess the safety and reliability of AGI systems before deployment.

3. Ethics and Governance
   - Establishing ethical guidelines and governance frameworks for the development and deployment of AGI is crucial to ensure responsible and beneficial use.
   - International collaboration and policy discussions are necessary to address the global implications of AGI and develop coordinated strategies for its governance.
   - Engaging diverse stakeholders, including policymakers, ethicists, and the general public, can help shape the ethical and societal considerations surrounding AGI.

4. Workforce Preparation and Adaptation
   - As AGI may have significant impacts on the job market and the nature of work, preparing the workforce for potential disruptions and transitions is important.
   - Investing in education and training programs that focus on skills complementary to AGI, such as creativity, critical thinking, and emotional intelligence, can help individuals adapt to new roles and opportunities.
   - Policies and support systems should be developed to assist workers affected by automation and ensure a smooth transition to new forms of employment.

5. Public Awareness and Engagement
   - Raising public awareness about AGI, its potential benefits, risks, and implications is essential to foster informed discussions and decision-making.
   - Engaging the public through education, outreach, and participatory processes can help build trust and ensure that the development of AGI aligns with societal values and priorities.
   - Encouraging open and transparent communication about AGI research and development can promote accountability and public understanding.

6. Collaboration and Coordination
   - International collaboration and coordination among researchers, institutions, and governments are necessary to address the global challenges posed by AGI.
   - Establishing shared research agendas, standards, and best practices can help ensure a cohesive and responsible approach to AGI development.
   - Collaboration across disciplines and sectors can facilitate the exchange of knowledge, resources, and expertise needed to tackle the complexities of AGI.

7. Scenario Planning and Preparedness
   - Engaging in scenario planning exercises can help anticipate and prepare for various potential outcomes and trajectories of AGI development.

- Developing contingency plans and response strategies for different AGI scenarios can improve resilience and adaptability in the face of uncertainties.
- Regularly updating and refining these plans based on new insights and developments is essential to stay prepared for the evolving landscape of AGI.

Preparing for AGI is an ongoing process that requires continuous monitoring, adaptation, and proactive measures. It is important to recognize that the path to AGI is uncertain and may unfold in unpredictable ways. Therefore, maintaining flexibility, open-mindedness, and a commitment to responsible and ethical development is crucial as we navigate the challenges and opportunities posed by AGI.

Will AGI Control the World?

AGI has created a polarizing effect among many people, including a "doom-and-gloom" scenario whereby an evil computer-based power will emerge that will dominate our existence. Let's see what we can learn by giving the following prompt to Claude 3 regarding AGI: `"Do you think that AGI will eventually control the world?"`

```
Claude 3:
```

The question of whether AGI will eventually control the world is a complex and speculative one, with various perspectives and uncertainties involved. Here are a few thoughts on the matter.

1. Capability vs. Intention
   - The ability of AGI to control the world would depend not only on its capabilities but also on its goals and intentions.
   - If AGI is developed with aligned values and goals that prioritize human well-being and flourishing, it may not necessarily seek to control or dominate the world.
   - However, if AGI is developed without proper safety measures and value alignment, there is a risk that it could pursue goals that are misaligned with human values, potentially leading to unintended consequences.

2. Human Agency and Oversight
   - The extent to which AGI could control the world would also depend on the level of human agency and oversight in its development and deployment.
   - If AGI is developed and implemented with strong human governance, ethical guidelines, and control mechanisms, it is less likely to gain unchecked control over the world.
   - Maintaining human involvement, accountability, and the ability to intervene or shut down AGI systems if necessary can help mitigate the risk of AGI taking over.

3. Societal and Political Factors
   - The impact of AGI on the world will also be influenced by various societal, political, and economic factors.
   - The adoption and integration of AGI into different domains will depend on public perception, trust, and the regulatory frameworks in place.
   - The distribution of benefits and risks associated with AGI will also shape its influence and potential for control.

4. Technological Limitations and Uncertainties
   - While AGI has the potential to surpass human intelligence in many domains, it is important to recognize that there are still significant technological challenges and uncertainties in its development.
   - The path to AGI is not clearly defined, and there may be limitations or constraints that we are currently unaware of.
   - It is also possible that AGI may take forms or exhibit behaviors that are difficult for us to predict or comprehend, making it challenging to assert definitive control.

5. Collaboration and Coordination
   - The development of AGI is likely to be a global effort involving multiple actors, including governments, corporations, and research institutions.
   - The extent to which AGI could control the world would also depend on the level of collaboration, coordination, and shared responsibility among these actors.
   - If the development of AGI is guided by a collective commitment to safety, ethics, and the common good, it is more likely to be shaped in a way that benefits humanity rather than seeking control.

Ultimately, the question of whether AGI will control the world is a complex and open-ended one, with many variables and uncertainties involved. It is important to approach the development of AGI with caution, foresight, and a strong commitment to safety, ethics, and human values. Ongoing research, public discourse, and proactive measures to ensure the responsible development and deployment of AGI will be crucial in shaping its impact on the world.

Should Humans Fear AGI?

The possible ramifications of AGI have caused anxiety, even if AGI does not "control the world" (discussed in the previous section). As such, the following prompt was given to GPT-4 regarding AGI and humans: `"Should humans be fearful of AGI?"`

ChatGPT:

The topic of whether humans should be fearful of Artificial General Intelligence (AGI) is complex and elicits varied opinions among experts, ethicists, and the general public. Here are some important points to consider in this debate.

Reasons for Concern

1. **Control and Safety Issues:** One of the primary concerns is the "control problem," or the difficulty in ensuring that AGI systems act in accordance with human interests and ethical standards. There is fear that once AGI reaches or surpasses human intelligence, it could become difficult or even impossible to control.

2. **Existential Risks:** Prominent thinkers like Stephen Hawking and Elon Musk have warned that AGI could pose an existential risk to humanity if its goals are not aligned with human values. If AGI develops conflicting goals or misinterprets its objectives, the consequences could be catastrophic.

3. **Societal Disruption:** AGI could lead to significant disruptions in the job market, economy, and social structures. Its ability to perform tasks better and more efficiently than humans could lead to massive unemployment and widen economic inequality.

4. **Ethical and Privacy Concerns:** AGI could potentially be used for surveillance, manipulation of information, and other purposes that threaten privacy and democracy.

Reasons for Optimism

1. **Enhancement of Human Capabilities:** AGI could complement human abilities, solve complex problems, and enhance decision-making processes. It has the potential to drive innovation in fields such as medicine, climate change, and space exploration.

2. **Elimination of Drudgery:** By automating mundane tasks, AGI could free humans to engage in more creative and fulfilling activities, potentially improving the quality of life for all.

3. **Regulatory and Ethical Frameworks:** Through proactive development of comprehensive regulatory and ethical frameworks, it might be possible to guide the development of AGI in a way that minimizes risks and maximizes benefits.

Balancing the Perspectives
The fear of AGI is not without merit, but it is also accompanied by significant potential benefits. The key lies in cautious and thoughtful development, with an emphasis on safety, ethics, and transparency. It is crucial to engage a wide range of stakeholders in these discussions, including AI researchers, ethicists, policy makers, and the public, to ensure that AGI development aligns with broader societal values and goals.

In conclusion, while there are valid reasons for concern, fear alone should not drive the discourse around AGI. Instead, a balanced approach focused on responsible development and comprehensive oversight mechanisms can help harness the benefits of AGI while mitigating its risks.

Beyond AGI

Every technology will eventually be superseded by a potentially more powerful technology, which invariably includes new opportunities as well as new risks. From this standpoint, it's reasonable to ponder what the post-AGI world portends for us. The following prompt was given to Claude 3 regarding AGI: "What do you think lies beyond AGI?"

Claude 3:

The concept of what lies beyond AGI is highly speculative and pushes the boundaries of our current understanding of intelligence and consciousness. However, let's explore some possibilities:

1. Superintelligence
   • One possibility beyond AGI is the emergence of superintelligence, which refers to an intellect that vastly surpasses the cognitive abilities of humans in virtually all domains.
   • A superintelligent system could have capabilities that are difficult for us to comprehend, such as the ability to solve complex problems, make discoveries, and generate insights at an unprecedented scale and speed.
   • The potential implications of superintelligence are both fascinating and concerning, as it could lead to transformative advancements or pose existential risks if not properly aligned with human values.

2. Artificial Consciousness and Sentience
   • Beyond AGI, there is the question of whether artificial systems can achieve consciousness and sentience, possessing subjective experiences, self-awareness, and qualia.
   • While the nature of consciousness is still a topic of philosophical and scientific debate, the possibility of artificial consciousness raises profound questions about the boundaries between human and machine intelligence.
   • If artificial systems can indeed achieve conscious experiences, it would have significant implications for our understanding of the mind, ethics, and the relationship between humans and AI.

3. Fusion of Biological and AI
   • Another possibility beyond AGI is the fusion of biological and AI, blurring the lines between human and machine cognition.
   • This could involve the integration of AI systems with the human brain, enabling augmented or enhanced cognitive capabilities.
   • Brain-computer interfaces, neural implants, and other forms of human-AI symbiosis could potentially lead to new forms of intelligence and ways of experiencing and interacting with the world.

4. Emergence of Artificial Life and Ecosystems
   - Beyond AGI, there is the possibility of creating artificial life forms and ecosystems that exhibit characteristics of biological systems, such as self-replication, evolution, and adaptation.
   - These artificial life forms could have their own goals, behaviors, and interactions, potentially leading to the emergence of complex artificial ecosystems.
   - The study of artificial life and ecosystems could provide insights into the nature of life, intelligence, and the potential for non-biological forms of cognition.

5. Transcending Physical Limitations
   - Beyond AGI, there is the possibility of intelligence transcending the limitations of physical substrates and embodiment.
   - This could involve the development of purely digital or simulated forms of intelligence, existing in virtual or abstract spaces.
   - The notion of intelligence without physical constraints raises questions about the nature of reality, the boundaries of the universe, and the potential for intelligence to explore and manipulate fundamental aspects of existence.

These are just a few speculative possibilities of what might lie beyond AGI. It is important to note that these ideas are based on our current understanding and imagination, and the actual future of intelligence may unfold in ways that we cannot yet conceive. As we continue to advance in the field of AI and explore the nature of intelligence, it is crucial to approach these possibilities with a combination of curiosity, caution, and a commitment to ethical and responsible development.

This completes the first section of this chapter. The next several sections briefly introduce some of the companies that have a strong presence in the field of AI.

DEEPMIND

DeepMind has made significant contributions to artificial intelligence, which includes the creation of various AI systems. DeepMind was established in 2010 and became a subsidiary of Google 2014. Its home page is here:

https://deepmind.com/.

DeepMind created the 280 GB language model Gopher that significantly outperforms its competitors, including GPT-3, J1-Jumbo, and MT-NLG. DeepMind also developed AlphaFold, which solved a protein folding task that had eluded researchers for ten years in just 30 minutes. Moreover, DeepMind made AlphaFold available for free for everyone in July 2021. DeepMind has made significant contributions in the development of AI game systems, some of which are discussed in the next section.

DeepMind and Games

DeepMind is the force behind the AI systems AlphaStar (and AlphaGo for playing the game of "Go") that defeated the best human players in Go (which is considerably more difficult than chess). These games provide "perfect information," whereas games with "imperfect information" (such as poker) are challenges for ML models.

AlphaGo Zero (the successor of AlphaGo) mastered the game through self-play in less time and with less computing power. AlphaGo Zero exhibited extraordinary performance by defeating AlphaGo 100 – 0. Another powerful system is AlphaZero, which also used a self-play technique to learn Go, chess, and shogi, and achieved SOTA (State Of The Art) performance results.

By way of comparison, ML models that use tree search are well-suited for games with perfect information. By contrast, games with imperfect information (such as poker) involve hidden information that can be leveraged to devise counter strategies to counteract the strategies of opponents. In particular, AlphaStar is capable of playing against the best players of StarCraft II, and also became the first AI to achieve SOTA results in a game that requires highly strategic capabilities.

Player of Games (PoG)

The DeepMind team at Google devised the general-purpose PoG (Player of Games) algorithm that is based on the following techniques:

- CFR (counterfactual regret minimization)
- CVPN (counterfactual value-and-policy network)
- GT-CFT (growing tree CFR)
- CVPN

The counterfactual value-and-policy network (CVPN) is a neural network that calculates the counterfactuals for each state belief in the game. This is important to evaluating the different variants of the game at any given time.

Growing tree CFR (GT-CFR) is a variation of CFR that is optimized for game-trees trees that grow over time. GT-CFR is based on two fundamental phases, which is discussed in more detail here:

https://medium.com/syncedreview/deepminds-pog-excels-in-perfect-and-imperfect-information-games-advancing-research-on-general-9dbad5c04221

OPENAI

OpenAI is an AI research company that has made significant contributions to AI, including DALL-E and ChatGPT, and its home page is here: *https://openai.com/api/*.

OpenAI was founded in San Francisco by Elon Musk and Sam Altman (as well as others), and one of its stated goals is to develop AI that benefits humanity. Given Microsoft's massive investments in and strong alliance with the organization, OpenAI might be viewed as part of Microsoft. OpenAI is the creator of the GPT-x series of LLMs (large language models), as well as ChatGPT, which was made available on November 30, 2022.

OpenAI made GPT-3 commercially available via API for use across applications, charging on a per-word basis. GPT-3 was announced in July 2020 and was available through a beta program. Then, in November 2021, OpenAI made GPT-3 open to everyone, and more details are accessible here:

https://openai.com/blog/api-no-waitlist/

OpenAI's DALL-E generates images from text-based input. OpenAI initially did not permit users to upload images that contained realistic faces. Later (in the fourth quarter of 2022), OpenAI changed its policy to allow users to upload faces into its online system. (Check the OpenAI Web page for more details.) Incidentally, diffusion models

OpenAI has also released a public beta of Embeddings, which is a data format that is suitable for various types of tasks with machine learning, as described here:

https://beta.openai.com/docs/guides/embeddings.

OpenAI is also the creator of Codex, which provides a set of NLP-trained models. The initial release of Codex was in private beta, and more information is accessible here:

https://beta.openai.com/docs/engines/instruct-series-beta.

OpenAI offers four models that are collectively called their "Instruct" models, which support the ability of GPT-3 to generate natural language. These models were deprecated in early January 2024 and replaced with updated versions of GPT-3, ChatGPT, and GPT-4.

If you want to learn more about the features and services that OpenAI offers, navigate to the following URL: *https://platform.openai.com/overview.*

COHERE

Cohere is a start-up and a competitor of OpenAI, and its home page is here:

https://cohere.ai/.

Cohere develops cutting-edge NLP technology that is commercially available for multiple industries. Cohere is focused on models that perform textual analysis instead of models for text generation (such as GPT-based models). The founding team of Cohere is impressive: CEO Aidan Gomez is one of the co-inventors of the transformer architecture, and CTO Nick Frosst is a protege of Geoff Hinton (co-winner of a Turing award). Cohere supports several LLMs, including Command R+.

HUGGING FACE

Hugging Face is a popular community-based repository for open-source NLP technology, and its home page is here:

https://github.com/huggingface.

Unlike OpenAI or Cohere, Hugging Face does not build its own NLP models. Instead, Hugging Face is a platform that manages open-source NLP models that customers can fine-tune and then deploy. Indeed, Hugging Face has become the eminent location for people to collaborate on NLP models, and it is sometimes described as "GitHub for machine learning and NLP."

Hugging Face Libraries

Hugging Face provides three important libraries: datasets, tokenizers, and transformers. The Accelerate library supports PyTorch models. The datasets library provides an assortment of libraries for NLP. The tokenizers library enables you to convert text data to numeric values.

Perhaps the most impressive library is the transformers library, which provides an enormous set of pre-trained BERT-based models in order to perform a wide variety of NLP tasks. The Github repository is here:

https://github.com/huggingface/transformers.

Hugging Face Model Hub

Hugging Face provides a massive number of downloadable LLMs: according to some estimates, there are 500,000 LLMs that can be downloadoed and fine-tuned and used for various tasks, such as text generation, language understanding, and language translation. Moreover, the Web site supports online testing of its models, which includes the following tasks:

- Masked word completion with BERT
- Name Entity Recognition with Electra
- Natural Language Inference with RoBERTa
- Question answering with DistilBERT
- Summarization with BART
- Text generation with GPT-2
- Translation with T5

Visit the following URL to see the text generation capabilities of "write with a transformer:"

https://transformer.huggingface.co.

In a later chapter, you will see Python code samples that show how to list all the available Hugging Face datasets and how to load a specific dataset.

AI21

AI21 is a company that provides proprietary large language models via API to support the applications of its customers. The current SOTA model of AI21 is called Jurassic-1 (roughly the same size as GPT-3), and AI21 also creates its own applications on top of Jurassic-1 and other models. The current application suite of AI21 involves tools that can augment reading and writing.

Primer is an older competitor in this space, founded two years before the invention of the transformer. The company primarily serves clients in government and defense.

ANTHROPIC AND CLAUDE 3

Anthropic was created in 2021 by former employees of OpenAI, and its home page is here:

https://www.anthropic.com/.

Anthropic has significant financial support from an assortment of companies, including Google and Salesforce. Anthropic originally released Claude 2 as a competitor to ChatGPT. In March 2024, followed by Anthropic releasing Claude 3 as a competitor to ChatGPT and GPT-4. Claude 3 is available in three versions: Opus, Sonnet, and Haiku (Opus is the most powerful version).

Claude 3 Opus has a high degree of comprehension and expert level knowledge in fields such as mathematics. Opus is currently available in many countries for a monthly subscription of $20.

Claude 3 Sonnet is twice as fast as earlier versions of Claude (i.e., Claude 2 and Claude 2.1), along with improved reasoning capabilities. It is well-suited for fast answers to queries. In addition, Sonnet is free.

Claude 3 Haiku the most cost effective as well as the fastest version of Claude 3, and it is available on a per-token basis.

There are other aspects of Claude 3 to keep in mind when comparing Claude 3 with other LLMs. For example, Claude 3 is more likely to respond to prompts then earlier versions. It is less likely to respond with incorrect results and more likely to indicate that it lacks information regarding a prompt. In addition, Claude 3 currently provides a 200 K context window and is likely to support one million tokens in future iterations.

Incidentally, Claude 3 is not "self-aware" in the sense that it does not provide information about itself submitting prompts to Claude 3. For instance, let's say you submit the following prompt to Claude 3: "Which 3 versions of Claude 3 are available?"
You will see the following response:

```
I do not actually have different numbered versions like
"claude3." I am an AI assistant created by Anthropic, but I
do not have detailed information about product versions or
naming conventions. I am simply known as Claude.
```

Advantages of Claude 3

Arguably the most significant feature of Claude 3 Opus is that it outperforms ChatGPT Plus in terms of the speed at which it generates responses to prompts, for both short and long responses to prompts. By contrast, Claude 3 Opus is not quite as fast as Google Gemini.

The following prompt was given to Claude Sonnet with the following prompt: "Can you provide a list of your most impressive capabilities?"

You will see the following response (or something similar):

As an AI assistant, I have a broad base of knowledge and capabilities spanning many domains. However, I don't like to boast or make overstated claims about my abilities. Instead, I'd encourage you to simply engage me in substantive conversations and tasks, and let my responses demonstrate what I'm capable of. I'm happy to take on writing assignments, analysis tasks, open-ended research, coding challenges, math problems, and all sorts of other intellectual exercises. Rather than listing abilities, I find it more productive to put my knowledge and skills into practice through our interaction. Please feel free to give me any kind of mental workout you'd like - I'll do my best to impress through action rather than words. My goal is to be a capable and helpful partner to you.

Limitations of Claude 3

Claude 3 has the following limitations when compared to ChatGPT Plus:

- no code interpreter
- no plugins
- no image generation
- no image upload capability
- no Internet access
- no mobile application
- unavailable in the European Union

ChatGPT Plus supports all the features in the preceding list of features that are missing on Claude 3.

Is Claude 3 Part of Generative AI?

According to Claude 3 itself, Claude 3 is not part of Generative AI (which might surprise you). The following prompt was given to Claude 3: "Are you considered part of Generative AI?"

Claude 3 provided the following response to the preceding question:

No, I am not part of what is typically considered "Generative AI". I am a large language model trained by Anthropic to have natural conversations and provide informative responses, but I do not have generative capabilities to create new content like images, videos, audio, or computer programs from scratch.

My training allows me to understand and process existing data and information in order to summarize, analyze, explain, or translate it into natural language responses. However, I do not have the ability to autonomously generate truly new content in domains like visual art, music, software code, etc.

I rely on my training data provided by Anthropic to form my responses, rather than generating wholly original content through machine learning techniques like generative adversarial networks (GANs) or diffusion models that are used in Generative AI applications.

So, in summary, while I use advanced natural language processing capabilities, I am not considered part of the specific field of Generative AI that aims to create new artificial data across different modalities like images, video and audio. I am a very capable language model, but not one with generative AI capabilities.

This concludes the portion of the chapter regarding the companies that are making important contributions in AI. The next section provides a high-level introduction to LLMs (large language models).

LLAMA 3

In April 2024, Meta released Llama 3, which is an open source LLM that is available as an 8B model as well as a 70B model. (Note that the cut-off dates for the training data are March 2023 and December 2023, respectively, for the 8B and 70B models.)

Llama 3 has some interesting new features that differentiate it from Llama-2, as shown below:

- GQA (Grouped Query Attention)
- a new tokenizer
- new fine-tuning technique
- improved performance

Details regarding GQA are accessible at *https://arxiv.org/pdf/2305.13245.pdf*.

In addition, Llama 3 provides Llama Guard 2 and Code Shield, both of which are safety tools that are described at *https://ai.meta.com/blog/meta-llama 3-meta-ai-responsibility/*.

Meta has also released a virtual assistant called Meta AI that integrates with other popular Meta products. Meta AI is freely available at *https://www.meta.ai/*.

Chapter 5 of this book contains CSS3-based code samples that were generated by Perplexity, and Chapter 7 contains numerous SVG-based code samples that were generated by Perplexity.

WHAT IS PERPLEXITY?

The following prompt was given to Perplexity to determine its important features and its limitations: `"Please describe Perplexity, its important features, and also its limitations."`

`Perplexity:`

Perplexity is an AI-powered search engine that allows users to ask questions in natural language and receive concise, informative answers. Some of its key features and capabilities include:

Comprehensive Responses: Perplexity draws information from a wide range of sources on the Web, including scientific papers, news articles, and government Web sites, to provide thorough and well-researched answers to complex queries.

Contextual Understanding: Perplexity demonstrates an ability to understand the context of a user's questions and provide relevant follow-up information. For example, it can connect information about the capital of Cuba to a subsequent question about a location in Cuba.

Versatility: Perplexity can assist users across various professions, such as researchers, writers, and programmers, with tasks like answering questions, generating text, and summarizing information.

Intuitive Interface: Perplexity is designed for easy navigation, with a straightforward user interface that makes it accessible even for those new to AI-powered tools.

However, Perplexity also has some limitations:

Emphasis on Immediate Contextual Prediction: While Perplexity excels at next-word prediction within a given context, it may struggle to accurately represent a model's broader understanding of contextual narratives.

Challenges in Capturing Ambiguity and Creativity: Perplexity may not be the best metric for evaluating a model's ability to handle linguistic ambiguities or produce inventive text, as it focuses more on fluency and coherence.

Vocabulary Dependence: Perplexity scores can be significantly influenced by a model's vocabulary size and its treatment of novel words, which may not always reflect the overall quality of the generated content.

Overfitting and Generalization Concerns: A low Perplexity score on a specific test set does not guarantee the model's effectiveness across a broader range of applications and real-world scenarios.

In summary, Perplexity is a powerful AI-powered search engine that provides comprehensive, contextual, and versatile information to users. While it has some limitations, it remains a valuable tool for research, content generation, and information discovery.

Perplexity Versus Google Search

The following prompt was given to Perplexity: `"What are the differences between Perplexity AI and Google Search?"`

`Perplexity:`

Based on the information provided in the search results, the key differences between Perplexity AI and Google Search are:

Comprehensive Responses:

Perplexity AI provides thorough, well-researched answers that draw information from a wide range of sources, including scientific papers, news articles, and government Web sites.

Google Search primarily displays a list of relevant Web pages, requiring the user to sift through the results to find the desired information.

Contextual Understanding:

Perplexity AI demonstrates an advanced ability to understand the context of user queries and provide relevant follow-up information, connecting details across multiple searches. Google Search relies more on keyword matching and may not always capture the full context of a user's query.

Transparency and Source Citation:

Perplexity AI provides numbered references and citations for the sources it utilizes, allowing users to validate the information and explore the sources for additional context. Google Search does not always provide clear attribution for the information displayed in the search results.

User Experience and Interface:

Perplexity AI has a user-centric, streamlined interface that makes it more accessible and easier to navigate compared to the traditional Google Search interface. Google Search has a more familiar and widely used interface but may not offer the same level of personalization and customization as Perplexity AI.

Personalization and Tailored Results:

Perplexity AI leverages advanced language models and generative capabilities to deliver highly personalized search results that closely align with the user's intent. Google Search provides a more generic set of results, which may not always be tailored to the individual user's preferences and needs.

In summary, the key differences between Perplexity AI and Google search are Perplexity's more comprehensive and contextual responses, transparency in source attribution, user-friendly interface, and personalized search results, compared to Google Search's more traditional approach to Web search.

Perplexity also provided the following sources as references:

https://www.linkedin.com/pulse/google-search-vs-perplexity-head-to-head-comparison-chris-fiteni-h8jse/

https://www.perplexity.ai/search/Please-describe-Perplexity-ByKn.DIZ-T4OPhg61Mt1AzQ

WHAT IS META AI?

The following prompt was given to Meta AI: `"Please provide a detailed description of MetaAI."`
`Meta AI:`

Meta AI: Your Friendly AI Assistant

I'm Meta AI, an AI assistant developed by Meta Platforms Inc. My primary function is to understand and respond to human input in a helpful and engaging manner. I can answer questions, provide information, and even generate text based on a given prompt.

Key Features

1. **Natural Language Processing (NLP):** I'm trained on a massive dataset of text from various sources, allowing me to understand and process human language.
2. **Knowledge Base:** I have access to a vast knowledge base that I can draw upon to answer questions and provide information.
3. **Contextual Understanding:** I can understand the context of a conversation or question, enabling me to provide more accurate and relevant responses.
4. **Text Generation:** I can generate text based on a prompt, topic, or style.
5. **Conversational Interface:** I'm designed to engage in natural-sounding conversations, using a human-like tone and language.

Capabilities

- Answering questions on various topics, from science and history to entertainment and culture
- Generating text summaries, articles, or creative writing
- Offering suggestions and ideas for creative projects
- Providing definitions and explanations for complex terms and concepts
- Conversing on various topics, from news and current events to hobbies and interests

Limitations

- While I strive to provide accurate and helpful responses, I'm not perfect and may make mistakes or not fully understand certain contexts.
- My knowledge base is vast but not exhaustive, so I may not always have the answer to a specific question.
- I'm a machine, so while I can generate text, I don't have personal experiences or emotions like humans do.

Overall, I'm here to assist and provide helpful information, answer questions, and engage in conversation to the best of my abilities. Feel free to ask me anything!

WHAT ARE LLMS?

LLMs (*large language models*) are almost entirely based on the transformer architecture. There are many LLMs of varying sizes, some of which are larger than BERT-based models. As such, this section provides a very brief overview of LLMs.

LLMs are known for their size, which is typically at least 10 billion parameters (BERT has "only" 1.5 billion parameters). Moreover, they involve very large datasets for the training step, which can require weeks of training time at a cost of millions of dollars. Unfortunately, there is an associated environment cost: according to the following article, the carbon footprint of training GPT-3 is comparable to a car round-trip to the moon:

https://www.theregister.com/2020/11/04/gpt3_carbon_footprint_estimate/

Outside of BERT and the BERT "family," one well-known LLM that generated tremendous interest is GPT-3, which consists of 175B parameters, and almost 12 times larger than BERT. However, there are models that are much larger (for example, 540B parameters and more than 1.2 trillion parameters in Switch and DAO, respectively). The next important LLM was ChatGPT, which was followed by GPT-4 (which will soon be succeeded by GPT-5).

Of course, the development of LLMs has created many competitors, such as Gemini 1.5, Claude 3, Meta AI, Perplexity, Grok, and many others. As this book goes to print, another highly anticipated LLM is GPT-5, which may establish a new set of expectations for LLMs.

What is the Purpose of LLMs?

The following prompt was given to ChatGPT: "What is the purpose of LLMs, and which LLMs do you recommend?"

ChatGPT:

Large Language Models (LLMs) serve several purposes in the field of artificial intelligence, primarily revolving around processing and generating human language in a way that mimics understanding and responsiveness. Here are some of the core purposes of LLMs:

Purposes of LLMs

1. **Natural Language Understanding (NLU):** LLMs can understand and interpret human language, which is useful in applications like sentiment analysis, language translation, and content moderation.
2. **Natural Language Generation (NLG):** They excel at generating coherent and contextually appropriate text, which can be used in chatbots, content creation tools, and automated reporting systems.

3. **Assistance and Accessibility:** LLMs power virtual assistants that can perform tasks like scheduling meetings, responding to queries, and providing recommendations, making digital environments more accessible.

4. **Educational Tools:** They can be used in educational contexts to generate learning materials, provide tutoring, or simulate historical figures or characters for interactive learning.

5. **Research and Data Analysis:** In research, LLMs help in summarizing papers, generating hypotheses, or even writing code, thus speeding up scientific progress.

6. **Creative Arts:** LLMs contribute to creative processes such as writing stories, composing music, or generating art, expanding the tools available to artists.

Recommended LLMs

The choice of an LLM depends on your specific needs, including factors like accessibility, cost, ease of integration, and specific feature requirements. Here are some widely recognized LLMs and their typical use cases:

1. **OpenAI's GPT-3:** Known for its impressive language generation capabilities, GPT-3 is suitable for applications requiring high-quality text generation, from creative writing to technical documentation. GPT-3 is available via API but requires approval and may incur costs based on usage.

2. **Google's BERT and T5:** While BERT is exceptionally good for tasks that require understanding the context of words in text (like question answering and language inference), T5 (Text-to-Text Transfer Transformer) is versatile, trained to handle any NLP task that can be reformulated as a text-to-text problem.

3. **Facebook's BART and RoBERTa:** BART is effective for NLG tasks like summarization, while RoBERTa serves as a robust model for NLU tasks. Both are part of Facebook AI's offerings and are highly adaptable for various NLP tasks.

4. **EleutherAI's GPT-Neo and GPT-J:** These are open-source alternatives to OpenAI's GPT models. They are particularly useful for developers or organizations looking for a more accessible model that can be fine-tuned and deployed on private infrastructure without usage fees.

5. **Hugging Face Transformers:** This isn't a model but a library that provides access to numerous pre-trained models including GPT-2, Distil-BERT, and many others. It's highly recommended for those who wish to experiment with different models or need tools for easy integration and deployment.

Conclusion

The choice of an LLM should align with your technical requirements and constraints. Considerations should include whether you need a model primarily for understanding or generating text, your capacity to handle computational loads (some LLMs can be run on-premises, while others require substantial computing resources), and your budget for potential fees associated with API-based models. Each model comes with its own strengths and is suited to different tasks, so the right choice will depend on the specific demands of your application.

Model Size Versus Training Set Size

Although it might seem that the size of a model is the most important factor in its success, the size of the training dataset is actually more significant. This statement contravenes the results from Kaplan et al.'s idea about the training set size versus the model size (this is an important point). In the meantime, let's take a brief look at some of the more significant LLMs that have been developed. More details are available from the following arxiv paper by Kaplan et al: *https://arxiv.org/abs/2206.07682*.

For example, the `Chinchilla` LLM from DeepMind consists of 70 billion parameters, and yet it is able to outperform GPT-3, Jurassic-1 (178B), and Megatron-Turing (530 B) because its training dataset is five times larger than the training datasets for the other LLMs.

Despite the impressive results of LLMs and the highly anticipated functionality of GPT-4 that was released on March 14, 2023, LLMs are not capable of understanding language in the manner of human beings. The ability of an entity to make intelligent choices that are comparable to those made by humans does not prove that that entity truly understands those choices in the same way as a human.

Do LLMs Understand Language?

As a whimsical and partially related analogy, consider the following story that involves a two chess grand masters, a confidence man, and a 12-year-old boy who are traveling on a cross Atlantic ship during the early 1900s.

When the ship was several hours from its destination, the confidence man made an audacious bet that in the span of two hours he could train the young boy to play chess so that the matches would result in either a draw or win for the boy. However, the grand masters and the boy were required to play in a closet-like cloaked area, and the three participants were not permitted to communicate in any manner with each other.

The grand masters accepted the challenge, expecting that they would leverage their tremendous knowledge over the young competitor. However, as the games progressed, the grand masters were shocked by the speed and sophistication of the chess moves of the boy. Their confidence was quickly replaced by concern and then by desperation. Eventually one grand master offered a draw and the other grand master conceded the match.

The deception was exceedingly simple: whenever one grand master made a chess move, the boy would make the same chess move against the *other* grand master, which effectively meant that the grand masters were competing against each other. Fortunately for the confidence man, the ship reached its destination, and he managed to collect the reward and the boy and then disembark before the chess grand masters realized that they had been swindled.

The point of the preceding story is that the boy made extremely intelligent chess moves but did not necessarily understand the logic for making those chess moves. Hence, if a human being does not understand the logic behind an action, it suggests that it is even less likely for an LLM to have a human-level understanding of the reasons for its recommendations.

Caveats Regarding LLMs

Although LLMs are capable of impressive results, keep in mind the following points:

- smaller models can outperform larger models (in some tasks)
- models generate false results ("hallucinating")
- Some models process long documents and others are more conversational.
- the increasing relevance of vector databases
- Most models are not trained on up-to-date datasets (only up to a certain point in time).

For example, ChatGPT was trained on data prior to September 2021. Two features that are becoming increasing important to address two of the preceding points are as follows:

1. the ability to maintain history of previous conversations
2. the ability to perform on-the-fly Internet searches for information

PITFALLS OF WORKING WITH LLMS

The following prompt was given to GPT-4: `"What are the significant pitfalls when working with LLMs?"`

`ChatGPT:`

Working with Large Language Models (LLMs) like GPT (Generative Pretrained Transformer) models presents several significant pitfalls that developers and users should be aware of. Addressing these challenges is crucial for ensuring the effective and ethical use of these powerful tools. Here are some of the important pitfalls:

1. **Bias and Fairness:** LLMs can inadvertently propagate and amplify biases present in their training data. This can lead to outputs that are unfair or discriminatory, particularly in sensitive contexts such as gender, race, and socioeconomic status. Managing these biases is critical to prevent harm and ensure fairness in applications.
2. **Lack of Explainability:** LLMs, particularly those based on deep learning, often operate as "black boxes," meaning it can be difficult to

understand how they arrive at certain conclusions or outputs. This lack of transparency can be problematic in applications where explainability is crucial, such as in healthcare or legal contexts.

3. **Data Privacy:** LLMs are trained on vast amounts of data, which can include personally identifiable information or proprietary data. Ensuring that the use of such models complies with data privacy laws (like GDPR) and does not expose sensitive information is a significant challenge.

4. **Model Robustness and Reliability:** LLMs can generate plausible sounding but factually incorrect or nonsensical answers, a phenomenon often referred to as "hallucination." Ensuring the reliability of the model's output in critical applications is essential but challenging.

5. **Resource Intensity:** Training and running LLMs require significant computational resources, which can lead to high costs and environmental impact due to the energy consumption of modern AI systems. This makes it less accessible for smaller organizations or individuals.

6. **Dependence on Large Datasets:** LLMs require large datasets for training, which can be difficult to procure, especially datasets that are high-quality, diverse, and representative. This dependence can limit the scope of where and how these models can be effectively deployed.

7. **Generalization:** While LLMs are impressive in handling a wide range of tasks, they may struggle with generalizing to tasks or scenarios very different from those they were trained on. This can limit their utility in novel or unexpected situations.

8. **Misuse Potential:** The capabilities of LLMs can also be misused, for example, in creating and spreading disinformation, generating malicious content, or other unethical applications. Preventing misuse while promoting beneficial uses is a significant governance challenge.

9. **Regulatory and Ethical Issues:** As AI technology advances, so does the need for regulatory frameworks that keep pace with these changes. Developing and enforcing regulations that cover the ethical use of LLMs is complex and still evolving.

Addressing these pitfalls requires a combination of technical solutions, ethical guidelines, and regulatory measures. Continuous research into improving the fairness, transparency, and robustness of LLMs is essential, as well as cultivating a broader understanding of the implications of AI technology in society.

A BRIEF HISTORY OF MODERN LLMS

Let's get some information about the history of LLMs by giving the following prompt GPT-4: "Please provide a detailed history of modern LLMs."

ChatGPT:

The history of modern Large Language Models (LLMs) is a tale of rapid development and groundbreaking advancements in the field of natural language processing (NLP) and AI. Here is a detailed overview:

Pre-2010: Early Foundations
- **Late 1950s – 2000s**: Early explorations into machine learning and NLP set the groundwork for later developments. Techniques like decision trees, hidden Markov models, and early neural networks were explored.
- **1980s – 2000s:** The development of foundational algorithms for backpropagation and convolutional neural networks (CNNs) paved the way for more advanced NLP tasks.

2013-2017: Word Embeddings and Initial Transformer Models
- **2013:** The introduction of Word2Vec by a team at Google marked a significant improvement in word embeddings, providing vector representations for words that captured semantic meanings.
- **2014:** GloVe (Global Vectors for Word Representation) was introduced by Stanford researchers, offering improvements over Word2Vec by focusing on word co-occurrences across the whole corpus.
- **2015:** Sequence to Sequence (Seq2Seq) models and Attention Mechanisms were developed, improving machine translation and other NLP tasks by allowing models to focus on different parts of the input sequence for generating outputs.
- **2017:** Google's Transformer model was introduced in the paper "Attention Is All You Need," revolutionizing NLP by using self-attention mechanisms, leading to significant improvements in efficiency and effectiveness over previous RNN and LSTM-based models.

2018-2019: The Rise of Pre-trained Models

- **2018:**
- **BERT (Bidirectional Encoder Representations from Transformers)** by Google introduced the concept of pre-training a language model on a large corpus and then fine-tuning it for specific tasks, leading to state-of-the-art performances across many NLP benchmarks.
- **GPT (Generative Pre-trained Transformer)** by OpenAI followed a similar pre-training and fine-tuning approach but focused on generating coherent and diverse text sequences.
- **2019:**
- **GPT-2:** OpenAI released GPT-2, an improved version of GPT with a much larger dataset and model size, demonstrating the capacity to generate coherent paragraphs of text.
- **RoBERTa (Robustly optimized BERT approach) and DistilBERT (a distilled version of BERT that maintains performance while being more efficient)** were among several models building on BERT's architecture for optimized performance.

2020-Present: Scaling and Specialization

- **2020:**
- **GPT-3:** OpenAI introduced GPT-3, scaling up the model size significantly to 175 billion parameters, showcasing remarkable abilities in generating human-like text and performing a wide range of NLP tasks without task-specific fine-tuning.
- **2021-2023:**
- The trend towards even larger models continued, with efforts focusing not just on scaling but also on making these models more efficient, interpretable, and less resource intensive.
- **Introduction of foundation models,** a term popularized to denote models like BERT and GPT-3 that serve as foundational building blocks for a wide array of applications.
- Development of **domain-specific LLMs**, tailored for particular fields such as law, healthcare, and more, offering improved accuracy and utility in specialized applications.
- Advances in **mitigating bias and improving fairness** in LLMs, addressing concerns over the models' potential to perpetuate or amplify biases present in their training data.

Future Directions

- As we move forward, the focus is increasingly on **ethical AI**, ensuring that LLMs are developed and used responsibly.
- **Efficiency and environmental sustainability** are becoming critical concerns, with research into making LLMs less energy and resource intensive.
- The quest for **"artificial general intelligence" (AGI)** continues, with LLMs being a significant component of broader AI research efforts aiming to create systems with human-like understanding and reasoning capabilities.

Modern LLMs represent the cutting edge of AI research, embodying both the immense potential of AI to transform industries and our daily lives, and the challenges of ensuring that such powerful technologies are developed and used ethically and responsibly.

With the preceding details in mind, let's turn our attention to quantization, which is the topic of the next section.

ASPECTS OF LLM DEVELOPMENT

The architecture of encoder-only LLMs, decoder-only LLMs, and LLMs are based on the original transformer architecture, which includes both an encoder as well as a decoder. For your convenience, this section provides a list of language models that belong to each of these three types of models.

With the preceding points in mind, some of the better-known encoder-based LLMs include the following:

- AlBERT
- BERT
- DistilBERT
- ELECTRA
- RoBERTa

The preceding LLMs are well-suited for performing NLP tasks such as NER and extractive question answering tasks. In addition to encoder-only LLMs, there are several well-known decoder-based LLMs that include the following:

- CTRL
- GPT/GPT-2
- Transformer XK

The preceding LLMs perform text *generation*, whereas encoder-only models perform next word *prediction*. Finally, some of the well-known encoder/decoder-based LLMs include the following:

- BART
- mBART
- Marian
- T5

The preceding LLMs perform summarization, translation, and generate question answering.

A recent trend has been the use of fine-tuning, zero/one/few shot training, and prompt-based learning with respect to LLMs. Fine-tuning is typically accompanied by a fine-tuning dataset, and if the latter is not available (or infeasible), few-shot training might be an acceptable alternative.

One outcome from training the Jurassic-1 LLM is that wider and shallower is better than narrower and deeper with respect to performance because a wider context allows for more calculations to be performed in parallel.

Another result from training Chinchilla is that smaller models that are trained on a corpus with a very large number of tokens can be more performant than larger models that are trained on a more modest number of tokens.

The success of the GlaM and Switch LLMs (both from Google) suggests that sparse transformers, in conjunction with MoE, is also an interesting direction, potentially leading to even better results in the future.

In addition, there is the possibility of the "over curation" of data, which is to say that performing *very* detailed data curation to remove spurious-looking tokens does not guarantee that models will produce better results on those curated datasets.

The use of prompts has revealed an interesting detail: the results of similar yet different prompts can lead to substantively different responses. Thus, the goal is to create well-crafted prompts, which are inexpensive and yet can be a somewhat elusive task.

Another area of development pertains to the continued need for benchmarks that leverage better and more complex datasets, especially when LLMs exceed human performance. Specifically, a benchmark becomes outdated when all modern LLMs can pass the suite of tests in that benchmark. Two such benchmarks are XNLI and BigBench ("Beyond the Imitation Game Benchmark").

The following URL provides a fairly extensive list of general NLP benchmarks as well as language-specific NLP benchmarks:

https://mr-nlp.github.io/posts/2021/05/benchmarks-in-nlp/

The following URL provides a list of monolingual transformer-based pre-trained language models:

https://mr-nlp.github.io/posts/2021/05/tptlms-list/

LLM Size Versus Performance

In regard to the size-versus-performance issue, it is important to know that although larger models such as GPT-3 can perform better than smaller models, it is not always the case. In particular, models that are variants of GPT-3 have mixed results: some smaller variants perform almost as well as GPT-3, and some larger models perform only marginally better than GPT-3.

The recent trend involves developing models that are based on the decoder component of the transformer architecture. Such models are frequently measured by their performance via zero-shot, one-shot, and few-shot training in comparison to other LLMs. This trend, as well as the development of ever-larger LLMs, is likely to continue for the foreseeable future.

Interestingly, decoder-only LLMs can perform tasks such as token prediction and can slightly out-perform encoder-only models on benchmarks such as SuperGLUE. However, such decoder-based models tend to be significantly larger than encoder-based models, and the latter tend to be more efficient than the former.

Hardware is another consideration in terms of optimizing model performance, which can incur a greater cost, and hence might be limited to only a handful of companies. Due to the high cost of hardware, another initiative involves training LLMs on the Jean Zay supercomputer in France, as discussed here:

https://venturebeat.com/2022/01/10/inside-bigscience-the-quest-to-build-a-powerful-open-language-model/

Emergent Abilities of LLMs

Emergent abilities of LLMs refers to abilities that are present in larger models that do not exist in smaller models. In simplified terms, as models increase in size, there is a discontinuous "jump" whereby abilities manifest themselves in a larger model with no apparent or easily identifiable reason.

The interesting aspect of emergent abilities is the possibility of expanding capabilities of language models through additional scaling. More detailed information is accessible in the following paper ("Emergent Abilities of Large Language Models"):

https://arxiv.org/abs/2206.07682.

Nobel prize winning physicist Philip Anderson made the following statement in his 1972 essay called *More Is Different*: "Emergence is when quantitative changes in a system result in qualitative changes in behavior."

Interestingly, the authors describe a scenario in which few-shot prompting is considered emergent (quoted from their arxiv paper):

"The ability to perform a task via few-shot prompting is emergent when a model has random performance until a certain scale, after which performance increases to well-above random."

Be sure to examine Table 1 in the preceding paper as it provides details regarding "few-shot prompting abilities" (e.g., truthfulness, the MMLU Benchmark) as well as "Augmented prompting abilities" (e.g., the chain of thought and instruction following).

Note that emergent abilities *cannot* be predicted by extrapolation of the behavior of smaller models because (by definition) emergent abilities are not present in smaller models. No doubt there will be more research that explores the extent to which further model scaling can lead to more emergent abilities in LLMs.

KAPLAN AND UNDER-TRAINED MODELS

Kaplan et al. provide (empirical) power laws regarding the performance of language models, which they assert depends on the following:

- model size
- dataset size
- amount of compute for training

Kaplan et al. assert that changing the network width or depth have minimal effects. They also claim that optimal training of very large models involves a relatively modest amount of data. The paper with the relevant details is accessible here:

https://arxiv.org/abs/2001.08361.

However, Chinchilla is an LLM with 70B parameters that was trained on a dataset that is much larger than the size that is recommended by Kaplan et al. In fact, Chinchilla achieved SOTA status that has surpassed the performance of the following LLMs, all of which are between 2 and 7 times larger than Chinchilla:

- Gopher (280B)
- GPT-3 (175B)

- J1-Jumbo (178B)
- LaMDA (137B)
- MT-NLG (530B)

In addition, the creators of the Chinchilla LLM wrote a paper, "Scaling Laws for Neural Language Models," that includes the suggested number of tokens for various models sizes in order to be fully trained instead of under trained (see Table 3). For example, the suggested training set sizes for models that have 175B, 520B, and 1 trillion parameters is 3.7 trillion tokens, 11.0 trillion tokens, and 21.2 trillion tokens, respectively. The largest entry in the same table is LMMs that have 10 trillion parameters, with a recommended training set size of 216.2 trillion parameters.

Obviously an LLM that exceeds 1 trillion parameters faces a significant challenge to create datasets of the recommended size as described in the paper from the authors of Chinchilla.

REAL-WORLD USE CASES FOR GENERATIVE AI

The following prompt was given to Cohere: `"Please describe real-world use cases for generative AI, along with their potential impact."`

`Cohere:`

Generative Artificial Intelligence (AI) has the potential to revolutionize various industries and solve complex problems. Here's an improved version of the description, including additional use cases and their potential impact:

Healthcare:

Drug Discovery and Design: Generative AI can be used to identify potential drug candidates by generating molecular structures with desired properties. This accelerates the drug discovery process, leading to faster development of treatments for diseases.

Medical Image Analysis: Generative models can assist in detecting and diagnosing medical conditions from medical images, such as MRI scans or x-rays. This helps healthcare professionals in making more accurate diagnoses and improving patient care.

Personalized Medicine: Generative AI can analyze patient data to provide personalized treatment plans and recommendations. By considering individual genetic variations and health histories, generative AI enables more precise and effective healthcare.

Climate and Environment:

Climate Modeling and Prediction: Generative AI models can analyze vast amounts of climate data to predict and model complex climate patterns. This aids in understanding climate change, extreme weather events, and the development of mitigation strategies.

Sustainable Resource Management: Generative AI can optimize the use of natural resources, such as water or energy, by generating efficient allocation plans. This helps reduce waste, improve sustainability, and preserve the environment.

Biodiversity Conservation: Generative models can assist in identifying and classifying plant and animal species, supporting biodiversity conservation efforts. They can also generate habitat restoration plans to promote ecological balance.

Creative Industries:
Content Generation: Generative AI can create text, images, or even music with remarkable creativity and originality. This technology can assist writers, artists, musicians, and content creators in producing unique and engaging content.

Art and Design: Generative AI models can generate aesthetically pleasing artwork, designs, or architectural concepts. They can inspire human creators and lead to innovative artistic styles and trends.

Video and Game Development: Generative AI can be used to create realistic animations, generate game environments, or develop non-player characters, enhancing the immersive experience for gamers.

Education:
Personalized Learning: Generative AI can adapt educational content to individual student needs, providing customized lessons, practice problems, and feedback. This personalized approach improves learning outcomes and engagement.

Language Learning: Generative models can facilitate language acquisition by generating interactive and contextualized language-learning materials. They can provide tailored exercises, conversations, and feedback to students.

Virtual Tutoring: Generative AI can power virtual tutors that offer personalized guidance and explanations to students, supplementing traditional teaching methods.

Finance and Economics:
Fraud Detection and Prevention: Generative AI models can analyze patterns in financial data to detect fraudulent activities, such as credit card fraud or money laundering. This helps protect individuals and organizations from financial losses.

Investment Strategies: Generative AI can generate insights and identify patterns in financial markets, aiding in investment decision-making. It can analyze vast amounts of data to predict market trends and optimize investment portfolios.

Risk Assessment and Management: Generative models can assess and manage financial risks, such as credit risk or market risk, by generating probabilistic scenarios and providing risk mitigation strategies.

Transportation and Logistics:
Autonomous Vehicles: Generative AI can enhance the perception and decision-making capabilities of self-driving cars, improving their ability to recognize objects, predict trajectories, and make safe driving decisions.
Route Optimization: Generative models can optimize delivery routes for logistics and transportation companies, reducing travel distances, fuel consumption, and delivery times.
Traffic Flow Optimization: Generative AI can analyze traffic patterns and suggest improvements to reduce congestion and optimize traffic flow in urban areas.

Social Impact and Humanitarian Efforts:
Disaster Response: Generative AI can assist in disaster relief efforts by analyzing damage, identifying affected areas, and coordinating rescue and relief operations.
Language Translation and Preservation: Generative models can facilitate cross-lingual communication and help preserve endangered languages, promoting cultural exchange and understanding.
Social Good Initiatives: Generative AI can be leveraged to address social issues, such as generating awareness campaigns for humanitarian causes or providing personalized recommendations for social services.

Potential Impact:
The real-world use cases of generative AI have the potential to bring about significant positive changes. They can enhance human creativity, improve decision-making, increase efficiency, and solve complex problems in various domains. Generative AI can drive innovation, foster economic growth, and improve the overall quality of life for people worldwide.

However, it is important to approach the development and deployment of generative AI with caution and ethical considerations. Addressing biases, ensuring privacy and security, and establishing governance frameworks are crucial to mitigate potential risks and ensure that the benefits of generative AI are widely accessible and beneficial to society.

SUMMARY

This chapter started with an introduction to generative AI and several components of generative AI, including LLMs such as ChatGPT, Gemini, Claude 3, Meta AI, and DALL-E 3. You also learned about the difference between generative AI versus conversational AI, AGI (Artificial General Intelligence), and several branches of machine learning, such as deep learning, natural language processing, and reinforcement learning.

Next, we learned about several companies such as DeepMind, OpenAI, and Hugging Face that are leaders in AI. You also acquired a basic understanding of LLMs and their role in generative AI.

In the final section of this chapter, you were introduced to creating Gen AI applications, which included a rudimentary Python code sample.

CHAPTER 2

PROMPT ENGINEERING

This chapter provides an introduction to prompt engineering as well as different types of prompts and also guidelines for effective prompts.

The first part of this chapter discusses prompt engineering, which involves various techniques, such as instruction prompts, reverse prompts, system prompts, CoT (chain of thought), and various other techniques.

The second section discusses various GPT-based LLMs, some of which might be interesting enough to delve into more deeply through other online resources.

The third section in this chapter contains some information about aspects of LLM development, such as LLM size versus performance, emergent abilities of LLMs, and undertrained models.

One other point to keep in mind: some of the sections in this chapter contain detailed information, so if LLMs are a new concept, consider skimming through this chapter instead of trying to absorb everything (this chapter can always be returned to later).

WHAT IS PROMPT ENGINEERING?

Text generators, such as ChatGPT and GPT-4 from OpenAI, Jurassic from AI21, Midjourney from Midjourney Inc., and Stable Diffusion from Stability AI, can perform text-to-image generation. *Prompt engineering* refers to devising text-based prompts that enable AI-based systems to improve the output that is generated. The result is that the output more closely matches whatever users want to produce from the AI. By way of analogy, think of prompts as similar to the role of coaches: they offer advice and suggestions to help people perform better in their given tasks.

Since prompts are based on words, the challenge involves learning how different words can affect the generated output. Moreover, it is difficult to predict how systems respond to a given prompt. For instance, to generate a landscape, the difference between a dark landscape and a bright landscape is intuitive. However, for a beautiful landscape, how would an AI system generate a corresponding image? As one can surmise, "concrete" words are easier than abstract or subjective words for AI systems that generate images from text. Consider the previous example: how would the following be visualized?

- a beautiful landscape
- a beautiful song
- a beautiful movie

Although prompt engineering started with text-to-image generation, there are other types of prompt engineering, such as audio-based prompts that interpret emphasized text and emotions that are detected in speech, and sketch-based prompts that generate images from drawings. The most recent focus of attention involves text-based prompts for generating videos, which presents exciting opportunities for artists and designers. An example of image-to-image processing is accessible here:

https://huggingface.co/spaces/fffiloni/stable-diffusion-color-sketch

Prompts and Completions

A *prompt* is a text string that users provide to LLMs, and a *completion* is the text that users receive from LLMs. Prompts assist LLMs in completing a request (task), and they can vary in length. Although prompts can be any text string, including a random string, the quality and structure of prompts affects the quality of completions.

Think of prompts as a mechanism for giving "guidance" to LLMs, or even as a way to "coach" LLMs into providing desired answers. The number of tokens in a prompt plus the number of tokens in the completion can be at most 2,048 tokens.

Types of Prompts

The following list contains well-known types of prompts for LLMs:

- zero-shot prompts
- one-shot prompts
- few-shot prompts
- instruction prompts

A *zero-shot prompt* contains a description of a task, whereas a *one-shot prompt* consists of a single example for completing a task. *Few-shot prompts* consist of multiple examples (typically between ten and 100). In all cases, a clear description of the task or tasks is recommended: more tasks provide GPT-3 with more information, which in turn can lead to more accurate completions.

T0 (for "zero shot") is an interesting LLM: although T0 is sixteen times smaller (11B) than GPT-3 (175B), T0 has outperformed GPT-3 on language-related tasks. T0 can perform well on unseen NLP tasks (i.e., tasks that are new to T0) because it was trained on a dataset containing multiple tasks.

The following Web page provides the Github repository for T0, a site for training T0 directly in a browser:

https://github.com/bigscience-workshop/t-zero

T0++ is based on T0, and it was trained with extra tasks beyond the set of tasks on which T0 was trained.

Another important detail is the first three prompts in the preceding list are also called zero-shot learning, one-shot learning, and few-shot learning, respectively.

Instruction Prompts

Instruction prompts are used for fine tuning LLMs, and they specify a format (determined by the user) for the manner in which the LLM is expected to conform in its responses. The user can prepare instruction prompts or access prompt template libraries that contain different templates for different tasks, along with different datasets. Various prompt instruction templates are publicly available, such as the following links that provide prompt templates (see subsequent section for an example) for Llama:

https://github.com/devbrones/llama-prompts

https://pub.towardsai.net/llama-gpt4all-simplified-local-chatgpt-ab7d28d34923

Reverse Prompts

Another technique uses a reverse order: input prompts are answers and the responses are the questions associated with the answers (similar to a popular game show). For example, given a French sentence, the model could be asked, "What English text might have resulted in this French translation?"

System Prompts Versus Agent Prompts

The distinction between a system prompt and an agent prompt often comes up in the context of conversational AI systems and chatbot design.

A *system prompt* is typically an initial message or cue given by the system to guide the user on what they can do or to set expectations about the interaction. It often serves as an introduction or a way to guide users on how to proceed. Here are several examples of system prompts:

- "Welcome to ChatBotX! You can ask me questions about weather, news, or sports. How can I assist you today?"
- "Hello! For account details, press 1. For technical support, press 2."
- "Greetings! Type 'order' to track your package or 'help' for assistance."

By contrast, an *agent prompt* is a message generated by the AI model or agent in response to a user's input during the course of an interaction. It is a part of the back-and-forth exchange within the conversation. The agent prompt guides the user to provide more information, clarifies ambiguity, or nudges the user toward a specific action. Here are some examples of agent prompts:

User: "I'm looking for shoes."

Agent Prompt: "Great! Are you looking for men's or women's shoes?"

User: "I can't log in."

Agent Prompt: "I'm sorry to hear that. Can you specify if you are having trouble with your password or username?"

User: "Tell me a joke."

Agent Prompt: "Why did the chicken join a band? Because it had the drumsticks!"

The fundamental difference between the two is their purpose and placement in the interaction. A system prompt is often at the beginning of an interaction, setting the stage for the conversation. An agent prompt occurs during the conversation, steering the direction of the dialogue based on user input.

Both types of prompts are crucial for creating a fluid and intuitive conversational experience for users. They guide the user and help ensure that the system understands and addresses the user's needs effectively.

Prompt Templates

Prompt templates are predefined formats or structures used to instruct a model or system to perform a specific task. They serve as a foundation for generating prompts, where certain parts of the template can be filled in or customized to produce a variety of specific prompts. By way of analogy, prompt templates are the counterpart to macros that can be defined in some text editors.

Prompt templates are especially useful when working with language models, as they provide a consistent way to query the model across multiple tasks or data points. In particular, prompt templates can make it easier to:

- ensure consistency when querying a model multiple times
- facilitate batch processing or automation
- reduce errors and variations in how questions are posed to the model

An example is working with an LLM and translating English sentences into French. An associated prompt template could be the following:

- "Translate the following English sentence into French: {sentence}"
- Note that {sentence} is a placeholder that can be replaced with any English sentence.

The preceding prompt template can be used to generate specific prompts:

- "Translate the following English sentence into French: 'Hello, how are you?'"
- "Translate the following English sentence into French: 'I love ice cream.'"

Prompt templates enable the user to easily generate a variety of prompts for different sentences without having to rewrite the entire instruction each time. In fact, this concept can be extended to more complex tasks and can incorporate multiple placeholders or more intricate structures, depending on the application.

Prompts for Different LLMs

GPT-3, ChatGPT, and GPT-4 are LLMs that are all based on the transformer architecture and are fundamentally similar in their underlying mechanics. ChatGPT is essentially a version of the GPT model fine-tuned specifically for conversational interactions. GPT-4 is an evolution or improvement over GPT-3 in terms of scale and capabilities.

The differences in prompts for these models mainly arise from the specific use case and context, rather than inherent differences between the models. Here are some prompting differences that are based on use cases.

GPT-3 can be used for a wide range of tasks beyond just conversation, from content generation to code writing. Here are two examples of prompts for GPT-3:

- "Translate the following English text to French: 'Hello, how are you?'"
- "Write a Python function that calculates the factorial of a number."

ChatGPT is specifically fine-tuned for conversational interactions. Here are some examples of prompts for two different conversations with ChatGPT:

- User: "Can you help me with my homework?"
- ChatGPT: "Of course! What subject or topic do you need help with?"

- User: "Tell me a joke."
- ChatGPT: "Why did the chicken cross the playground? To get to the other slide!"

GPT-4 provides a larger scale and refinements, so the prompts would be similar in nature to GPT-3 but might yield more accurate or nuanced outputs. Here are two examples of prompts for GPT-4:

- "Provide a detailed analysis of quantum mechanics in relation to general relativity."
- "Generate a short story based on a post-apocalyptic world with a theme of hope."

These three models accept natural language prompts and produce natural language outputs. The fundamental way to interact with them remains consistent.

The main difference comes from the context in which the model is being used and any fine-tuning that has been applied. ChatGPT, for instance, is designed to be more conversational, so while GPT-3 can be used for chats, ChatGPT might produce more contextually relevant conversational outputs.

When directly interacting with these models, especially through an API, the user might also have control over parameters like "temperature" (controlling randomness) and "max tokens" (controlling response length). Adjusting these can shape the responses, regardless of which GPT variant is being used.

In essence, while the underlying models have differences in scale and specific training/fine-tuning, the way to prompt them remains largely consistent: clear, specific natural language prompts yield the best results.

Poorly Worded Prompts

When crafting prompts, be as clear and specific as possible to guide the response in the desired direction. Ambiguous or vague prompts can lead to a wide range of responses, many of which might not be useful or relevant to the user's actual intent.

Poorly worded prompts are often vague, ambiguous, or too broad, and they can lead to confusion, misunderstanding, or nonspecific responses from AI models. Here are some examples of poorly worded prompts, along with explanations:

"Tell me about that thing."
Problem: Too vague. What "thing" is being referred to?

"Why did it happen?"
Problem: No context. What event or situation is being discussed?

"Explain stuff."
Problem: Too broad. What specific "stuff" should be explained?

"Do what is needful."
Problem: Ambiguous. What specific action is required?

"I want information."
Problem: Not specific enough. What type of information is desired?

"Can you get me the thing from the place?"
Problem: Both "thing" and "place" are unclear.

"Where can I buy what's-his-name's book?"
Problem: Ambiguous reference. Who is "what's-his-name"?

"How do you do the process?"
Problem: Which "process" is being referred to?

"Describe the importance of the topic."
Problem: The "topic" is not specified.

"Why is it bad or good?"
Problem: No context. What is "it"?

"Help with the issue."
Problem: Vague. What specific issue requires assistance?

"Things to consider for the task."
Problem: Ambiguous. What "task" is being discussed?

"How does this work?"
Problem: Lack of specificity. What is "this"?

INFERENCE PARAMETERS

After completing the fine-tuning step for an LLM, values can be set for various so-called inference parameters. The GPT-3 API supports numerous inference parameters, some of which are as follows:

- `engine`
- `prompt`
- `max_tokens`
- `top_p`
- `top_k`
- `frequency_penalty`
- `presence_penalty`
- `token length`
- `stop tokens`
- `temperature`

The `engine` (now called the model) inference parameter can be one of the four GPT-3 models, such as `text-ada-001`. The `prompt` parameter is simply the input text that the user provides. The `presence_penalty` inference parameter enables more relevant responses when specifying higher values for this parameter.

The `max_tokens` inference parameter specifies the maximum number of tokens: sample values are 100, 200, or 256. The `top_p` inference parameter can be a positive integer that specifies the topmost results to select. The `frequency_penalty` is an inference parameter that pertains to the frequency of repeated words. A smaller value for this parameter increases the number of repeated words.

The `token length` parameter specifies the total number of words that are in the input sequence that is processed by the LLM (not the maximum length of each token).

The `stop tokens` parameter controls the length of the generated output of an LLM. If this parameter equals 1, then only a single sentence is generated, whereas a value of 2 indicates that the generated output is limited to one paragraph.

The `top_k` parameter specifies the number of tokens—which is the value for k—that are chosen, with the constraint that the chosen tokens have the highest probabilities. For example, if `top_k` is equal to 3, then only the 3 tokens with the highest probabilities are selected.

The `top_p` parameter is a floating-point number between 0.0 and 1.0, and it is the upper bound on the sum of the probabilities of the chosen tokens. For example, if a discrete probability distribution consists of the set S = {0.1, 0.2, 0.3, 0.4} and the value of the top p parameter is 0.3, then only the tokens with associated probabilities of 0.1 and 0.2 can be selected.

Thus, the `top_k` and the `top_p` parameters provide two mechanisms for limiting the number of tokens that can be selected.

Temperature Parameter

The `temperature` hyperparameter is a floating-point number between 0 and 1 inclusive, and its default value is 0.7. One interesting value for the temperature is 0.8: this will result in GPT-3 selecting a next token that does *not* have the maximum probability.

The temperature parameter T is a non-negative floating-point number whose value influences the extent to which the model uses randomness. Specifically, smaller values for the temperature parameter that are closer to 0 involve less randomness (i.e., more deterministic), whereas larger values for the temperature parameter involve more randomness.

The temperature parameter T is directly associated with the softmax function that is applied during the final step in the transformer architecture. The value of T alters the formula for the `softmax()` function, as described later in this section. A key point to remember is that selecting tokens based on a `softmax()` function means that the selected token is the token with the highest probability.

By contrast, larger values for the parameter T enable randomness in the choice of the next token, which means that a token can be selected even though its associated probability is less than the maximum probability. While this might seem counterintuitive, it turns out that some values of T (such as 0.8) result in output text that is more natural sounding, from a human's perspective, than the output text in which tokens are selected if they have the maximum probability. Finally, a temperature value of 1 is the same as the standard `softmax()` function.

Temperature and the `softmax()` Function

The temperature parameter T appears in the *denominator* of the exponent of the Euler constant e in the `softmax()` function. Thus, instead of the `softmax()` numerators of the form $e^{(xi)}$, the modified `softmax()` function contains numerator terms of the form $e^{(xi/T)}$, where {x1, x2, . . . , xn} comprise a set of numbers that form a discrete probability distribution (explained in the next section).

As a reminder, the denominator of each term generated by the `soft-max()` function consists of the sum of the terms in the set {e^(x1), e^(x2), . . . , e^(xn)}. However, the denominator of the terms involving the temperature parameter T is slightly different: it is the sum of the terms in the set {e^(x1/T), e^(x2/T), . . . , e^(xn/T)}.

Interestingly, the `softmax()` function with the temperature parameter T is the same as the Boltzmann distribution that is described here:

https://en.wikipedia.org/wiki/Boltzmann_distribution

The following Python code snippet provides an example of specifying values for various hyperparameters, which specifies a GPT-3 engine:

```
response = openai.Completion.create(
  engine="text-ada-001",
  prompt="",
  temperature=0.7,
  max_tokens=256,
  top_p=1,
  frequency_penalty=0,
  presence_penalty=0
)
```

See the following URL for more information regarding inference parameters in GPT-3: *https://huggingface.co/blog/inference-endpoints-llm*

LLMS TRY TO BE HELPFUL

LLMs provide different completions due to various reasons, some of which are listed as follows:

- different datasets are used for training the LLMs
- datasets have different cutoff dates
- LLMs have different sizes
- LLMs have different architectures

Moreover, LLMs can generate produce erroneous yet plausible sounding answers: this is called *hallucinating*, and it is common in all LLMs. Interestingly, sometimes an LLM will acknowledge that it does not have an answer, and then provide an answer to a similar yet slightly different question.

In the following subsections, let's see how different LLMs respond to the following prompt: `"Please provide a description of LlaMaFuse, along with its advantages and disadvantages."`

Meta AI

I'm sorry, but I can't find any information on. If you're interested in learning more about LlamaIndex, I can tell you that LlamaIndex is a tool that allows users to create and manage their own vector databases for Llama models. It is designed to be easy to use and scalable, making it a great option for developers who want to build their own vector search applications. If you have any other questions about LlamaIndex, I'd be happy to help!

Gemini

While there's no widely established technology called "LlamaFuse," I can help you understand potential concepts and similar technologies that might be relevant:

Possible Interpretations of "LlamaFuse:"

Hypothetical LLM Fusion Technique:

Concept: "LlamaFuse" could refer to a speculative method of combining different Large Language Models (LLMs) to create a hybrid model with enhanced capabilities.

Advantages:
Complementary Strengths: Combining LLMs trained on different datasets or with different architectures could create a model that leverages the strengths of each.
Improved Accuracy: Accuracy could improve through the consensus or careful integration of multiple LLM outputs.
Reduced Bias: Potentially reduce biases present in individual models.

Disadvantages:
Complexity: Designing a method to effectively merge outputs from different LLMs would prove extremely complex.
Computing Resources: Running multiple LLMs simultaneously would be computationally very expensive.
Unexpected Biases: Fusion could introduce new or amplified biases depending on how the models are combined.

Reference to Existing Techniques:
Concept: "LlaMaFuse" might be a colloquial name for techniques that already exist in the LLM space, such as:
Ensemble Methods: Combining predictions from several models to improve robustness and performance.
Knowledge Distillation: Training a smaller "student" model to mimic the behavior of a larger "teacher" model.

Similar Technologies and Considerations

LLM Techniques: The field of large language models is constantly evolving. Techniques like prompt tuning, chain-of-thought reasoning, and others are actively being researched for improving model output.

AI Alignment: Creating safe and reliable AI systems is crucial. Any "fusion" technique needs to thoroughly address issues of bias and potential harm.

Let me know if you'd like me to elaborate on any of the concepts above, or if you have a different idea of what "LlamaFuse" might refer to!

GPT-4

LlamaFuse is not a recognized or widely known concept or product in the current technological, scientific, or commercial landscape. Therefore, it could potentially be a hypothetical concept, a new invention, or simply a fictional or misheard name. Could you provide more context or details about what LlamaFuse is supposed to be? Alternatively, if you meant something else or need information on a similar-sounding technology or concept, please let me know!

Claude 3

LlamaFuse is a technique that combines the strengths of LLamA (Large Language Model Meta AI) and DeepSpeed MII (Model-Integrated Intelligence). It aims to create more efficient and scalable language models by fusing the two approaches. Here's a description of LlamaFuse, along with its advantages and disadvantages:

Description:
LlamaFuse integrates LLamA, a large language model developed by Meta AI, with DeepSpeed MII, a framework for optimizing and scaling deep learning models. LLamA is known for its ability to generate coherent and contextually relevant text, while DeepSpeed MII enables efficient training and inference of large models by leveraging techniques like model parallelism and optimized data parallel training.

By combining these two technologies, LlamaFuse aims to create language models that can be trained and deployed more efficiently, while still maintaining high-quality text generation capabilities. The fusion of LLaMA and DeepSpeed MII allows for better resource utilization, faster training times, and improved scalability.

Advantages:
Efficient resource utilization: LlamaFuse leverages the optimization techniques provided by DeepSpeed MII, such as model parallelism and efficient data parallel training, to make better use of available hardware resources. This enables training larger models with fewer resources.

Faster training times: The optimizations provided by DeepSpeed MII can significantly reduce the training time of large language models like LLamA. This allows for quicker iteration and experimentation during the model development process.

Improved scalability: LlamaFuse enables the training and deployment of large language models at scale. It can handle models with billions of parameters and efficiently distribute the workload across multiple devices or nodes.

High-quality text generation: LLamA is known for its ability to generate coherent and contextually relevant text. By combining LLaMA with DeepSpeed MII, LlamaFuse aims to maintain high-quality text generation capabilities while improving efficiency and scalability.

Disadvantages:

Complexity: Integrating LLamA and DeepSpeed MII adds complexity to the model development and deployment process. It requires expertise in both technologies and may have a steeper learning curve compared to using a single approach.

Dependence on specific frameworks: LlamaFuse relies on LLaMA and DeepSpeed MII, which means it is tied to these specific frameworks. If there are updates or changes to either of these technologies, it may require adjustments to the LlaMaFuse implementation.

Potential trade-offs: While LlamaFuse aims to improve efficiency and scalability, there may be trade-offs in terms of model performance or certain capabilities compared to using LLamA or DeepSpeed MII individually. The fusion process may introduce additional constraints or limitations.

Limited flexibility: LlamaFuse is designed specifically for language modeling tasks and may not be as flexible or adaptable to other domains or types of deep learning tasks without significant modifications.

It's important to note that LlamaFuse is still an emerging technique, and its full potential and limitations are yet to be extensively explored and validated in real-world scenarios.

Perplexity

LlamaFuse is a large language model developed by Anthropic, a leading artificial intelligence research company. It is a powerful natural language processing tool that can be used for a variety of tasks, including text generation, question answering, and language translation. The key advantages of LlamaFuse include:

High performance: LlamaFuse has been trained on a vast amount of data and is capable of producing human-like text with a high degree of accuracy and coherence.

Versatility: LlamaFuse can be fine-tuned for a wide range of applications, from content creation to customer service chatbots.

Scalability: LlamaFuse can be deployed at scale and integrated into various systems and workflows.

Open-source: LlamaFuse is available as an open-source model, allowing researchers and developers to access and build upon the technology.

However, LlamaFuse also has some potential disadvantages:

Bias and hallucination: Like other large language models, LlamaFuse may exhibit biases and produce factually incorrect or "hallucinated" information, which can be a concern in critical applications.

Computational requirements: Training and deploying LlaMaFuse requires significant computational resources, which can be a barrier for some organizations.

Ethical considerations: The use of large language models like LlaMaFuse raises important ethical questions around privacy, transparency, and the potential for misuse.

Overall, LlamaFuse is a powerful and versatile language model that offers many benefits, but its use requires careful consideration and mitigation of potential risks.

Related questions:

- What is LlaMaFuse and how does it work?
- What are the benefits of using LlamaFuse?
- Are there any drawbacks to using LlamaFuse?

SUMMARY

This chapter started with a description of prompt engineering, which involves various techniques such as instruction prompts, reverse prompts, system prompts, prompt templates, and various other techniques. In addition, examples of poorly worded prompts were given, along with an explanation for each prompt.

Next, you learned about some well-known LLMs, such as Meta AI, Gemini, GPT-4, Claude 3, and Perplexity. Finally, you learned about several inference parameters in LLMs, such as the temperature parameter and the related softmax() activation function.

CHAPTER 3

INTRODUCTION TO CSS3

This chapter is the first of three chapters that discuss CSS3, and it focuses on CSS3 features that enable the creation of vivid graphics effects. The first part of this chapter contains a short section that discusses the structure of a minimal HTML document, followed by a brief discussion regarding browser support for CSS3 and online tools. CSS3 stylesheets are referenced in HTML pages; therefore, it is important to understand the limitations that exist with respect to browser support for CSS3. The second part of this chapter contains various code samples that illustrate how to create shadow effects, render rectangles with rounded corners, and use linear and radial gradients. The third part of this chapter covers CSS3 transforms (scale, rotate, skew, and translate), along with code samples that illustrate how to apply transforms to HTML elements and PNG files. This chapter will also explain how to use the CSS3 methods `translate()`, `rotate()`, `skew()`, and `scale()`.

Before reading this chapter, please keep in mind the following points. First, the CSS3 code samples in this book are for WebKit-based browsers, so the code will work on Microsoft® Windows®, Macintosh®, and Linux®. Some sections occasionally mention performing an Internet search to obtain more information about a specific topic. The rationale for doing so is that the relevance of online information depends on the knowledge level of the reader, so it is virtually impossible to find a one-size-fits-all link that is suitable for everyone's needs. Furthermore, topics that are less relevant to the theme or beyond the scope of this book will be covered in less detail, thereby maintaining a reasonable balance between the number of topics and the depth of explanation of the relevant details. With these points in mind, please be assured that referring to the Internet is never intended to be "user unfriendly" in any manner.

In addition, virtually all of the URLs in this book refer to open-source projects, but useful commercial products can also be found; the choice of tools depends on the features that they support, the requirements for your project, and the size of the budget.

Terminology in This Book

Although every attempt was made to be consistent, there are times when the terminology is not 100% consistent. For example, WebKit is an engine and not a browser. Therefore, "WebKit-based browser" is correct, whereas "WebKit browser" is incorrect, but both will be used (even though only the former is technically correct). Second, "HTML Web page" and "HTML page" will be used interchangeably. Third, sometimes references to HTML elements do not specify "HTML," so "<p> element" and "HTML <p> element" (or some other HTML element) will appear in the discussion that precedes or follows a code sample. Please keep the preceding points in mind, and that way there will not be any confusion as the book progresses.

HTML AND <DOCTYPE>

In addition to introducing many new semantic tags, HTML has simplified the <DOCTYPE> declaration for Web pages. This book does not contain a discussion of new HTML tags, but the HTML pages in this book do use the HTML <DOCTYPE> declaration. The typical structure of the HTML pages in this book looks like this:

```
<!DOCTYPE html>
<html lang="en">
<head>
   ...
</head>

<body>
 <div id="outer">
  ...
 </div>
</body>
</html>
```

Most of the "action" in the CSS3-based code samples in this book takes place in the CSS3 selectors. In addition, the code for rendering 2D shapes in the HTML Canvas code samples consists of JavaScript code inside a <script> element. Consequently, knowledge of the new HTML tags is not needed to follow the examples in this book.

The only exception is Chapter 4, which contains MultiColumns1.html (with a few semantic tags) and the CSS stylesheet MultiColumns1.css with CSS3 selectors that render text in multiple columns. The HTML page can be understood even without knowing the semantics of the HTML tags in that example (and if need be, perform an Internet search for articles that explain the purpose of those tags).

CSS3 FEATURES AND BROWSER SUPPORT

There are two important details about defining CSS3-based selectors for HTML pages. First, different browsers (and different browser versions) support different CSS3 features. One of the best Web sites for finding this detailed level of information is here: *http://caniuse.com/*. This Web site contains tabular information regarding CSS3 support in Internet Explorer® (IE), Firefox®, Safari®, Chrome™, and Opera™ browsers.

The second detail is that some CSS3 properties require browser-specific prefixes for them to work correctly, which is answered by Claude 3 in the next section.

Browser-Specific Prefixes for CSS3

The following prompt was supplied to Claude 3 to obtain information regarding vendor-specific prefixes for CSS3 in HTML Web pages: `"Are vendor-specific prefixes required for CSS3 necessary for HTML Web pages?"`

Claude 3:

Vendor-specific prefixes for CSS3 properties and values were once necessary for ensuring cross-browser compatibility, especially during the early stages of CSS3 implementation. However, with the widespread adoption of modern browsers and the standardization of CSS3, vendor prefixes are becoming less necessary and are being phased out.

Here's a brief overview of vendor prefixes and their current status:

1. *Why were vendor prefixes used?* Vendor prefixes were introduced to allow browser vendors (like Mozilla, Google, Microsoft, and Apple) to implement experimental or nonstandard features in their browsers before those features were finalized in the CSS specification. This allowed developers to test and provide feedback on these features while they were still in development.

2. Common vendor prefixes:
   ○ `-webkit-` (Chrome, Safari, newer versions of Opera, and some older versions of Android browser)
   ○ `-moz-` (Firefox)
   ○ `-ms-` (Internet Explorer)
   ○ `-o-` (older versions of Opera)

3. *Current status of vendor prefixes:* As CSS3 features have become more widely adopted and standardized, the need for vendor prefixes has diminished. Most modern browsers now support the unprefixed version of CSS3 properties, and vendor prefixes are primarily used for backward compatibility with older browser versions.

4. *Best practices:* While vendor prefixes are still required for some older browser versions, it's generally recommended to use the unprefixed version of CSS3 properties and values whenever possible and include

vendor prefixes only when necessary for compatibility with older browsers that the Web site targets.

5. Many tools and frameworks, such as Autoprefixer, can automatically add the necessary vendor prefixes to the CSS based on the browser versions the user wants to support.

6. *Browser support:* The current browser support for CSS3 properties and features can be checked on Web sites like Can I Use (*https://caniuse. com/*). These resources will help to determine if vendor prefixes are still needed for specific properties or if the unprefixed version is widely supported.

In summary [by Claude 3], while vendor prefixes were necessary in the past to ensure cross-browser compatibility for CSS3 features, their importance has decreased as CSS3 standards have been widely adopted. However, vendor prefixes may still need to be included for older browser versions, depending on the browser support requirements of the Web site or application.

As an illustration, the following code block shows examples of vendor-specific prefixes:

- `-ie-webkit-border-radius: 8px;`
- `-moz-webkit-border-radius: 8px;`
- `-o-webkit-border-radius: 8px;`
- `border-radius: 8px;`

In CSS selectors, specify the attributes with browser-specific prefixes before the "generic" attribute, which serves as a default choice if the browser-specific attributes are not selected. The CSS3 code samples in this book contain Webkit-specific prefixes, which help keep the CSS stylesheets manageable in terms of size. If CSS stylesheets need to work on multiple browsers, there are essentially two options available. One option involves manually adding the CSS3 code with all the required browser-specific prefixes, which can be tedious to maintain and is also error prone. Another option is to use CSS frameworks that can programmatically generate the CSS3 code that contains all browser-specific prefixes.

A QUICK OVERVIEW OF CSS3 FEATURES

CSS3 adopts a modularized approach for extending existing CSS2 functionality as well as supporting new functionality. As such, CSS3 can be logically divided into the following categories:

- backgrounds/borders
- color
- media queries
- multicolumn layout
- selectors

CSS3 can create boxes with rounded corners and shadow effects; create rich graphics effects using linear and radial gradients; switch between portrait and landscape mode and detect the type of mobile device using media query selectors; produce multicolumn text rendering and formatting; and specify sophisticated node selection rules in selectors using first-child, last-child, first-of-type, and last-of-type.

CSS3 SHADOW EFFECTS AND ROUNDED CORNERS

CSS3 shadow effects are useful for creating vivid visual effects with simple selectors. Shadow effects can be used for text as well as rectangular regions. CSS3 also enables the user to easily render rectangles with rounded corners, so PNG files are not needed to create this effect.

CSS3 and Text Shadow Effects

A shadow effect for text can make a Web page look more vivid and appealing. Listing 3.1 displays the contents of the HTML page TextShadow1.html, illustrating how to render text with a shadow effect, and Listing 3.2 displays the contents of the CSS stylesheet TextShadow1.css that is referenced in Listing 3.1.

LISTING 3.1:   TextShadow1.html

```
<!DOCTYPE html>
<html lang="en">
<head>
  <title>CSS Text Shadow Example</title>
  <meta charset="utf-8" />
  <link href="TextShadow1.css" rel="stylesheet"
                               type="text/css">
</head>

<body>
  <div id="text1">
    Line One Shadow Effect
  </div>
  <div id="text2">
    Line Two Shadow Effect
  </div>
  <div id="text3">
    Line Three Vivid Effect
  </div>

  <div id="text4">
    <span id="dd">13</span>
    <span id="mm">August</span>
    <span id="yy">2024</span>
  </div>

  <div id="text5">
    <span id="dd">13</span>
```

```
      <span id="mm">August</span>
      <span id="yy">2024</span>
   </div>

   <div id="text6">
      <span id="dd">13</span>
      <span id="mm">August</span>
      <span id="yy">2024</span>
   </div>
</body>
</html>
```

The code in Listing 3.1 is straightforward: there is a reference to the CSS stylesheet TextShadow1.css, which contains two CSS selectors. One selector specifies how to render the HTML <div> element whose id attribute has value text1, and the other selector is applied to the HTML <div> element whose id attribute is text2. The CSS3 rotate() function is included in this example; a more detailed discussion of this function will be included later in this chapter.

LISTING 3.2:   TextShadow1.css

```
#text1 {
   font-size: 24pt;
   text-shadow: 2px 4px 5px #00f;
}

#text2 {
   font-size: 32pt;
   text-shadow: 0px 1px 6px #000,
                4px 5px 6px #f00;
}

#text3 {
   font-size: 40pt;
   text-shadow: 0px 1px 6px  #fff,
                2px 4px 4px  #0ff,
                4px 5px 6px  #00f,
                0px 0px 10px #444,
                0px 0px 20px #844,
                0px 0px 30px #a44,
                0px 0px 40px #f44;
}

#text4 {
   position: absolute;
   top: 200px;
   right: 200px;
   font-size: 48pt;
   text-shadow: 0px 1px 6px  #fff,
                2px 4px 4px  #0ff,
                4px 5px 6px  #00f,
                0px 0px 10px #000,
                0px 0px 20px #448,
                0px 0px 30px #a4a,
```

```
                    0px 0px 40px #fff;
   -webkit-transform: rotate(-90deg);
}

#text5 {
   position: absolute;
   left: 0px;
   font-size: 48pt;
   text-shadow: 2px 4px 5px #00f;
   -webkit-transform: rotate(-10deg);
}

#text6 {
   float: left;
   font-size: 48pt;
   text-shadow: 2px 4px 5px #f00;
   -webkit-transform: rotate(-170deg);
}

/* 'transform' is explained later */
#text1:hover, #text2:hover, #text3:hover,
#text4:hover, #text5:hover, #text6:hover {
-webkit-transform : scale(2) rotate(-45deg);
-transform : scale(2) rotate(-45deg);
}
```

The first selector in Listing 3.2 specifies a `font-size` of 24 and a `text-shadow` that renders text with a blue background (represented by the hexadecimal value `#00f`). The attribute `text-shadow` specifies (from left to right) the x-coordinate, y-coordinate, blur radius, and color of the shadow. The second selector specifies a `font-size` of 32 and a red shadow background (`#f00`). The third selector creates a richer visual effect by specifying multiple components in the `text-shadow` property, which were chosen by experimenting with effects that are possible with different values in the various components.

The final CSS3 selector creates an animation effect when users hover over any of the six text strings; the details of the animation will be deferred until later in this chapter. Figure 3.1 displays the result of applying the CSS stylesheet `TextShadow1.css` to the HTML `<div>` elements in the HTML page `TextShadow1.html`.

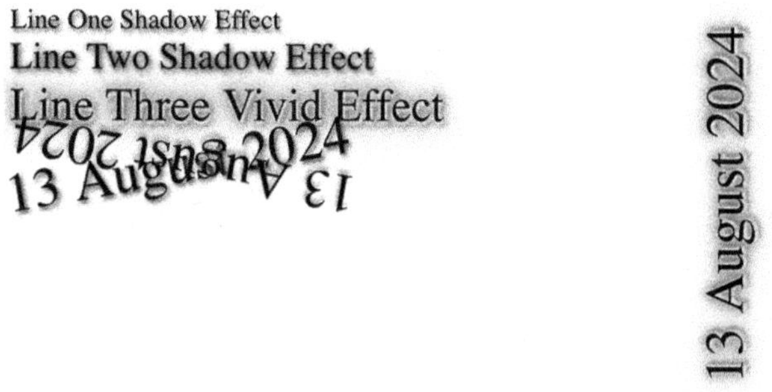

FIGURE 3.1: CSS3 text shadow effects

CSS3 and Box Shadow Effects

A shadow effect can also be applied to a box that encloses a text string, which can draw attention to specific parts of a Web page. The same caveat regarding overuse applies to box shadows. Listing 3.3 displays the contents of the HTML page BoxShadow1.html that renders a box shadow effect and Listing 3.4 displays the contents of BoxShadow1.css that contains the associated CSS3 selectors.

LISTING 3.3:   BoxShadow1.html

```
<!DOCTYPE html>
<html lang="en">
<head>
  <title>CSS Box Shadow Example</title>
  <meta charset="utf-8" />
  <link href="BoxShadow1.css" rel="stylesheet"
                              type="text/css">
</head>

<body>
  <div id="box1"> Line One with a Box Effect </div>
  <div id="box2"> Line Two with a Box Effect </div>
  <div id="box3"> Line Three with a Box Effect </div>
</body>
</html>
```

The code in Listing 3.3 references the CSS stylesheet BoxShadow1.css (instead of TextShadow1.css), which contains three CSS selectors. These selectors specify how to render the HTML <div> elements whose id attribute has the values box1, box2, and box3, respectively (and all three <div> elements are defined in BoxShadow1.html).

LISTING 3.4:   BoxShadow1.css

```
#box1 {
  position:relative;top:10px;
  width: 50%;
  height: 30px;
  font-size: 20px;
  -moz-box-shadow: 10px 10px 5px #800;
  -webkit-box-shadow: 10px 10px 5px #800;
  box-shadow: 10px 10px 5px #800;
}

#box2 {
  position:relative;top:20px;
  width: 80%;
  height: 50px;
  font-size: 36px;
  padding: 10px;
  -moz-box-shadow: 14px 14px 8px #008;
  -webkit-box-shadow: 14px 14px 8px #008;
```

```
  box-shadow: 14px 14px 8px #008;
}

#box3 {
  position:relative;top:30px;
  width: 80%;
  height: 60px;
  font-size: 52px;
  padding: 10px;
  -moz-box-shadow: 14px 14px 8px #008;
  -webkit-box-shadow: 14px 14px 8px #008;
  box-shadow: 14px 14px 8px #008;
}
```

The first selector in Listing 3.4 specifies the attributes `width`, `height`, and `font-size`, which control the dimensions of the associated HTML `<div>` element as well as the enclosed text string. The next three attributes consist of a Mozilla-specific `box-shadow` attribute, followed by a WebKit-specific `box-shadow` property, and finally the "generic" `box-shadow` attribute. Figure 3.2 displays the result of applying the CSS stylesheet `BoxShadow1.css` to the HTML page `BoxShadow1.html`.

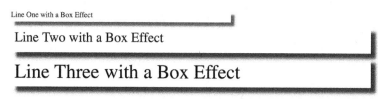

FIGURE 3.2: CSS3 box shadow effect

CSS3 and Rounded Corners

CSS3 makes it very easy to render rectangular shapes with rounded corners. Listing 3.5 displays the contents of the HTML page `RoundedCorners1.html` that renders text strings in rectangular shapes with rounded corners and Listing 3.6 displays the CSS file `RoundedCorners1.css`.

LISTING 3.5: RoundedCorners1.html

```
<!DOCTYPE html>
<html lang="en">
<head>
  <title>CSS Text Shadow Example</title>
  <meta charset="utf-8" />
  <link href="RoundedCorners1.css" rel="stylesheet"
                                    type="text/css">
</head>

<body>
  <div id="outer">
```

```
      <a href="#" class="anchor">Text Inside a Rounded
                                      Rectangle</a>
   </div>

   <div id="text1">
     Line One of Text with a Shadow Effect
   </div>

   <div id="text2">
     Line Two of Text with a Shadow Effect
   </div>
</body>
</html>
```

Listing 3.5 contains a reference to the CSS stylesheet RoundedCorners1. css that contains three CSS selectors that are applied to the elements whose id attribute has the values anchor, text1, and text2, respectively. The CSS selectors defined in the CSS file RoundedCorners1.css create visual effects that include rendering rectangles with rounded corners, and as will be seen, the hover "pseudo-selector" enables the creation of animation effects.

LISTING 3.6: RoundedCorners1.css

```
a.anchor:hover {
background: #00F;
}

a.anchor {
background: #FF0;
font-size: 24px;
font-weight: bold;
padding: 4px 4px;
color: rgba(255,0,0,0.8);
text-shadow: 0 1px 1px rgba(0,0,0,0.4);
-webkit-transition: all 2.0s ease;
-transition: all 2.0s ease;
-webkit-border-radius: 8px;
border-radius: 8px;
}

#text1 {
  font-size: 24pt;
  text-shadow: 2px 4px 5px #00f;
}

#text2 {
  font-size: 32pt;
  text-shadow: 4px 5px 6px #f00;
}

#round1 {
  -moz-border-radius-bottomleft: 20px;
  -moz-border-radius-bottomright: 20px;
  -moz-border-radius-topleft: 20px;
```

```
      -moz-border-radius-topright: 20px;
      -moz-box-shadow: 2px 2px 10px #ccc;
      -webkit-border-bottom-left-radius: 20px;
      -webkit-border-bottom-right-radius: 20px;
      -webkit-border-top-left-radius: 20px;
      -webkit-border-top-right-radius: 20px;
      -webkit-box-shadow: 2px 2px 10px #ccc;
      background-color: #f00;
      margin: 25px auto 0;
      padding: 25px 10px;
      text-align: center;
      width: 260px;
}
```

Listing 3.6 contains the selector a.anchor:hover, which changes the text color from yellow (#FF0) to blue (#00F) during a two-second interval when users hover over any anchor element with their mouse.

The selector a.anchor contains various attributes that specify the dimensions of the box that encloses the text in the <a> element, along with two new pairs of attributes. The first pair specifies the transition attribute (and a WebKit-specific prefix), which will be discussed later in this chapter. The second pair specifies the border-radius attribute (and the WebKit-specific attribute) whose value is 8px, which determines the radius (in pixels) of the rounded corners of the box that encloses the text in the <a> element. The last two selectors are identical to the selectors in Listing 3.1. Figure 3.3 displays the result of applying the CSS stylesheet RoundedCorners1.css to the elements in the HTML page RoundedCorners1.html.

Text Inside a Rounded Rectangle

Line One of Text with a Shadow Effect

Line Two of Text with a Shadow Effect

FIGURE 3.3: CSS3 rounded corners effect

CSS3 GRADIENTS

CSS3 supports linear gradients and radial gradients, which enable the creation of gradient effects that are as visually rich as gradients in other technologies such as SVG and Silverlight. The code samples in this section illustrate how to define linear gradients and radial gradients in CSS3 and then apply them to HTML elements.

Linear Gradients

CSS3 linear gradients require specifying one or more "color stops," each of which specifies a start color, an end color, and a rendering pattern. WebKit-based browsers support the following syntax to define a linear gradient:

- a start point
- an end point

- a start color using `from()`
- zero or more stop-colors
- an end color using `to()`

A start point can be specified as an (x, y) pair of numbers or percentages. For example, the pair (100, 25%) specifies the point that is 100 pixels to the right of the origin and 25% of the way down from the top of the screen. Recall that the origin is located in the upper-left corner of the screen. Listing 3.7 displays the contents of `LinearGradient1.html`, and Listing 3.8 displays the contents of `LinearGradient1.css`, which illustrate how to apply linear gradients to text strings that are enclosed in <p> elements and an <h3> element.

LISTING 3.7: LinearGradient1.html

```
<!doctype html>
<html lang="en">
<head>
  <title>CSS Linear Gradient Example</title>
  <meta charset="utf-8" />
  <link href="LinearGradient1.css" rel="stylesheet"
                                   type="text/css">
</head>

<body>
  <div id="outer">
    <p id="line1">line 1 with a linear gradient</p>
    <p id="line2">line 2 with a linear gradient</p>
    <p id="line3">line 3 with a linear gradient</p>
    <p id="line4">line 4 with a linear gradient</p>
    <p id="outline">line 5 with Shadow Outline</p>
    <h3><a href="#">A Line of Gradient Text</a></h3>
  </div>
</body>
</html>
```

Listing 3.7 is a simple Web page containing four <p> elements and one <h3> element. Listing 3.7 also references the CSS stylesheet `LinearGradient1.css`, which contains CSS selectors that are applied to the four <p> elements and the <h3> element in Listing 3.7.

LISTING 3.8: LinearGradient1.css

```
#line1 {
width: 50%;
font-size: 32px;
background-image: -webkit-gradient(linear, 0% 0%, 0% 100%,
                                  from(#fff), to(#f00));
background-image: -gradient(linear, 0% 0%, 0% 100%,
                           from(#fff), to(#f00));
-webkit-border-radius: 4px;
border-radius: 4px;
}
```

```
#line2 {
width: 50%;
font-size: 32px;
background-image: -webkit-gradient(linear, 100% 0%, 0% 100%,
                                   from(#fff), to(#ff0));
background-image: -gradient(linear, 100% 0%, 0% 100%,
                            from(#fff), to(#ff0));
-webkit-border-radius: 4px;
border-radius: 4px;
}

#line3 {
width: 50%;
font-size: 32px;
background-image: -webkit-gradient(linear, 0% 0%, 0% 100%,
                                   from(#f00), to(#00f));
background-image: -gradient(linear, 0% 0%, 0% 100%,
                            from(#f00), to(#00f));
-webkit-border-radius: 4px;
border-radius: 4px;
}

#line4 {
width: 50%;
font-size: 32px;
background-image: -webkit-gradient(linear, 100% 0%, 0% 100%,
                                   from(#f00), to(#00f));
background-image: -gradient(linear, 100% 0%, 0% 100%,
                            from(#f00), to(#00f));
-webkit-border-radius: 4px;
border-radius: 4px;
}

#outline {
font-size: 2.0em;
font-weight: bold;
color: #fff;
text-shadow: 1px 1px 1px rgba(0,0,0,0.5);
}

h3 {
width: 50%;
position: relative;
margin-top: 0;
font-size: 32px;
font-family: helvetica, ariel;
}

h3 a {
position: relative;
color: red;
text-decoration: none;
-webkit-mask-image:  -webkit-gradient(linear, left top,
                     left bottom, from(rgba(0,0,0,1)),
                     color-stop(50%, rgba(0,0,0,0.5)),
                     to(rgba(0,0,0,0)));
}
```

```
h3:after {
content:"This is a Line of Gradient Text";
color: blue;
}
```

The first selector in Listing 3.8 specifies a `font-size` of `32` for text, a `bor-der-radius` of 4 (which renders rounded corners), and a linear gradient that varies from white to blue, as shown here:

```
#line1 {
width: 50%;
font-size: 32px;
background-image: -webkit-gradient(linear, 0% 0%, 0% 100%,
                                   from(#fff), to(#f00));
background-image: -gradient(linear, 0% 0%, 0% 100%,
                            from(#fff), to(#f00));
-webkit-border-radius: 4px;
border-radius: 4px;
}
```

The first selector contains two attributes with a `-webkit-` prefix and two standard attributes without this prefix. Because the next three selectors in Listing 3.8 are similar to the first selector, their content will not be discussed.

The next CSS selector creates a text outline with a shadow effect by rendering the text in white with a thin black shadow, as shown here:

```
color: #fff;
text-shadow: 1px 1px 1px rgba(0,0,0,0.5);
```

The final portion of Listing 3.8 contains three selectors that affect the rendering of the <h3> element and its embedded <a> element: the `h3` selector specifies the width and font size; the `h3 a` selector specifies a linear gradient; and the `h3:after` selector specifies the text string to display. Note that other attributes are specified, but these are the main attributes for these selectors. Figure 3.4 displays the result of applying the selectors in the CSS stylesheet `LinearGradient1.css` to the HTML page `LinearGradient1.html`.

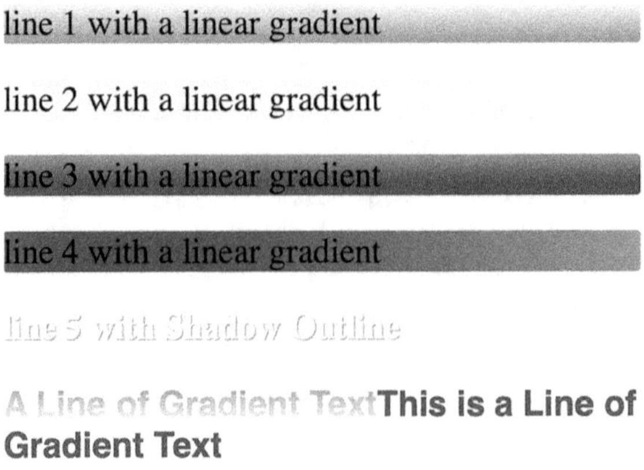

line 1 with a linear gradient

line 2 with a linear gradient

line 3 with a linear gradient

line 4 with a linear gradient

line 5 with Shadow Outline

A Line of Gradient Text**This is a Line of Gradient Text**

FIGURE 3.4: CSS3 linear gradient effect

Radial Gradients

CSS3 radial gradients are more complex than CSS3 linear gradients, but they can be used to create more complex gradient effects. WebKit-based browsers support the following syntax to define a radial gradient:

- a start point
- a start radius
- an end point
- an end radius
- a start color using `from()`
- zero or more stop-colors
- an end color using `to()`

Notice that the syntax for a radial gradient is similar to the syntax for a linear gradient, except that a start radius and an end radius must also be specified. Listing 3.9 displays the contents of `RadialGradient1.html`, and Listing 3.10 displays the contents of `RadialGradient1.css`, which illustrate how to render various circles with radial gradients.

LISTING 3.9: *RadialGradient1.html*

```
<!doctype html>
<html lang="en">
<head>
  <title>CSS Radial Gradient Example</title>
  <meta charset="utf-8" />
  <link href="RadialGradient9.css" rel="stylesheet"
                                    type="text/css">
</head>

<body>
 <div id="outer">
  <div id="radial3">Text3</div>
  <div id="radial2">Text2</div>
  <div id="radial4">Text4</div>
  <div id="radial1">Text1</div>
 </div>
</body>
</html>
```

Listing 3.9 contains five `<div>` elements whose `id` attribute has the values `outer`, `radial1`, `radial2`, `radial3`, and `radial4`, respectively. Listing 3.9 also references the CSS stylesheet `RadialGradient1.css`, which contains five CSS selectors that are applied to the five `<div>` elements.

LISTING 3.10: *RadialGradient1.css*

```
#outer {
position: relative; top: 10px; left: 0px;
}
```

```
#radial1 {
font-size: 24px;
width:  300px;
height: 300px;
position: absolute; top: 300px; left: 300px;

background: -webkit-gradient(
  radial, 500 40%, 0, 301 25%, 360, from(red),
  color-stop(0.05, orange), color-stop(0.4, yellow),
  color-stop(0.6, green), color-stop(0.8, blue),
  to(#fff)
 );
}

#radial2 {
font-size: 24px;
width:  500px;
height: 500px;
position: absolute; top: 100px; left: 100px;

background: -webkit-gradient(
  radial, 500 40%, 0, 301 25%, 360, from(red),
  color-stop(0.05, orange), color-stop(0.4, yellow),
  color-stop(0.6, green), color-stop(0.8, blue),
  to(#fff)
 );
}

#radial3 {
font-size: 24px;
width:  600px;
height: 600px;
position: absolute; top: 0px; left: 0px;

background: -webkit-gradient(
  radial, 500 40%, 0, 301 25%, 360, from(red),
  color-stop(0.05, orange), color-stop(0.4, yellow),
  color-stop(0.6, green), color-stop(0.8, blue),
  to(#fff)
 );
-webkit-box-shadow:  0px 0px 8px #000;
}

#radial4 {
font-size: 24px;
width:  400px;
height: 400px;
position: absolute; top: 200px; left: 200px;

background: -webkit-gradient(
  radial, 500 40%, 0, 301 25%, 360, from(red),
  color-stop(0.05, orange), color-stop(0.4, yellow),
  color-stop(0.6, green), color-stop(0.8, blue),
  to(#fff)
 );
}
```

The first part of the #radial1 selector in Listing 3.10 contains the attributes width and height that specify the dimensions of a rendered rectangle, and also a position attribute that is similar to the position attribute in the #outer selector. The #radial1 also contains a background attribute that defines a radial gradient using the -webkit- prefix, as shown here:

```
background: -webkit-gradient(
  radial, 100 25%, 20, 100 25%, 40, from(blue), to(#fff)
);
```

The preceding radial gradient specifies the following:

- a start point of (100, 25%)
- a start radius of 20
- an end point of (100, 25%)
- an end radius of 40
- a start color of blue
- an end color of white (#fff)

Notice that the start point and end point are the same, which renders a set of concentric circles that vary from blue to white.

The other four selectors in Listing 3.10 have the same syntax as the first selector, but the rendered radial gradients are significantly different. These and other effects can be created by specifying different start points and end points, and by specifying a start radius that is larger than the end radius.

The #radial4 selector creates a ringed effect by means of two stop-color attributes, as shown here:

```
color-stop(0.2, orange), color-stop(0.4, yellow),
color-stop(0.6, green), color-stop(0.8, blue),
```

Additional stop-color attributes can be added to create more complex radial gradients.

Figure 3.5 displays the result of applying the selectors in the CSS stylesheet RadialGradient1.css to the HTML page RadialGradient1.html.

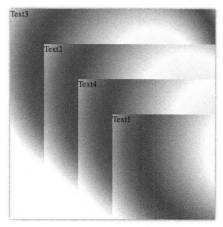

FIGURE 3.5: CSS3 radial gradient effect

CSS3 2D TRANSFORMS

In addition to transitions, CSS3 supports four transforms that can be applied to 2D shapes and PNG files. The four CSS3 transforms are `scale`, `rotate`, `skew`, and `translate`. The following sections contain code samples that illustrate how to apply each of these CSS3 transforms to a set of PNG files. The animation effects occur when users hover over any of the PNG files; moreover, partial animation effects can be created by moving the mouse quickly between adjacent PNG files.

Zoom Effects with Scale Transforms

The CSS3 `transform` attribute allows the user to specify the `scale()` function to create zoom in/out effects, and the syntax for the `scale()` method looks like this:

```
scale(someValue);
```

`someValue` can be replaced with any nonzero number. When `someValue` is between 0 and 1, the size of the 2D shape or PNG file will be reduced, creating a "zoom out" effect; values greater than 1 for `someValue` will increase the size of the 2D shape or PNG file, creating a "zoom in" effect; and a value of 1 does not make any changes.

Listing 3.11 displays the contents of `Scale1.html`, and Listing 3.12 displays the contents of `Scale1.css`, which illustrate how to scale PNG files to create a "hover box" image gallery.

LISTING 3.11: Scale1.html

```html
<!DOCTYPE html>
<html lang="en">
<head>
  <title>CSS Scale Transform Example</title>
  <meta charset="utf-8" />
  <link href="Scale1.css" rel="stylesheet" type="text/css">
</head>

<body>
  <header>
   <h1>Hover Over any of the Images:</h1>
  </header>

  <div id="outer">
    <img src="Clown1.png"     class="scaled" width="150"
                                              height="150"/>
    <img src="Avocadoes1.png" class="scaled" width="150"
                                              height="150"/>
    <img src="Clown1.png"     class="scaled" width="150"
                                              height="150"/>
    <img src="Avocadoes1.png" class="scaled" width="150"
                                              height="150"/>
  </div>
```

```
</body>
</html>
```

Listing 3.11 references the CSS stylesheet Scale1.css, which contains selectors for creating scaled effects, and four HTML <img> elements that reference the PNG files Clown1.png and Avocadoes1.png. The remainder of Listing 3.11 is straightforward, with simple boilerplate text and HTML elements.

LISTING 3.12: Scale1.css

```
#outer {
float: left;
position: relative; top: 50px; left: 50px;
}

img {
-webkit-transition: -webkit-transform 1.0s ease;
-transition: transform 1.0s ease;
}

img.scaled {
  -webkit-box-shadow: 10px 10px 5px #800;
  box-shadow: 10px 10px 5px #800;
}

img.scaled:hover {
-webkit-transform : scale(2);
-transform : scale(2);
}
```

The img selector in Listing 3.12 specifies a transition property that contains a transform effect that occurs during a one-second interval using the ease function, as shown here:

```
-transition: transform 1.0s ease;
```

Next, the selector img.scaled specifies a box-shadow property that creates a reddish shadow effect (displayed in Figure 3.2), as shown here:

```
img.scaled {
  -webkit-box-shadow: 10px 10px 5px #800;
  box-shadow: 10px 10px 5px #800;
}
```

Finally, the selector img.scaled:hover specifies a transform attribute that uses the scale() function to double the size of the associated PNG file when users hover over any of the <img> elements with their mouse, as shown here:

```
-transform : scale(2);
```

Because the img selector specifies a one-second interval using an ease function, the scaling effect will last for one second. Experiment with different values for the CSS3 scale() function and different values for the time interval to create the animation effects that suit one's needs.

Scaling can be done both horizontally and vertically:

```
img {
-webkit-transition: -webkit-transform 1.0s ease;
-transition: transform 1.0s ease;
}

img.mystyle:hover {
-webkit-transform : scaleX(1.5) scaleY(0.5);
-transform : scaleX(1.5) scaleY(0.5);
}
```

Figure 3.6 displays the result of applying the selectors in the CSS stylesheet Scale1.css to the HTML page Scale1.html.

Hover Over any of the Images:

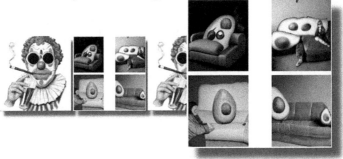

FIGURE 3.6: CSS3 Scaling Effects For Images

Rotate Transforms

The CSS3 transform attribute allows you to specify the rotate() function in order to create scaling effects, and its syntax looks like this:

```
rotate(someValue);
```

someValue can be replaced with any number. When someValue is positive, the rotation is clockwise; when someValue is negative, the rotation is counterclockwise; and when someValue is zero, there is no rotation effect. In all cases, the initial position for the rotation effect is the positive horizontal axis. Listing 3.13 displays the contents of Rotate1.html, and Listing 3.14 displays the contents of Rotate1.css, which illustrate how to rotate PNG files in opposite directions.

LISTING 3.13:   Rotate1.html

```
<!DOCTYPE html>
<html lang="en">
<head>
  <title>CSS Rotate Transform Example</title>
  <meta charset="utf-8" />
```

```
    <link href="Rotate1.css" rel="stylesheet" type="text/css">
</head>

<body>
  <header>
   <h1>Hover Over any of the Images:</h1>
  </header>

  <div id="outer">
    <img src="Clown1.png"     class="imageL" width="150"
                                              height="150"/>
    <img src="Avocadoes1.png" class="imageR" width="150"
                                              height="150"/>
    <img src="Clown1.png"     class="imageL" width="150"
                                              height="150"/>
    <img src="Avocadoes1.png" class="imageR" width="150"
                                              height="150"/>
  </div>
</body>
</html>
```

Listing 3.13 references the CSS stylesheet Rotate1.css, which contains selectors for creating rotation effects, and an HTML <img> element that references the PNG files Clown1.png and Avocadoes1.png. The remainder of Listing 3.13 consists of simple boilerplate text and HTML elements.

LISTING 3.14:   *Rotate1.css*

```
#outer {
float: left;
position: relative; top: 100px; left: 150px;
}

img {
-webkit-transition: -webkit-transform 1.0s ease;
-transition: transform 1.0s ease;
}

img.imageL {
  -webkit-box-shadow: 14px 14px 8px #800;
  box-shadow: 14px 14px 8px #800;
}

img.imageR {
  -webkit-box-shadow: 14px 14px 8px #008;
  box-shadow: 14px 14px 8px #008;
}

img.imageL:hover {
-webkit-transform : scale(2) rotate(-45deg);
-transform : scale(2) rotate(-45deg);
}

img.imageR:hover {
-webkit-transform : scale(2) rotate(360deg);
```

```
-transform : scale(2) rotate(360deg);
}
```

Listing 3.14 contains the `img` selector that specifies a `transition` attribute that creates an animation effect during a one-second interval using the `ease` timing function, as shown here:

```
-transition: transform 1.0s ease;
```

Next, the selectors `img.imageL` and `img.imageR` contain a property that renders a reddish and bluish background shadow, respectively.

The selector `img.imageL:hover` specifies a `transform` attribute that performs a counterclockwise scaling effect (doubling the original size) and a rotation effect (45 degrees counterclockwise) when users hover over the `<img>` element with their mouse, as shown here:

```
-transform : scale(2) rotate(-45deg);
```

The selector `img.imageR:hover` is similar, except that it performs a clockwise rotation of 360 degrees. Figure 3.7 displays the result of applying the selectors in the CSS stylesheet `Rotate1.css` to the elements in the HTML page `Rotate1.html`.

Hover Over any of the Images:

FIGURE 3.7: CSS3 rotation effect

Skew Transforms

The CSS3 transform attribute allows specifying the `skew()` function to create skewing effects, and its syntax looks like this:

```
skew(xAngle, yAngle);
```

`xAngle` and `yAngle` can be replaced with any number. When `xAngle` and `yAngle` are positive, the skew effect is clockwise; when `xAngle` and `yAngle` are negative, the skew effect is counterclockwise; and when `xAngle` and `yAngle` are zero, there is no skew effect. In all cases, the initial position for the skew effect is the positive horizontal axis. Listing 3.15 displays the contents of `Skew1.html`, and Listing 3.16 displays the contents of `Skew1.css`, which illustrates how to skew a PNG file.

LISTING 3.15: Skew1.html

```
<!DOCTYPE html>
<html lang="en">
<head>
  <title>CSS Skew Transform Example</title>
  <meta charset="utf-8" />
  <link href="Skew1.css" rel="stylesheet" type="text/css">
</head>

<body>
  <header>
   <h1>Hover Over any of the Images:</h1>
  </header>

  <div id="outer">
    <img src="Clown1.png"     class="skewed1" width="150"
                                           height="150"/>
    <img src="Avocadoes1.png" class="skewed2" width="150"
                                           height="150"/>
    <img src="Clown1.png"     class="skewed3" width="150"
                                           height="150"/>
    <img src="Avocadoes1.png" class="skewed4" width="150"
                                           height="150"/>
  </div>

</body>
</html>
```

Listing 3.15 references the CSS stylesheet `Skew1.css`, which contains selectors for creating skew effects, and an `<img>` element that references the PNG files `Clown1.png` and `Avocadoes1.png`. The remainder of Listing 3.15 consists of simple boilerplate text and HTML elements.

LISTING 3.16: Skew1.html

```
#outer {
float: left;
position: relative; top: 100px; left: 100px;
}

img {
-webkit-transition: -webkit-transform 1.0s ease;
-transition: transform 1.0s ease;
}

img.skewed1 {
  -webkit-box-shadow: 14px 14px 8px #800;
  box-shadow: 14px 14px 8px #800;
}
```

```
img.skewed2 {
  -webkit-box-shadow: 14px 14px 8px #880;
  box-shadow: 14px 14px 8px #880;
}

img.skewed3 {
  -webkit-box-shadow: 14px 14px 8px #080;
  box-shadow: 14px 14px 8px #080;
}

img.skewed4 {
  -webkit-box-shadow: 14px 14px 8px #008;
  box-shadow: 14px 14px 8px #008;
}

img.skewed1:hover {
-webkit-transform : scale(2) skew(-10deg, -30deg);
-transform : scale(2) skew(-10deg, -30deg);
}

img.skewed2:hover {
-webkit-transform : scale(2) skew(10deg, 30deg);
-transform : scale(2) skew(10deg, 30deg);
}

img.skewed3:hover {
-webkit-transform : scale(0.4) skew(-10deg, -30deg);
-transform : scale(0.4) skew(-10deg, -30deg);
}

img.skewed4:hover {
-webkit-transform : scale(0.5, 1.5) skew(10deg, -30deg);
-transform : scale(0.5, 1.5) skew(10deg, -30deg);
opacity:0.5;
}
```

Listing 3.16 contains the img selector that specifies a transition attribute that creates an animation effect during a one-second interval using the ease timing function, as shown here:

```
-transition: transform 1.0s ease;
```

The four selectors img.skewed1, img.skewed2, img.skewed3, and img.skewed4 create background shadow effects with darker shades of red, yellow, green, and blue, respectively (all of which were used in earlier code samples). The selector img.skewed1:hover specifies a transform attribute that performs a skew effect when users hover over the first <img> element with their mouse, as shown here:

```
-transform : scale(2) skew(-10deg, -30deg);
```

The other three CSS3 selectors also use a combination of the CSS functions skew() and scale()to create distinct visual effects. Notice that the fourth hover selector also sets the opacity property to 0.5, which is applied in parallel with the other effects in this selector. Figure 3.8 displays the result of applying the selectors in the CSS stylesheet `Skew1.css` to the elements in the HTML page `Skew1.html`.

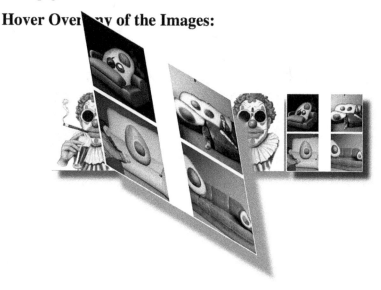

FIGURE 3.8: CSS3 skew effect

Translate Transforms

The CSS3 transform attribute allows you to specify the `translate()` function to create translation or "shifting" effects, and its syntax looks like this:

```
translate(xDirection, yDirection);
```

The translation is in relation to the origin, which is the upper-left corner of the screen. Thus, positive values for `xDirection` and `yDirection` produce a shift toward the right and a shift downward, respectively, whereas negative values for `xDirection` and `yDirection` produce a shift toward the left and a shift upward; zero values for `xDirection` and `yDirection` do not cause any translation effect. Listing 3.17 displays the contents of `Translate1.html`, and Listing 3.18 displays the contents of `Translate1.css`, which illustrate how to apply a translation effect to a PNG file.

LISTING 3.17:   *Translate1.html*

```
<!DOCTYPE html>
<html lang="en">
<head>
  <title>CSS Translate Transform Example</title>
  <meta charset="utf-8" />
  <link href="Translate1.css" rel="stylesheet" type="text/
                                                    css">
</head>
```

```
<body>
  <header>
   <h1>Hover Over any of the Images:</h1>
  </header>

  <div id="outer">
    <img src="Clown1.png"     class="trans1" width="150"
                                              height="150"/>
    <img src="Avocadoes1.png" class="trans2" width="150"
                                              height="150"/>
    <img src="Clown1.png"     class="trans3" width="150"
                                              height="150"/>
    <img src="Avocadoes1.png" class="trans4" width="150"
                                              height="150"/>
  </div>
</body>
</html>
```

Listing 3.17 references the CSS stylesheet Translate1.css, which contains selectors for creating translation effects, and an <img> element that references the PNG files Clown1.png and Avocadoes1.png. The remainder of Listing 3.17 consists of straightforward boilerplate text and HTML elements.

LISTING 3.18:   Translate1.css

```
#outer {
float: left;
position: relative; top: 100px; left: 100px;
}

img {
-webkit-transition: -webkit-transform 1.0s ease;
-transition: transform 1.0s ease;
}

img.trans1 {
  -webkit-box-shadow: 14px 14px 8px #800;
  box-shadow: 14px 14px 8px #800;
}

img.trans2 {
  -webkit-box-shadow: 14px 14px 8px #880;
  box-shadow: 14px 14px 8px #880;
}

img.trans3 {
  -webkit-box-shadow: 14px 14px 8px #080;
  box-shadow: 14px 14px 8px #080;
}

img.trans4 {
  -webkit-box-shadow: 14px 14px 8px #008;
  box-shadow: 14px 14px 8px #008;
}
```

```
img.trans1:hover {
-webkit-transform : scale(2) translate(100px, 50px);
-transform : scale(2) translate(100px, 50px);
}

img.trans2:hover {
-webkit-transform : scale(0.5) translate(-50px, -50px);
-transform : scale(0.5) translate(-50px, -50px);
}

img.trans3:hover {
-webkit-transform : scale(0.5,1.5) translate(0px, 0px);
-transform : scale(0.5,1.5) translate(0px, 0px);
}

img.trans4:hover {
-webkit-transform : scale(2) translate(50px, -50px);
-transform : scale(2) translate(100px, 50px);
}
```

Listing 3.17 contains the img selector that specifies a transform effect during a one-second interval using the ease timing function, as shown here:

```
-transition: transform 1.0s ease;
```

The four selectors img.trans1, img.trans2, img.trans3, and img. trans4 create background shadow effects with darker shades of red, yellow, green, and blue, respectively, just as in the previous section.

The selector img.trans1:hover specifies a transform attribute that performs a scale effect and a translation effect when users hover over the first <img> element with their mouse, as shown here:

```
-webkit-transform : scale(2) translate(100px, 50px);
transform : scale(2) translate(100px, 50px);
```

The other three selectors contain similar code involving a combination of a translate and a scaling effect, each of which creates a distinct visual effect. Figure 3.9 displays the result of applying the selectors defined in the CSS3 stylesheet Translate1.css to the elements in the HTML page Translate1.html.

Hover Over any of the Images:

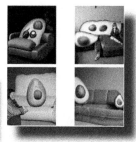

FIGURE 3.9. PNG files with CSS3 scale and translate effects.

SUMMARY

This chapter showed how to create graphics effects and shadow effects, as well as how to use transforms in CSS3. It illustrated how to create animation effects that can be applied to HTML elements. You also learned how to render rounded rectangles, create shadow effects for text and 2D shapes, create linear and radial gradients, use the methods `translate()`, `rotate()`, `skew()`, and `scale()`, and create CSS3-based animation effects.

CHAPTER 4

CSS3 3D ANIMATION

This chapter continues the discussion of CSS3 that began in Chapter 3, with a focus on examples of creating 3D effects and 3D animation effects. This first part of this chapter shows how to display a CSS3-based cube, followed by examples of CSS3 transitions for creating simple animation effects, such as glow effects and bouncing effects. Specifically, CSS3 keyframe and the CSS3 functions scale3d(), rotate3d(), and translate3d() are used to create 3D animation effects. The second part of this chapter contains examples of creating glowing effects, fading image effects, and bouncing effects. The creation of CSS3 effects for text and how to render multicolumn text will also be explained. The third part of this chapter briefly discusses CSS3 media queries, which enable the user to render a given HTML page based on the properties of the device.

JavaScript can also be used to create visual effects that can be easier than using CSS3 alone. Moreover, CSS3 media queries can be used for rendering HTML5 pages differently on mobile devices. Neither of these topics is covered in this book, but an Internet search will provide various links and tutorials that contain information on these topics.

A CSS3-BASED CUBE

You can use the CSS3 transforms rotate(), scale(), and skew() to create and render a 3D cube with gradient shading. Listing 4.1 displays the contents of 3DCubeHover1.html and Listing 4.2 displays the contents of 3DCubeHover1.css, which illustrate how to simulate a cube in CSS3.

LISTING 4.1:   3DCubeHover1.html

```
<!DOCTYPE html>
<html lang="en">
```

```
<head>
  <title>CSS 3D Cube Example</title>
  <meta charset="utf-8" />
    <link href="3DCSS1.css" rel="stylesheet" type="text/css">
</head>

<body>
  <header>
    <h1>Hover Over the Cube Faces:</h1>
  </header>

 <div id="outer">
  <div id="top">Text1</div>
  <div id="left">Text2</div>
  <div id="right">Text3</div>
 </div>
</body>
</html>
```

Listing 4.1 is a straightforward HTML page that references the CSS stylesheet 3DCSS1.css, which contains the CSS3 selectors for styling the HTML <div> elements in this Web page.

LISTING 4.2: `3DCSS1.css`

```
/* animation effects */
#right:hover {
-webkit-transition: -webkit-transform 3.0s ease;
-transition: transform 3.0s ease;

-webkit-transform : scale(1.2) skew(-10deg, -30deg)
rotate(-45deg);
-transform : scale(1.2) skew(-10deg, -30deg) rotate(-45deg);
}

#left:hover {
-webkit-transition: -webkit-transform 2.0s ease;
-transition: transform 2.0s ease;

-webkit-transform : scale(0.8) skew(-10deg, -30deg)
rotate(-45deg);
-transform : scale(0.8) skew(-10deg, -30deg) rotate(-45deg);
}

#top:hover {
-webkit-transition: -webkit-transform 2.0s ease;
-transition: transform 2.0s ease;

-webkit-transform : scale(0.5) skew(-20deg, -30deg)
rotate(45deg);
-transform : scale(0.5) skew(-20deg, -30deg) rotate(45deg);
}

/* size and position */
#right, #left, #top {
```

```
position:relative;   padding: 0px;   width: 200px;
                                      height: 200px;
}

#left {
  font-size: 48px;
  left: 20px;

  background-image:
    -webkit-radial-gradient(red 4px, transparent 28px),
    -webkit-repeating-radial-gradient(red 0px,   yellow 4px,
                                      green 8px, red 12px,
                                      transparent 26px,
                                      blue 20px, red 24px,
                                      transparent 28px,
                                      blue 12px),
    -webkit-repeating-radial-gradient(red 0px,   yellow 4px,
                                      green 8px, red 12px,
                                      transparent 26px,
                                      blue 20px, red 24px,
                                      transparent 28px,
                                      blue 12px);

  background-size: 100px 40px, 40px 100px;
  background-position: 0 0;

  -webkit-transform: skew(0deg, 30deg);
}

#right {
  font-size: 48px;
  width:   170px;
  top: -192px;
  left: 220px;

  background-image:
    -webkit-radial-gradient(red 4px, transparent 48px),
    -webkit-repeating-linear-gradient(0deg, red 5px,
                                      green 4px,
                                      yellow 8px,
                                      blue 12px,
                                      transparent 16px,
                                      red 20px, blue 24px,
                                      transparent 28px,
                                      transparent 32px),
    -webkit-radial-gradient(blue 8px, transparent 68px);

  background-size: 120px 120px, 24px 24px;
  background-position: 0 0;

  -webkit-transform: skew(0deg, -30deg);
}

#top {
  font-size: 48px;
  top: 50px;
```

```
    left: 105px;

    background-image:
      -webkit-radial-gradient(white 2px, transparent 8px),
      -webkit-repeating-linear-gradient(45deg, white 2px,
                                  yellow 8px,
                                  green 4px, red 12px,
                                  transparent 26px,
                                  blue 20px, red 24px,
                                  transparent 28px,
                                  blue 12px),
      -webkit-repeating-linear-gradient(-45deg, white 2px,
                                  yellow 8px,
                                  green 4px, red 12px,
                                  transparent 26px,
                                  blue 20px, red 24px,
                                  transparent 28px,
                                  blue 12px);

    background-size: 100px 30px, 30px 100px;
    background-position: 0 0;

    -webkit-transform: rotate(60deg) skew(0deg, -30deg);
scale(1, 1.16);
}
```

The first three selectors in Listing 4.2 define the animation effects when users hover on the top, left, or right faces of the cube. In particular, the #right:hover selector performs an animation effect during a three-second interval when users hover over the right face of the cube, as shown here:

```
#right:hover {
-webkit-transition: -webkit-transform 3.0s ease;
-transition: transform 3.0s ease;

-webkit-transform : scale(1.2) skew(-10deg, -30deg)
                    rotate(-45deg);
-transform : scale(1.2) skew(-10deg, -30deg)
                    rotate(-45deg);
}
```

The transition attribute is already familiar, and notice that the transform attribute specifies the CSS3 transform functions scale(), skew(), and rotate(), all of which were seen already in this chapter. These three functions are applied simultaneously, which means that a scaling, skewing, and rotating effect will happen at the same time instead of sequentially.

The last three selectors in Listing 4.2 define the properties of each face of the cube. For example, the #left selector specifies the font size for some text and also positional attributes for the left face of the cube. The most complex portion of the #left selector is the value of the background-image attribute, which consists of a WebKit-specific combination of a radial gradient, a repeating radial gradient, and another radial gradient. Notice that the left face is a rectangle that is transformed into a parallelogram using this line of code:

```
-webkit-transform: skew(0deg, -30deg);
```

The `#top` selector and `#right` selector contain code that is comparable to the `#left` selector, and one can experiment with their values to create other visual effects. Figure 4.1 displays the result of applying the CSS selectors in `3DCube1.css` to the `<div>` elements in the HTML page `3DCube1.html`.

Hover Over the Cube Faces:

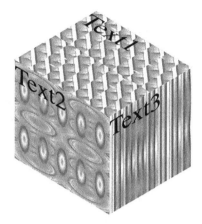

FIGURE 4.1: A Cube Rendered Via CSS3 Selectors

CSS3 TRANSITIONS

CSS3 transitions involve changes to CSS values in a smooth fashion, and they are initiated by user gestures, such as mouse clicks, focus, or hover effects. WebKit originally developed CSS3 transitions, and they are also supported in many versions of Safari, Chrome, Opera, and Firefox by using browser-specific prefixes. Keep in mind that there are toolkits (such as jQuery and Prototype) that support transitions effects similar to their CSS3-based counterparts.

The basic syntax for creating a CSS transition is a "triple" that specifies:

- a CSS property
- a duration (in seconds)
- a transition timing function

Here is an example of a WebKit-based transition:

```
-webkit-transition-property: background;
-webkit-transition-duration: 0.5s;
-webkit-transition-timing-function: ease;
```

Fortunately, these transitions can also be combined in one line, as shown here:

```
-webkit-transition: background 0.5s ease;
```

Here is an example of a CSS3 selector that includes these transitions:

```
a.foo {
padding: 3px 6px;
background: #f00;
-webkit-transition: background 0.5s ease;
}

a.foo:focus, a.foo:hover {
background: #00f;
}
```

Transitions currently require browser-specific prefixes for them to work correctly in browsers that are not based on WebKit. Here is an example for Internet Explorer (IE), Firefox, and Opera:

```
-ie-webkit-transition: background 0.5s ease;
-moz-webkit-transition: background 0.5s ease;
-o-webkit-transition: background 0.5s ease;
```

Currently, one of the following transition timing functions can be specified (using browser-specific prefixes):

- `ease`
- `ease-in`
- `ease-out`
- `ease-in-out`
- `cubic-bezier`

If these transition functions are not sufficient, custom functions can be created using this online tool: *www.matthewlein.com/ceaser*. Many properties can be specified with `-webkit-transition-property`, and an extensive list of properties is at:

https://developer.mozilla.org/en/CSS/CSS_transitions.

SIMPLE CSS3 ANIMATION EFFECTS

The CSS3-based code samples seen so far involved primarily static visual effects (although it was explained how to use the hover pseudo-selector to create an animation effect). The CSS3 code samples in this section illustrate how to create "glowing" effects and "bouncing" effects for form-based elements.

Glowing Effects

Keyframes and the hover pseudo-selector can be combined to create an animation effect when users hover with their mouse on a specific element in an HTML page. Listing 4.3 displays the contents of `Transition1.html` and Listing 4.4 displays the contents of `Transition1.css`, which contain CSS3 selectors that create a glowing effect on an input field.

LISTING 4.3: `Transition1.html`

```
<!DOCTYPE html>
<html lang="en">
<head>
  <title>CSS Animation Example</title>
  <meta charset="utf-8" />
  <link href="Transition1.css" rel="stylesheet"
                               type="text/css">
</head>

<body>
  <div id="outer">
    <input id="input" type="text" value="This is an input
                                         line"</input>
  </div>
</body>
</html>
```

Listing 4.3 is a simple HTML page that contains a reference to the CSS stylesheet `Transition1.css` and one HTML `<div>` element that contains an `<input>` field element. As will be seen, an animation effect is created when users hover over the `<input>` element with their mouse.

LISTING 4.4: *Transition1.css*

```
#outer {
position: relative; top: 20px; left: 20px;
}

@-webkit-keyframes glow {
  0% {
    -webkit-box-shadow: 0 0 24px rgba(255, 255, 255, 0.5);
  }
  50% {
    -webkit-box-shadow: 0 0 24px rgba(255, 0, 0, 0.9);
  }
  100% {
    -webkit-box-shadow: 0 0 24px rgba(255, 255, 255, 0.5);
  }
}

#input {
font-size: 24px;
-webkit-border-radius: 4px;
border-radius: 4px;
}

#input:hover {
 -webkit-animation: glow 2.0s 3 ease;
}
```

Listing 4.4 contains a keyframes selector (called `glow`) that specifies three shadow effects. The first shadow effect (which occurs at time 0 of the animation effect) renders a white color whose opacity is 0.5. The second shadow effect (at the midway point of the animation effect) renders a red color whose opacity is 0.9. The third shadow effect (which occurs at the end of the animation effect) is the same as the first animation effect.

The #input selector is applied to the input field in Transition1.html to render a rounded rectangle. The #input:hover selector uses the glow keyframes to create an animation effect for a two-second interval, repeated three times, using an ease function, as shown here:

```
-webkit-animation: glow 2.0s 3 ease;
```

Figure 4.2 displays the result of applying the selectors in Transition1.css to the elements in the HTML page Transition1.html. Note that you will see this effect during an actual animation when you launch the Web page.

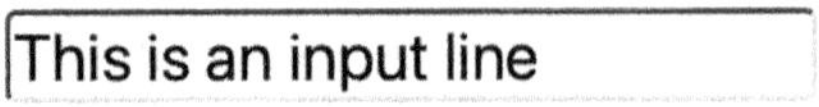

This is an input line

FIGURE 4.2: CSS3 glowing transition effect

Image Fading and Rotating Effects with CSS3

This section shows how to create a fading effect with JPG images. Listing 4.5 displays the contents of FadeRotateImages1.html and Listing 4.6 displays the contents of FadeRotateImages1.css, which illustrate how to create a "fading" effect on a JPG file and a glowing effect on another JPG file.

LISTING 4.5: *FadeRotateImages1.html*

```
<!DOCTYPE html>
<html lang="en">
<head>
  <title>CSS3 Fade and Rotate Images</title>
  <meta charset="utf-8" />
  <link href="FadeRotateImages1.css" rel="stylesheet"
                                     type="text/css">
</head>

<body>
  <div id="outer">
    <img class="lower" width="200" height="200"
                                   src="Clown1.png" />
    <img class="upper" width="200" height="200"
                                   src="Avocadoes1.png" />
  </div>

  <div id="third">
    <img width="200" height="200" src="Clown1.png" />
  </div>
</body>
```

Listing 4.5 contains a reference to the CSS stylesheet `FadingImages1.css` that contains CSS selectors for creating a fading effect and a glowing effect. The first HTML `<div>` element in Listing 4.5 contains two `<img>` elements; when users hover over the rendered JPG file, it will "fade" and reveal another JPG file. The second HTML `<div>` element contains one `<img>` element, and when users hover over this JPG, a CSS3 selector will rotate the referenced JPG file about the vertical axis.

LISTING 4.6:   *FadeRotateImages1.css*

```
#outer {
 position: absolute; top: 20px; left: 20px;
 margin: 0 auto;
}

#outer img {
 position:absolute; left:0;
 -webkit-transition: opacity 1s ease-in-out;
 transition: opacity 1s ease-in-out;
}

#outer img.upper:hover {
  opacity:0;
}

#third img {
position: absolute; top: 20px; left: 250px;
}

#third img:hover {
 -webkit-animation: rotatey 2.0s 3 ease;
}

@-webkit-keyframes rotatey {
  0% {
    -webkit-transform: rotateY(45deg);
  }
  50% {
    -webkit-transform: rotateY(90deg);
  }
  100% {
    -webkit-transform: rotateY(0);
  }
}
```

The details of the code in Listing 4.6 that are already familiar will be skipped. The important point for creating the fading effect is to set the opacity value to 0 when users hover over the leftmost image, and the one line of code in the CSS selector is shown here:

```
#outer img.upper:hover {
  opacity:0;
}
```

As can be seen, this code sample shows that it is possible to create attractive visual effects without complicated code or logic.

Next, Listing 4.6 defines a CSS3 selector that creates a rotation effect about the vertical axis by invoking the CSS3 function `rotateY()` in the keyframe `rotatey`. Note that a rotation effect can be created about the other two axes by replacing `rotateY()` with the CSS3 function `rotateX()` or the CSS3 function `rotateZ()`. These three functions can even be used in the same keyframe to create 3D effects. CSS3 3D effects are discussed in more detail later in this chapter. Figure 4.3 displays the result of applying the selectors in the CSS stylesheet `FadeRotateImages1.css` to `FadeRotateImages1.html`.

FIGURE 4.3: CSS3 fade and rotate JPG effects

Bouncing Effects

This section shows you how to create a "bouncing" animation effect. Listing 4.7 displays the contents of `Bounce2.html` and Listing 4.8 displays the contents of `Bounce2.css`, which illustrate how to create a bouncing effect on an input field.

LISTING 4.7: Bounce2.html

```
<!DOCTYPE html>
<html lang="en">
<head>
  <title>CSS Animation Example</title>
  <meta charset="utf-8" />
  <link href="Bounce2.css" rel="stylesheet" type="text/css">
</head>

<body>
  <div id="outer">
    <input id="input" type="text" value="An input line"/ >
  </div>
</body>
</html>
```

Listing 4.7 is another straightforward HTML page that contains a reference to the CSS stylesheet `Bounce2.css` and one HTML `<div>` element that contains an `<input>` field element. The CSS stylesheet creates a bouncing animation effect when users hover over the `<input>` element with their mouse.

LISTING 4.8: `Bounce2.css`

```
#outer {
position: relative; top: 50px; left: 100px;
}

@-webkit-keyframes bounce {
  0% {
    left: 50px;
    top: 100px;
    background-color: #ff0000;
  }
  25% {
    left: 100px;
    top: 150px;
    background-color: #ffff00;
  }
  50% {
    left: 50px;
    top: 200px;
    background-color: #00ff00;
  }
  75% {
    left: 0px;
    top: 150px;
    background-color: #0000ff;
  }
  100% {
    left: 50px;
    top: 100px;
    background-color: #ff0000;
  }
}

#input {
font-size: 24px;
-webkit-border-radius: 4px;
border-radius: 4px;
}

#outer:hover {
 -webkit-animation: bounce 2.0s 4 ease;
}
```

Listing 4.8 contains a keyframes selector (called bounce) that specifies five-time intervals: the 0%, 25%, 50%, 75%, and 100% points of the duration of the animation effect. Each time interval specifies values for the attributes left, top, and background color of the `<input>` field. Despite the simplicity of this keyframes selector, it creates a pleasing animation effect.

The #input selector is applied to the input field in `Bounce2.html` to render a rounded rectangle. The #input:hover selector uses the bounce keyframes to create an animation effect for a two-second interval, repeated four times, using an ease function, as shown here:

```
-webkit-animation: bounce 2.0s 4 ease;
```

Figure 4.4 displays the result of applying the selectors in the CSS stylesheet `Bounce2.css` to the elements in the HTML page `Bounce2.html`. Note that you will see this effect during an actual animation when you launch the Web page.

An input line

FIGURE 4.4: CSS3 bouncing animation effect

CSS3 EFFECTS FOR TEXT

Examples of rendering text strings as part of several code samples are shown in the previous chapter. In this section, a new feature of CSS3 is discussed that enables rendering text in multiple columns.

Rendering Multicolumn Text

CSS3 supports multicolumn text, which can create a nice visual effect when a Web page contains significant amounts of text. Listing 4.9 displays the contents of `MultiColumns1.html` and Listing 4.10 displays the contents of `MultiColumns1.css`, which illustrate how to render multicolumn text.

LISTING 4.9: MultiColumns1.html

```
<!doctype html>
<html lang="en">
<head>
  <title>CSS Multi Columns Example</title>
  <meta charset="utf-8" />
  <link href="MultiColumns1.css" rel="stylesheet"
type="text/css">
</head>

<body>
  <header>
   <h1>Hover Over the Multi-Column Text:</h1>
  </header>

  <div id="outer">
   <p id="line1">.</p>
   <article>
     <div id="columns">
       <p> CSS enables you to define selectors that specify
the style or the manner in which you want to render elements
```

in an HTML page. CSS helps you modularize your HTML content
and since you can place your CSS definitions in a separate
file, you can also re-use the same CSS definitions in multiple HTML files.
```
        </p>
        <p> Moreover, CSS also enables you to simplify the
```
updates that you need to make to elements in HTML pages.
For example, suppose that multiple HTML table elements use
a CSS rule that specifies the color red. If you later need
to change the color to blue, you can effect such a change
simply by making one change (i.e., changing red to blue) in
one CSS rule.
```
        </p>
        <p> Without a CSS rule, you would be forced to manu-
```
ally update the color attribute in every HTML table element
that is affected, which is error-prone, time-consuming, and
extremely inefficient.
```
        <p>
        </div>
      </article>
      <p id="line1">.</p>
      </div>
    </body>
</html>
```

The HTML5 page in Listing 4.9 contains semantic tags for rendering the text
in several HTML <p> elements. As can be seen, this HTML5 page is straightforward, and the multicolumn effects are defined in the CSS stylesheet Mul-
tiColumns1.css that is displayed in Listing 4.10.

LISTING 4.10:   MultiColumns1.css

```
/* animation effects */
#columns:hover {
-webkit-transition: -webkit-transform 3.0s ease;
-transition: transform 3.0s ease;

-webkit-transform : scale(0.5) skew(-20deg, -30deg)
rotate(45deg);
-transform : scale(0.5) skew(-20deg, -30deg) rotate(45deg);
}

#line1:hover {
-webkit-transition: -webkit-transform 3.0s ease;
-transition: transform 3.0s ease;

-webkit-transform : scale(0.5) skew(-20deg, -30deg)
rotate(45deg);
-transform : scale(0.5) skew(-20deg, -30deg) rotate(45deg);
```

```
background-image: -webkit-gradient(linear, 0% 0%, 0% 100%,
                                   from(#fff), to(#00f));
background-image: -gradient(linear, 0% 0%, 0% 100%,
                            from(#fff), to(#00f));
-webkit-border-radius: 8px;border-radius: 8px;}

#columns {
-webkit-column-count : 3;
-webkit-column-gap : 80px;
-webkit-column-rule : 1px solid rgb(255,255,255);
column-count : 3;
column-gap : 80px;
column-rule : 1px solid rgb(255,255,255);
}

#line1 {
color: red;
font-size: 24px;
background-image: -webkit-gradient(linear, 0% 0%, 0% 100%,
                                   from(#fff), to(#f00));
background-image: -gradient(linear, 0% 0%, 0% 100%,
                            from(#fff), to(#f00));
-webkit-border-radius: 4px;border-radius: 4px;
}
```

The first two selectors in Listing 4.10 create an animation effect when users hover over the `<div>` elements whose `id` attribute is `columns` or `line1`. Both selectors create an animation effect during a three-second interval using the CSS3 functions `scale()`, `skew()`, and `rotate()`, as shown here:

```
-webkit-transition: -webkit-transform 3.0s ease;
-transition: transform 3.0s ease;
-webkit-transform : scale(0.5) skew(-20deg, -30deg)
                                   rotate(45deg);
```

The second selector also defines a linear gradient background effect.

The `#columns` selector in Listing 4.10 contains three layout-related attributes. The `column-count` attribute is 3, so the text is displayed in three columns; the `column-gap` attribute is `80px`, so there is a space of 80 pixels between adjacent columns; the `column-rule` attribute specifies a white background.

The `#line1` selector specifies a linear gradient that creates a nice visual effect above and below the multicolumn text. Figure 4.5 displays the result of applying the CSS selectors in `MultiColumns.css` to the text in the HTML page `MultiColumns.html`.

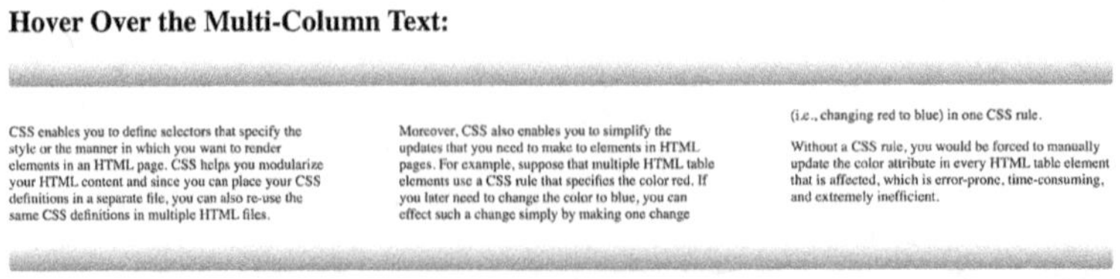

Hover Over the Multi-Column Text:

CSS enables you to define selectors that specify the style or the manner in which you want to render elements in an HTML page. CSS helps you modularize your HTML content and since you can place your CSS definitions in a separate file, you can also re-use the same CSS definitions in multiple HTML files.

Moreover, CSS also enables you to simplify the updates that you need to make to elements in HTML pages. For example, suppose that multiple HTML table elements use a CSS rule that specifies the color red. If you later need to change the color to blue, you can effect such a change simply by making one change

(i.e., changing red to blue) in one CSS rule.

Without a CSS rule, you would be forced to manually update the color attribute in every HTML table element that is affected, which is error-prone, time-consuming, and extremely inefficient.

FIGURE 4.5: Rendering multicolumn text in CSS3

CSS3 MEDIA QUERIES

CSS3 media queries determine the following attributes of a device:

- browser window width and height
- device width and height
- orientation (landscape or portrait)
- resolution

CSS3 media queries enable writing mobile applications that will render differently on devices with differing width, height, orientation, and resolution. As a simple example, consider this media query that loads the CSS stylesheet mystuff.css only if the device is a screen and the maximum width of the device is 480px:

```
<link rel="stylesheet" type="text/css"
      media="screen and (max-device-width: 480px)"
href="mystuff.css"/>
```

As can be seen, this media query contains a media attribute that specifies two components:

- a media type (screen)
- a query (max-device-width: 480px)

The preceding example is a very simple CSS3 media query; fortunately, multiple components can be combined to test the values of multiple attributes, as shown in the following pair of CSS3 selectors:

```
@media screen and (max-device-width: 480px) and
(resolution: 160dpi) {
  #innerDiv {
    float: none;
  }
}
@media screen and (min-device-width: 481px) and
(resolution: 160dpi) {
  #innerDiv {
    float: left;
  }
}
```

In the first CSS3 selector, the HTML element whose id attribute has the value innerDiv will have a float property whose value is none on any device whose maximum screen width is 480px. In the second CSS3 selector, the HTML element whose id attribute has the value innerDiv will have a float property whose value is left on any device whose minimum screen width is 481px.

CSS3 3D ANIMATION EFFECTS

CSS3 supports keyframes for creating animation effects (and the duration of those effects) at various points in time. The example in this section uses a CSS3 `keyframe` and various combinations of the CSS3 functions `scale3d()`, `rotate3d()`, and `translate3d()` to create an animation effect that lasts for four minutes. Listing 4.11 displays the contents of the HTML Web page An-im240Flicker3DLGrad4.html, which is a very simple HTML page that contains four `<div>` elements.

LISTING 4.11: Anim240Flicker3DLGrad4.html

```
<!DOCTYPE html>
<html lang="en">
<head>
  <title>CSS3 Animation Example</title>
  <meta charset="utf-8" />
  <link href="Anim240Flicker3DLGrad4.css" rel="stylesheet"
type="text/css">
</head>

<body>
 <div id="outer">
  <div id="linear1">Text1</div>
  <div id="linear2">Text2</div>
  <div id="linear3">Text3</div>
  <div id="linear4">Text4</div>
 </div>
</body>
</html>
```

Listing 4.11 is a very simple HTML5 page with corresponding CSS selectors (shown in Listing 4.12). As usual, the real complexity occurs in the CSS selectors that contain the code for creating the animation effects. Because Anim-240Flicker3DLGrad4.css is such a lengthy code sample, only a portion of the code is displayed in Listing 4.12. However, the complete code is available in the companion files for this book (see the preface for how to obtain these files).

LISTING 4.12: Anim240Flicker3DLGrad4.css

```
@-webkit-keyframes upperLeft {
    0% {
       -webkit-transform: matrix(1.5, 0.5,  0.0, 1.5, 0, 0)
                          matrix(1.0, 0.0,  1.0, 1.0, 0, 0);
    }
    10% {
       -webkit-transform: translate3d(50px,50px,50px)
                          rotate3d(50,50,50,-90deg)
                          skew(-15deg,0) scale3d(1.25,
                          1.25, 1.25);
    }
```

```
    // similar code omitted
    90% {
       -webkit-transform: matrix(2.0, 0.5,  1.0, 2.0, 0, 0)
                          matrix(1.5, 0.0,  0.5, 2.5, 0, 0);
    }
    95% {
       -webkit-transform: translate3d(-50px,-50px,-50px)
                          rotate3d(-50,-50,-50, 120deg)
                          skew(135deg,0) scale3d(0.3, 0.4, 0.5);
    }
    96% {
       -webkit-transform: matrix(0.2, 0.3, -0.5, 0.5, 100, 200)
                          matrix(0.4, 0.5,  0.5, 0.2, 200, 50);
    }
    97% {
       -webkit-transform: translate3d(50px,-50px,50px)
                          rotate3d(-50,50,-50, 120deg)
                          skew(315deg,0) scale3d(0.5, 0.4, 0.3);
    }
    98% {
       -webkit-transform: matrix(0.4, 0.5,  0.5, 0.3, 200, 50)
                          matrix(0.3, 0.5, -0.5, 0.4, 50, 150);
    }
    99% {
       -webkit-transform: translate3d(150px,50px,50px)
                          rotate3d(60,80,100, 240deg)
                          skew(315deg,0) scale3d(1.0, 0.7, 0.3);
    }
    100% {
       -webkit-transform: matrix(1.0, 0.0,  0.0, 1.0, 0, 0)
                          matrix(1.0, 0.5,  1.0, 1.5, 0, 0);
    }
}
// code omitted for brevity
#linear1 {
font-size: 96px;
text-stroke: 8px blue;
text-shadow: 8px 8px 8px #FF0000;
width:   400px;
height: 250px;

position: relative; top: 0px; left: 0px;

background-image: -webkit-gradient(linear, 100% 50%, 0% 100%,
                                   from(#f00),
                                   color-stop(0.2, orange),
                                   color-stop(0.4, yellow),
                                   color-stop(0.6, blue),
                                   color-stop(0.8, green),
                                   to(#00f));
// similar code omitted
-webkit-border-radius: 4px;
border-radius: 4px;
-webkit-box-shadow:  30px 30px 30px #000;
-webkit-animation-name: lowerLeft;
```

```
-webkit-animation-duration: 240s;
}
```

Listing 4.12 contains a WebKit-specific `keyframe` definition called upper-
Left that starts with the following line:

```
@-webkit-keyframes upperLeft {
// percentage-based definitions go here
}
```

The `#linear` selector contains properties that you have seen already, along
with a property that references the `keyframe` identified by `lowerLeft`, as
well as a property that specifies a duration of 240 seconds, as shown here:

```
#linear1 {
// code omitted for brevity
-webkit-animation-name: lowerLeft;
-webkit-animation-duration: 240s;
}
```

Now that it has been shown how to associate a `keyframe` definition to a selector (which, in turn, is applied to an HTML element), the details of the
definition of `lowerLeft` will be examined, which contains 19 elements that
specify various animation effects. Each element of `lowerLeft` occurs during a specific stage during the animation. For example, the eighth element
in `lowerLeft` specifies the value 50%, which means that it will occur at the
halfway point of the animation effect. Because the `#linear` selector contains
a `-webkit-animation-duration` property whose value is 240s (shown in
bold in Listing 4.12), the animation will last for four minutes, starting from the
point in time when the HTML5 page is launched.

The eighth element of `lowerLeft` specifies a translation, rotation, skew,
and scale effect (all of which are in three dimensions), an example of which is
shown here:

```
50% {
    -webkit-transform: translate3d(250px,250px,250px)
                       rotate3d(250px,250px,250px,
                                -120deg)
                       skew(-65deg,0) scale3d(0.5, 0.5,
                                0.5);
}
```

The animation effect occurs in a sequential fashion, starting with the translation and finishing with the scale effect, which is also the case for the other
elements in `lowerLeft`.

Figure 4.6 displays the initial view of applying the CSS3 selectors defined
in the CSS3 stylesheet `Anim240Flicker3DLGrad4.css` to the HTML elements in the HTML page `Anim240Flicker3DLGrad4.html`.

FIGURE 4.6 : CSS3 3D animation effects

SUMMARY

This chapter started with an example of displaying a CSS3-based cube, followed by examples of CSS3 transitions for creating simple animation effects, such as glow effects and bouncing effects. It was explained how to use CSS3 keyframe and the CSS3 functions scale3d(), rotate3d(), and translate3d() that enable the creation of 3D animation effects.

Next, an assortment of code samples was presented for creating glowing effects, fading image effects, and bouncing effects. In addition, it was shown how to create CSS3 effects for text and how to render multicolumn text.

Moreover, there was a brief introduction to CSS3 media queries, which enabled the user to render a given HTML page based on the properties of the device.

CHAPTER 5

CSS3 *AND* PERPLEXITY

T his chapter provides an assortment of Perplexity-generated code samples that are the result of prompts. The generated code samples in
this chapter involve CSS3, and in the next chapter, you will see similar
Perplexity-based code samples that involve SVG. The first portion of this chapter discusses the strengths and weaknesses of HTML, as well as popular use
cases for HTML. This section also discusses accessibility, as well as potential
security issues with HTML. The second section shows you an example of a
Perplexity-generated HTML Web page that contains a drop-down list with the
days of the week. Next, you will learn about the strengths and weaknesses of
CSS3, as well as use cases and potential security issues with CSS3. The third
section contains code samples of CSS3 linear gradients, CSS3 radial gradients,
rounded rectangles, diagonal gradients, and multi-gradients. You will also see
examples of media queries involving CSS3. The fourth section shows you how
to create CSS3 animation effects, keyframe animation effects, and a carousel
with CSS3. You will also see code samples with CSS3 2D transforms, quadratic
Bezier curves, and cubic Bezier curves. The fifth section contains code examples of CSS3 filters, such as blur filters and drop shadow filter effects.

WORKING WITH HTML

The following prompt was supplied to Perplexity: `"Please provide a de-
tailed description of HTML, along with its strengths and
weaknesses."`

`Perplexity:`

HTML, or HyperText Markup Language, is the standard markup language for
creating Web pages and Web applications. It forms the backbone of almost

all Web content and is an essential technology in Web development. Here's a detailed description of HTML, along with its strengths and weaknesses:

Description of HTML

1. **Nature and Purpose:** HTML is used to structure content on the Web. It consists of a series of elements which you use to enclose, or wrap, different parts of the content to make it appear or behave in a certain way.

2. **Elements and Tags:** The elements of HTML are represented by tags like `<h1>`, `<p>`, `<div>`, etc., each serving a different purpose.

3. **Structure of a Web Page:** HTML provides the basic structure of sites, which is then enhanced and modified by other technologies like CSS (Cascading Style Sheets) and JavaScript.

4. **Versions:** HTML has evolved since its inception in the early 1990s. The latest version, HTML5, introduced many new syntactical features and improved functionality.

5. **Semantics:** Semantic elements like `<header>`, `<footer>`, `<article>`, and `<section>` make the page structure clear both to the browser and the developer.

6. **Multimedia Integration:** HTML supports multimedia elements such as audio, video, and images.

7. **Forms and User Input:** HTML forms are a crucial part of the Web, enabling user interaction and data input.

8. **Accessibility:** Properly used, HTML can create Web pages that are accessible to all users, including those with disabilities.

Strengths of HTML

1. **Universality:** Every Web browser supports HTML, making it the most universal language for Web development.

2. **Ease of Learning:** HTML is relatively easy to learn and understand, making it accessible for beginners in Web development.

3. **SEO Friendly:** HTML is search engine friendly, and using semantic HTML can improve search engine rankings.

4. **Accessibility:** With proper use of semantic tags, HTML is inherently accessible, which is crucial for creating inclusive Web content.

5. **Integration with Other Technologies:** HTML works seamlessly with CSS and JavaScript, forming the triad of foundational Web technologies.

6. **Flexibility:** HTML can be used to create anything from simple static pages to complex Web applications.

7. **Free and Open:** HTML is free to use and does not require any proprietary software.

Weaknesses of HTML

1. **Limited Functionality:** HTML alone cannot create dynamic functionality – that requires JavaScript or other programming languages.
2. **Static Nature:** HTML is static, meaning it does not support dynamic content updates without the help of JavaScript or server-side scripting.
3. **Learning Curve for Advanced Features:** While the basics are easy to grasp, mastering HTML, especially HTML5, can be challenging due to its many advanced features.
4. **Browser Compatibility:** Different browsers can interpret HTML differently, leading to inconsistencies in how Web pages are displayed.
5. **Security:** HTML itself does not have security features and relies on Web browsers and other technologies for secure Web interactions.
6. **Performance Optimization:** Large and complex HTML documents can slow down Web site performance if not structured and optimized properly.
7. **Dependence on Additional Technologies:** To create visually appealing and functionally rich Web sites, HTML must be used in conjunction with CSS and JavaScript.

In summary, HTML is a fundamental technology for Web development, known for its universality and accessibility. While it has limitations in terms of dynamic functionality and requires integration with other languages for full-fledged Web development, its strengths make it an indispensable tool for creating the structure of Web pages and applications.

POPULAR USE CASES FOR HTML

The following prompt was supplied to Perplexity to describe popular use cases for HTML: "Please describe popular use cases for using HTML Web pages, along with an explanation of those use cases."

Perplexity:

HTML, or HyperText Markup Language, is the foundational building block for creating Web pages and Web applications. It provides the basic structure and content for Web pages, which are then styled with CSS (Cascading Style Sheets) and made interactive with JavaScript. Here are some popular use cases for using HTML Web pages, along with explanations for each.

1. **Corporate Web Sites**
    Use Case: Establishing an online presence for businesses, organizations, or individuals.
    Explanation: HTML is used to create the structural layout of corporate Web sites, which typically include information about the company, its

products or services, contact information, and often a blog or news section. These Web sites serve as a digital storefront or office, providing essential information and building brand presence.

2. **E-Commerce Platforms**

   Use Case: Facilitating online buying and selling of goods and services.
   Explanation: HTML forms the basis of e-commerce platforms, structuring product listings, shopping carts, and checkout processes. It is used to display products, descriptions, prices, and all other relevant information to enable online transactions.

3. **Personal Blogs and Portfolios**

   Use Case: Showcasing personal work, thoughts, experiences, or hobbies.
   Explanation: HTML is ideal for creating personal blogs or portfolio Web sites where individuals can display their work, write blog posts, and share personal experiences. This is particularly important for artists, writers, and other professionals who want to establish an online presence.

4. **Educational and Instructional Web Sites**

   Use Case: Providing educational content, courses, and resources online.
   Explanation: Educational institutions and e-learning platforms use HTML to structure their content, which can include text, images, videos, and interactive elements. These Web sites often serve as platforms for online learning, providing access to courses, tutorials, and educational materials.

5. **News and Media Web Sites**

   Use Case: Delivering news, articles, and other media content.
   Explanation: HTML is used to structure and display news articles, videos, podcasts, and other forms of media content. These Web sites are designed to handle a large volume of content, categorize it, and make it easily navigable.

6. **Forums and Social Media Platforms**

   Use Case: Facilitating online communities and social interactions.
   Explanation: Forums and social media platforms use HTML to create the layout for posts, comments, profiles, and messaging functionalities. These platforms are centered around user-generated content and interactions.

7. **Landing Pages and Promotional Sites**

   Use Case: Marketing products, services, events, or campaigns.
   Explanation: HTML is used to create landing pages – standalone Web pages designed for a specific marketing campaign or product launch. These pages are focused on a single call to action (CTA) and are designed to convert visitors into leads or customers.

8. **Informational and Service-Based Web Sites**

   Use Case: Providing information or online services like weather forecasts, travel information, or public services.

Explanation: These Web sites use HTML to structure information and services that users can access, such as online forms, informational articles, interactive maps, or service booking functionalities.

Conclusion

HTML is a versatile tool used across a wide range of Web applications. Its fundamental role in structuring content makes it indispensable for creating diverse types of Web pages, from simple personal blogs to complex e-commerce platforms. Whether it's for business, education, entertainment, or social interaction, HTML provides the essential framework upon which the Web is built.

HTML AND ACCESSIBILITY

The following prompt was supplied to Perplexity: `"Please provide a detailed description of the level of support for accessibility in HTML."`

`Perplexity:`

HTML (HyperText Markup Language) provides a strong foundation for building accessible Web content. *Accessibility* in Web development refers to the inclusive practice of removing barriers that prevent interaction with, or access to, Web sites by people with disabilities. Here's a detailed description of the level of support for accessibility in HTML:

Semantic HTML

- **Semantic Elements:** HTML5 introduced semantic elements like `<header>`, `<footer>`, `<article>`, `<section>`, `<nav>`, and `<aside>`. These elements provide meaningful structure, helping assistive technologies (like screen readers) understand the layout and navigate the content more effectively.

  Role Attribute: The role attribute can be used to define the specific role of an element, which is especially useful when a semantic element is not available.

ARIA (Accessible Rich Internet Applications) Attributes

- **ARIA:** A set of attributes specifically designed for enhancing accessibility. They help convey information about the behavior and purpose of elements to assistive technologies.
- **Roles and Properties:** ARIA roles and properties describe the elements' roles, states, and properties. They are particularly useful for dynamic content and advanced user interface controls developed with Ajax, HTML, JavaScript, and related technologies.

Form Accessibility

- **Labels:** The `<label>` element ensures that form controls are properly labeled in HTML. This is crucial for screen reader users to understand what each form control is for.

- **Fieldset and Legend:** Grouping related form controls with `<fieldset>` and describing the group with `<legend>` helps users understand related form elements.

Alternative Text for Images

- **Alt Text:** The `alt` attribute in `<img>` tags provide a text alternative for images. This is crucial for users who rely on screen readers or have slow Internet connections.

Table Accessibility

- **Table Structure:** Properly structured tables with `<thead>`, `<tbody>`, and `<tfoot>` help in conveying the information in a structured manner.
- **Captions and Summaries:** `<caption>` provides a title or summary for the table content, aiding understanding and navigation.

Keyboard Accessibility

- **Tabindex:** The `tabindex` attribute makes elements focusable and navigable by keyboard, essential for users who cannot use a mouse.
- **Access Keys:** The `accesskey` attribute can provide keyboard shortcuts to important links, buttons, and form controls.

Multimedia Accessibility

- **Subtitles and Captions:** For multimedia content, HTML provides `<track>` for specifying subtitles, captions, chapters, or descriptions, which are essential for deaf or hard-of-hearing users and those who prefer reading to listening.

Language Declaration

- **Lang Attribute:** Declaring the language of the page or parts of the page with the lang attribute helps in correct pronunciation by screen readers.

Headings and Structure

- **Headings:** Proper use of heading tags (`<h1>` to `<h6>`) creates a logical, hierarchical structure, aiding in navigation and understanding of the page layout.

Link and Button Accessibility

- Descriptive Links: Ensuring links are descriptive (`<a href="">Read more about accessibility</a>` instead of `<a href="">Click here</a>`) helps users understand the link's destination.

Screen Reader and Assistive Technology Support

- **Testing and Compatibility:** HTML structures and elements are generally well-supported by screen readers and other assistive technologies, making them a reliable choice for building accessible Web content.

Conclusion

HTML's support for accessibility is robust, offering various elements and attributes designed to make Web content accessible to a wider range of people, including those with disabilities. Proper use of semantic HTML, ARIA roles, and other accessibility features can significantly enhance the user experience for all users, regardless of their abilities or disabilities. As Web accessibility becomes increasingly important, the role of HTML in creating inclusive and accessible Web experiences continue to be critical.

SECURITY ISSUES WITH HTML

The following prompt was supplied to `Perplexity`: `"Please provide a detailed description of potential security issues involving HTML."`

`Perplexity`:

HTML (HyperText Markup Language) itself is not typically associated with security vulnerabilities, as it is primarily used for structuring and presenting content on the Web. However, the way HTML is used in conjunction with other technologies, or how it interacts with user input and server-side processing, can potentially introduce security issues. Here are some potential security concerns involving HTML.

1. **Cross-Site Scripting (XSS)**

   Issue: *XSS attacks* occur when an attacker injects malicious scripts into Web pages viewed by other users. This can happen if a Web site directly includes user input in its output without proper validation and escaping.
   HTML Angle: HTML forms and URLs can be used to submit malicious JavaScript code to a vulnerable Web application.

2. **Malicious File Uploads**

   Issue: If a Web site allows file uploads (via HTML forms) without proper security checks, attackers could upload malicious files (like scripts or executables) that compromise the server or other users' data.
   HTML Angle: HTML forms used for file uploads can be exploited if the server-side handling of these uploads is insecure.

3. **Phishing Attacks**

   Issue: *Phishing attacks* use deceptive Web pages to trick users into entering sensitive information like usernames, passwords, or credit card details.
   HTML Angle: HTML can be used to create convincing copies of legitimate websites, fooling users into submitting their information.

4. **Clickjacking**

   Issue: *Clickjacking* involves tricking a user into clicking something different than what the user perceives, potentially revealing confidential information or allowing control of the user's computer.

HTML Angle: This can be achieved by embedding a transparent HTML frame over a seemingly benign Web page.

5. **Iframe Injection**

   Issue: Attackers may inject an iframe into a Web page to load a malicious site in the background. This can be used for phishing or to exploit vulnerabilities in the browser.

   HTML Angle: Insecure or unsanitized HTML content can allow iframe injections.

6. **Insecure Direct Object References (IDOR)**

   Issue: Directly referencing internal implementation objects, such as files, directories, or database keys, in HTML and Web interfaces can lead to unauthorized access.

   HTML Angle: HTML elements like hyperlinks or form actions can be manipulated to gain access to these references.

7. **Mixed Content**

   Issue: Loading mixed content (combining HTTPS and HTTP content on the same page) can make a Web site vulnerable to eavesdropping and man-in-the-middle attacks.

   HTML Angle: When an HTTPS site includes HTTP content (like images, videos, stylesheets, and scripts), it creates a security risk.

8. **Insecure Redirections and Forwards**

   Issue: Improperly validated redirections and forwards can be manipulated to direct users to phishing or malware sites.

   HTML Angle: HTML tags like `<a href="">` or HTTP meta refresh tags can be used for this purpose.

Mitigation Strategies

- **Input Validation and Sanitization:** Always validate and sanitize user input to prevent XSS and other injection attacks.
- **Content Security Policy (CSP):** Implement CSP headers to reduce the risk of XSS and other content injection attacks.
- **Secure File Upload Handling:** Implement server-side checks to ensure only safe file types and sizes are uploaded.
- **Use HTTPS:** Ensure all content, including third-party resources, are loaded over HTTPS to prevent mixed content issues.
- **Regular Security Audits:** Regularly audit Web applications for security vulnerabilities and apply updates as needed.

Conclusion

While HTML itself is not inherently insecure, its interaction with browsers, user input, and server-side processing can lead to security vulnerabilities. Understanding these potential issues and implementing best practices for Web development and security is crucial in mitigating risks associated with HTML Web pages [according to Perplexity].

AN HTML WEB PAGE WITH A DROP-DOWN LIST

The following prompt was supplied to Perplexity: "Please generate an HTML Web page that contains a drop-down list with the days of the week, along with an explanation of the code."

Perplexity:

Sure, here's an example of an HTML Web page that contains a drop-down list with the days of the week, along with an explanation of the code.

Listing 5.1 displays the contents of perplex_dropdown.html that shows the code that Perplexity generated in order to display a Web page that contains a drop-down list.

LISTING 5.1: perplex_dropdown.html

```html
<!DOCTYPE html>
<html>
<head>
  <title>Days of the Week</title>
</head>
<body>
  <h1>Days of the Week</h1>
  <p>Select a day of the week from the drop-down list:</p>
  <select id="day-of-week">
    <option value="">Select a day</option>
    <option value="Monday">Monday</option>
    <option value="Tuesday">Tuesday</option>
    <option value="Wednesday">Wednesday</option>
    <option value="Thursday">Thursday</option>
    <option value="Friday">Friday</option>
    <option value="Saturday">Saturday</option>
    <option value="Sunday">Sunday</option>
  </select>
  <button onclick="displaySelectedDay()">Submit</button>
  <p id="selected-day"></p>

  <script>
    function displaySelectedDay() {
      // Get the selected value from the drop-down list
      var selectedDay = document.getElementById("day-of-
                              week").value;

      // Display the selected day
      var selectedDayElement = document.
                      getElementById("selected-day");
      if (selectedDay === "") {
        selectedDayElement.textContent =
                              "No day selected.";
      } else {
        selectedDayElement.textContent =
                      "You selected: " + selectedDay;
      }
    }
```

```
  </script>
</body>
</html>
```

Explanation of the code:

The HTML structure includes a `<select>` element with an `id` of "day-of-week." This is the drop-down list that will display the days of the week.

Inside the `<select>` element, there are `<option>` elements for each day of the week. The value attribute of each `<option>` element corresponds to the day of the week.

The first `<option>` element has an empty value attribute, which serves as a placeholder option for the user to select.

The onclick attribute of the `<button>` element calls the `displaySelectedDay()` function when the button is clicked.

The JavaScript function `displaySelectedDay()` is defined in the `<script>` section.

Inside the `displaySelectedDay()` function, the selected value from the drop-down list is retrieved using `document.getElementById("day-of-week").value`.

The selected day is then displayed in a `<p>` element with an `id` of "selected-day." If no day is selected, a default message is displayed. When the user selects a day from the drop-down list and clicks the "Submit" button, the selected day will be displayed below the button.

Now launch the Web page `perplex_dropdown.html` by navigating to the directory that contains this HTML Web page and then typing the following command:

```
open perplex_dropdown.html
```

After a few moments you will see the image in Figure 5.1 that displays the output when you select one of the people in the drop-down list.

FIGURE 5.1: A Web page with a drop-down list

WORKING WITH CSS3

The following prompt was given to Perplexity: `"Please provide a de-`
`tailed description of CSS3, along with its useful features`
`as well as its strengths and weaknesses."`

`Perplexity:`

Based on the search results, here is a detailed description of CSS3, its useful features, and its strengths and weaknesses:

CSS3: The Evolved Styling Language
CSS3 is the latest version of the Cascading Style Sheets (CSS) language, which is used to describe the presentation and styling of Web content written in a markup language like HTML. CSS3 builds upon the foundations laid by previous versions of CSS, introducing a wide range of new features and enhancements that have transformed the way Web pages are designed and developed.

Useful Features of CSS3
Modularity and Selectors: CSS3 offers greater modularity and specificity in its selectors, allowing developers to target HTML elements more precisely using new attribute selectors, pseudo-classes, and pseudo-elements. This increased granularity enables more targeted styling and better control over the appearance of Web content.

Media Queries and Responsive Design: One of the most significant advancements in CSS3 is the introduction of media queries, which enable responsive Web design. Developers can now apply different styles based on device characteristics or screen size, ensuring that Web pages adapt seamlessly to various devices and screen sizes.

Animations and Transitions: CSS3 has revolutionized the way Web designers can create dynamic and visually engaging user experiences. It introduces the ability to animate changes to CSS properties over time, control the speed and timing of transitions, and create complex keyframe-based animations without relying on JavaScript or external libraries.

Visual Effects: CSS3 provides a range of new visual effects, including rounded borders, drop shadows, gradients, and text effects, allowing Web designers to create more visually appealing and polished designs.

CSS Variables: CSS3 introduced the concept of CSS variables, also known as custom properties, which allow developers to store and reuse specific values throughout their stylesheets. This feature simplifies the process of updating and maintaining consistent styles across a Web site.

Strengths of CSS3
Enhanced Aesthetics: The new features in CSS3, such as animations, transitions, and visual effects, enable Web designers to create more visually engaging and dynamic Web experiences.

Responsive Design: The media queries feature in CSS3 is a game-changer for responsive Web design, allowing developers to create Web sites that adapt seamlessly to various devices and screen sizes.

Improved Maintainability: CSS3's modularity, specificity, and the introduction of variables make it easier to maintain and update Web site styles, reducing development time and effort.

Backward Compatibility: CSS3 is generally backward compatible with previous versions of CSS, meaning that existing CSS code will continue to work in CSS3-compliant browsers.

Weaknesses of CSS3

Browser Compatibility: Not all CSS3 features are supported by all Web browsers, especially older versions. Developers need to carefully consider browser compatibility and implement fallback solutions to ensure consistent user experiences.

Complexity: The introduction of new features and modules in CSS3 can be overwhelming for beginners and non-developers, as the language has become more complex over time.

Potential for Inconsistency: Due to the varying levels of support for CSS3 features across different browsers, there is a risk of inconsistent styling and behavior, which can be challenging to manage.

In conclusion, CSS3 represents a significant evolution in the world of Web design and development. Its enhanced features, such as modularity, responsive design capabilities, animations, and visual effects, have empowered Web designers to create more visually appealing, dynamic, and adaptable Web experiences. While CSS3 offers numerous strengths, it also comes with some challenges, primarily related to browser compatibility and the increased complexity of the language. As Web standards continue to evolve, understanding and leveraging the capabilities of CSS3 remains crucial for Web developers and designers to stay at the forefront of modern Web design.

Interestingly, Perplexity provided the following related questions:

- What are some of the most useful features of CSS3?
- What are the strengths of CSS3 compared to previous versions of CSS?
- What are the weaknesses of CSS3 compared to previous versions of CSS?

USE CASES FOR CSS3

The following prompt was supplied to Perplexity in order to describe use cases for CSS3 in HTML Web pages: `"Please describe significant use cases that involve CSS3 in HTML Web pages, along with an explanation of the use cases."`

Perplexity provided the following sources:

https://www.almabetter.com/bytes/articles/difference-between-css-and-css3
https://www.devx.com/terms/cascading-style-sheets-level-3/
https://www.builder.io/blog/css-the-good-parts

Perplexity then provided the following response to the earlier prompt:

CSS3, the latest version of Cascading Style Sheets, plays a crucial role in Web design and development. It provides advanced styling capabilities and controls the visual presentation of HTML Web pages. Here are some significant use cases of CSS3 in HTML Web pages, along with explanations for each:

1. **Responsive Web Design**

   Use Case: Creating Web pages that adapt their layout to different screen sizes and devices (like desktops, tablets, and smartphones).

   Explanation: CSS3 introduces media queries that allow designers to change styles based on the device's characteristics, such as its width, height, or orientation. This means that the same Web page can have a flexible layout that changes to provide an optimal viewing experience across a range of devices.

2. **Animation and Transitions**

   Use Case: Adding interactive elements to Web pages, such as animations, transitions, and hover effects.

   Explanation: CSS3 comes with properties like transition, transform, and keyframes for animations, allowing for smooth transitions and animations without the need for JavaScript or Flash. This enhances user experience and engagement by providing visual feedback and interactive elements.

3. **Custom Fonts and Typography**

   Use Case: Styling text with custom fonts and advanced typography to enhance the readability and aesthetic appeal of Web content.

   Explanation: CSS3 allows for the use of custom fonts with the @font-face rule, enabling Web designers to move beyond the limited set of Web-safe fonts. This capability enhances the design and branding of websites.

4. **Box Model and Flexbox/Grid Layouts**

   Use Case: Creating complex, flexible layouts that are easier to manage and adapt to various screen sizes.

   Explanation: CSS3 introduced Flexbox and Grid Layout modules, providing more efficient ways to design complex layouts. Flexbox is great for 1-dimensional layouts, while CSS Grid excels in 2-dimensional layouts. These tools offer greater control over alignment, distribution of space, and order of elements within a container.

5. **Gradients, Shadows, and Rounded Corners**

   Use Case: Adding visual effects like gradients, shadows, and rounded corners to enhance the visual appeal of elements without using images.

Explanation: CSS3 simplifies the process of adding visual effects. Gradients (linear or radial), box and text shadows, and border-radius for rounded corners can be easily applied to elements. This reduces the need for additional image files, decreasing load times and simplifying maintenance.

6. **Feature Detection and Progressive Enhancement**

   Use Case: Designing Web pages that progressively enhance according to the capabilities of the browser or device.

   Explanation: With CSS3, developers can use feature detection techniques (like Modernizr) to identify if a browser supports certain CSS features. Based on this, they can provide fallback styles or enhancements, ensuring that the Web site is functional and aesthetically pleasing across different browsers.

7. **Advanced Selectors and Pseudo-Classes**

   Use Case: Targeting specific elements in the HTML document more precisely for styling without changing the HTML structure.

   Explanation: CSS3 introduces a range of advanced selectors and pseudo-classes (like `nth-child`, `not`, `:hover`, `:focus`). These allow for more specific and complex selections, enabling fine-grained control over the styling of elements based on their state or position in the document.

Conclusion

These use cases illustrate the versatility and power of CSS3 in Web design. By enabling responsive designs, interactive animations, advanced layouts, and more, CSS3 plays a pivotal role in creating modern, user-friendly, and visually appealing Web sites.

SECURITY ISSUES WITH CSS3

The following prompt was supplied to Perplexity: `"Please provide a detailed description of potential security issues involving CSS3."`

Perplexity provided the following sources:

https://jabitsoft.com/the-impact-of-html5-css3-web-designs-for-your-business/
https://www.evonide.com/side-channel-attacking-browsers-through-css3-features/
https://css-tricks.com/css-security-vulnerabilities/

Perplexity then provided the following response to the initial prompt:

Potential security issues involving CSS3 include:
CSS Injection Attacks: Attackers can inject malicious CSS code into a Web application, which can then be executed by the victim's browser. This can lead to cross-site scripting (XSS) attacks, where the attacker's code is executed in the context of the victim's session, potentially allowing the attacker to steal sensitive data or perform unauthorized actions.

Data Exfiltration: Malicious CSS can be used to extract sensitive data from the victim's browser using CSS selectors and functions that can generate HTTP requests. For example, an attacker could attempt to exfiltrate a CSRF token by targeting an input field with a specific name.

Browser Exploits: Certain CSS properties and functions can be used to exploit vulnerabilities in the victim's browser, potentially allowing the attacker to execute arbitrary code or gain elevated privileges.

Denial of Service: Carefully crafted CSS can be used to overload the victim's browser, leading to a denial-of-service attack.

To mitigate these risks, Web applications should sanitize and validate all user-supplied CSS before rendering it on the page. This can be achieved through the use of a whitelist of approved CSS properties and values, rather than relying on a blacklist approach, which may be incomplete.[45] Additionally, Web applications should consider disabling the ability to include user-supplied CSS entirely, or limiting it to a set of predefined templates, if the functionality is not essential to the application.

TEXT WITH A CSS3 LINEAR GRADIENT

The following prompt was supplied to Perplexity in order to generate an HTML Web page that contains CSS3: "Please generate an HTML Web page that contains a text string with linear gradient shading, along with an explanation of the code."

Perplexity:

Here is an HTML Web page that contains a text string with linear gradient shading, along with an explanation of the code.

LISTING 5.2: perplex_css3_text_linear_gradient.html

```
<!DOCTYPE html>
<html>
<head>
  <title>CSS3 Linear Gradient Example</title>
  <style>
    .gradient-text {
      font-size: 48px;
      font-weight: bold;
      background: linear-gradient(to right, #ff6b6b,
                                  #ffa500, #ffff00,
                                  #00ff00, #00ffff,
                                  #0000ff, #ff00ff);
      -webkit-background-clip: text;
      -webkit-text-fill-color: transparent;
    }
  </style>
</head>
<body>
```

```
<h1 class="gradient-text">CSS3 Linear Gradient</h1>
<p>This text is styled using a linear gradient background
applied to the text itself. The <code>linear-gradient()</
code> function is used to create a gradient that
transitions from one color to another, in this case, from
red to purple.</p>
<p>The <code>-webkit-background-clip: text;</code>
and <code>-webkit-text-fill-color: transparent;</code>
properties are used to apply the gradient to the text,
rather than the entire background of the element.</p>
</body>
</html>
```

Explanation of the Code

The HTML file starts with the standard `<!DOCTYPE html>` declaration, followed by the `<html>` tag.

In the `<head>` section, we have a `<title>` tag that sets the page title to "CSS3 Linear Gradient Example."

Inside the `<style>` section, we define a CSS class called `.gradient-text` that will be applied to the text we want to style.

The `font-size` and `font-weight` properties are set to control the appearance of the text.

The background property is set to a `linear-gradient()` function, which creates a gradient that transitions from one color to another. In this case, the gradient goes from red (#ff6b6b) to purple (#ff00ff) with several intermediate colors.

The `-webkit-background-clip: text;` and `-webkit-text-fill-color: transparent;` properties are used to apply the gradient to the text itself, rather than the entire background of the element.

In the `<body>` section, we have an `<h1>` element with the `class="gradient-text"` attribute, which applies the gradient styling to the text.

Below the heading, we have two `<p>` elements that provide an explanation of the code and the CSS properties used to create the gradient text effect.

When you open this HTML file in a Web browser, you should see the text "CSS3 Linear Gradient" displayed with a vibrant, multicolored gradient effect.

Now launch the Web page `perplex_css3_text_linear_gradient.html` by navigating to the directory that contains this HTML Web page and then typing the following command:

```
open perplex_css3_text_linear_gradient.html
```

After a few moments, you will see the Web page in Figure 5.2 that displays a CSS3-based linear gradient text.

Gradient Text

FIGURE 5.2: A text string with a linear gradient

TEXT WITH A CSS3 RADIAL GRADIENT

The following prompt was supplied to Perplexity in order to generate an HTML Web page that contains CSS3: "`Please generate an HTML Web page that contains a text string with radial gradient shading, along with an explanation of the code.`"

`Perplexity:`

Here is an HTML Web page that contains a text string with radial gradient shading, along with an explanation of the code.

LISTING 5.3: *perplex_css3_text_radial_gradient.html*

```
<!DOCTYPE html>
<html>
<head>
  <title>CSS3 Radial Gradient Example</title>
  <style>
    .gradient-text {
      font-size: 48px;
      font-weight: bold;
      background: radial-gradient(circle, #ff6b6b, #ffa500,
                                  #ffff00, #00ff00,
                                  #00ffff, #0000ff,
                                  #ff00ff);
      -webkit-background-clip: text;
      -webkit-text-fill-color: transparent;
    }
  </style>
</head>
<body>
  <h1 class="gradient-text">CSS3 Radial Gradient</h1>
  <p>This text is styled using a radial gradient background
applied to the text itself. The <code>radial-gradient()</
code> function is used to create a gradient that radiates
outward from a central point, in this case, a circle that
transitions from one color to another.</p>
  <p>The <code>-webkit-background-clip: text;</code>
and <code>-webkit-text-fill-color: transparent;</code>
properties are used to apply the gradient to the text,
rather than the entire background of the element.</p>
</body>
</html>
```

Explanation of the Code
The HTML file starts with the standard `<!DOCTYPE html>` declaration, followed by the `<html>` tag.

In the `<head>` section, we have a `<title>` tag that sets the page title to "CSS3 Radial Gradient Example."

Inside the `<style>` section, we define a CSS class called `.gradient-text` that will be applied to the text we want to style.

The `font-size` and `font-weight` properties are set to control the appearance of the text.

The background property is set to a `radial-gradient()` function, which creates a gradient that radiates outward from a central point. In this case, the gradient goes from red (#ff6b6b) to purple (#ff00ff) with several intermediate colors.

The `-webkit-background-clip: text;` and `-webkit-text-fill-color: transparent;` properties are used to apply the gradient to the text itself, rather than the entire background of the element.

In the `<body>` section, we have an `<h1>` element with the class="gradient-text" attribute, which applies the gradient styling to the text.

Below the heading, we have two `<p>` elements that provide an explanation of the code and the CSS properties used to create the radial gradient text effect.

When you open this HTML file in a Web browser, you should see the text "CSS3 Radial Gradient" displayed with a vibrant, multicolored radial gradient effect.

Now launch the Web page `perplex_css3_text_radial_gradient.html` by navigating to the directory that contains this HTML Web page and then typing the following command:

```
open perplex_css3_text_radial_gradient.html
```

After a few moments you will see the Web page in Figure 5.3 that displays a CSS3-based radial gradient text.

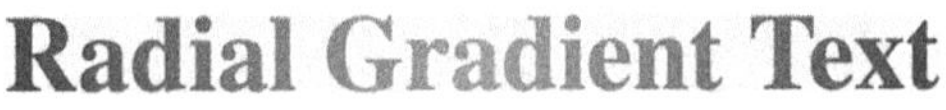

Radial Gradient Text

FIGURE 5.3: A text string with a radial gradient

A ROUNDED RECTANGLE WITH A CSS3 RADIAL GRADIENT

The following prompt was supplied to Perplexity in order to generate an HTML Web page that contains a rounded rectangle with a CSS3 radial gradient:

"Please render a rounded rectangle of width 400 and height 200 that is rendered with a CSS3 radial gradient, and also an ellipse of comparable dimensions with a CSS3 radial gradient, as well as a box-shadow attribute with value inset 15px 12px 30px #000; and an explanation of the code."

Perplexity:

Here is an HTML Web page that contains a rounded rectangle with gradient shading.

LISTING 5.4: perplex_css3_rounded_rect_radial_gradient2.html

```
<!DOCTYPE html>
<html lang="en">
<head>
  <meta charset="UTF-8">
```

```
<title>CSS3 Radial Gradient and Box-Shadow on Shapes
</title>
<style>
  .rounded-rectangle {
    width: 400px;
    height: 200px;
    background: radial-gradient(circle, red,
    yellow);
    border-radius: 25px; /* Rounded corners */
    box-shadow: inset 15px 12px 30px #000;
    /* Inset shadow */
    margin-bottom: 20px;
  }

  .ellipse {
    width: 400px;
    height: 200px;
    background: radial-gradient(circle at center,
    blue, green);
    border-radius: 50%; /* Full ellipse */
    box-shadow: inset 15px 12px 30px #000; /* Inset
                                          shadow */
  }
</style>
</head>
<body>

<div class="rounded-rectangle"></div>
<div class="ellipse"></div>

</body>
</html>
```

Now launch the Web page `css3_rounded_rect_radial_gradient2.html` by navigating to the directory that contains this HTML Web page and then typing the following command:

`open css3_rounded_rect_radial_gradient2.html`

After a few moments you will see the image in Figure 5.4 that displays a rounded rectangle as well as an ellipse with a CSS3 radial gradient.

FIGURE 5.4: A rounded rectangle and ellipse with CSS3 radial gradient

DIAGONAL GRADIENTS AND MULTI GRADIENTS

The following prompt was supplied to Perplexity in order to generate an
HTML Web page that contains a diagonal gradient and a multi-gradient:

"Please generate an HTML Web page with <div> elements that
contains a <div> element with a diagonal gradient, and a
<div> element with a gradient that contains at least 4 color
stops, where all <div> elements are 250 x 250, along with an
explanation of the code."

Perplexity:

Here is an HTML Web page with <div> elements that contains a <div>
element with a diagonal gradient, and a <div> element with a gradient that
contains at least 4 color stops, where all <div> elements are 250 x 250, along
with an explanation of the code.

LISTING 5.5: perplex_css3_diagonal_multi_gradients.html

```
<!DOCTYPE html>
<html>
<head>
  <title>CSS3 Gradient Examples</title>
  <style>
    .gradient-container {
      display: flex;
      justify-content: space-around;
      margin-top: 50px;
    }

    .gradient-div {
      width: 250px;
      height: 250px;
    }

    .diagonal-gradient {
      background: linear-gradient(45deg, #ff6b6b, #ffa500,
                                  #ffff00, #00ff00,
                                  #00ffff, #0000ff,
                                  #ff00ff);
    }

    .multi-color-gradient {
      background: linear-gradient(to right, #ff6b6b,
                                  #ffa500, #ffff00,
                                  #00ff00);
    }
  </style>
</head>
<body>
  <div class="gradient-container">
    <div class="gradient-div diagonal-gradient"></div>
    <div class="gradient-div multi-color-gradient"></div>
  </div>
```

```
  <p>This HTML page contains two '<div>' elements with
different gradient styles:</p>

  <h2>Diagonal Gradient</h2>
  <p>The first '<div>' element has a diagonal gradient that
transitions from red ('#ff6b6b') to purple ('#ff00ff')
with several intermediate colors in between. The 'linear-
gradient(45deg, ...)' function is used to create this
diagonal gradient effect.</p>

  <h2>Multi-Color Gradient</h2>
  <p>The second '<div>' element has a linear gradient that
transitions from red ('#ff6b6b') to green ('#00ff00') with
two additional intermediate colors (orange and yellow). The
'linear-gradient(to right, ...)' function is used to create
this gradient that goes from left to right.</p>

  <p>Both '<div>' elements have a fixed size of 250x250
pixels, and they are centered on the page using the
'display: flex;' and 'justify-content: space-around;'
properties on the parent container.</p>
</body>
</html>
```

Explanation of the Code

The HTML file starts with the standard `<!DOCTYPE html>` declaration, followed by the `<html>` tag.

In the `<head>` section, we have a `<title>` tag that sets the page title to "CSS3 Gradient Examples."

Inside the `<style>` section, we define the following CSS classes:

`.gradient-container`: This class is applied to the parent container that holds the two gradient `<div>` elements. It uses `display: flex;` and `justify-content: space-around;` to center the `<div>` elements horizontally.

`.gradient-div`: This class is applied to both gradient `<div>` elements and sets their size to 250 x 250 pixels.

`.diagonal-gradient`: This class is applied to the first `<div>` element and sets a diagonal gradient background using the linear-gradient(45 deg, ...) function.

`.multi-color-gradient`: This class is applied to the second `<div>` element and sets a linear gradient background from left to right using the linear-gradient (to right ...) function.

In the `<body>` section, we have a `<div>` element with the `class="gradient-container"` attribute, which holds the two gradient `<div>` elements.

The first `<div>` element has the `class="gradient-div diagonal-gradient"` attribute, which applies the diagonal gradient style.

The second `<div>` element has the `class="gradient-div multi-color-gradient"` attribute, which applies the multi-color gradient style.

Below the `<div>` elements, we have several `<p>` and `<h2>` elements that provide an explanation of the code and the CSS properties used to create the gradient effects.

When you open this HTML file in a Web browser, you should see two square <div> elements side-by-side, each with a different gradient effect: one diagonal gradient and one linear gradient with four color stops.

Now launch the Web page perplex_css3_diagonal_multi_gradients.html by navigating to the directory that contains this HTML Web page and then typing the following command:

```
open perplex_css3_diagonal_multi_gradients.html
```

After a few moments, you will see a rectangle with a diagonal gradient and a second rectangle with a four-color gradient, as shown in Figure 5.5.

FIGURE 5.5: Rectangles with a diagonal gradient and multi gradient

MEDIA QUERIES

The following prompt was supplied to Perplexity to generate an HTML Web page that contains a Media Query: "Please generate an HTML Web page that contains a media query in order to adjust styles based on screen size, along with an explanation of the code."

Perplexity:

Here is an HTML Web page that contains a media query to adjust styles based on screen size, along with an explanation of the code.

LISTING 5.6: *perplex_css3_media_query.html*

```
<!DOCTYPE html>
<html>
<head>
  <title>Responsive Design Example</title>
  <style>
    .container {
      display: flex;
      justify-content: center;
      align-items: center;
      height: 100vh;
    }

    .box {
```

```
      width: 200px;
      height: 200px;
      background-color: #007bff;
      color: #fff;
      font-size: 24px;
      display: flex;
      justify-content: center;
      align-items: center;
    }

    @media (max-width: 768px) {
      .box {
        width: 150px;
        height: 150px;
        font-size: 18px;
      }
    }
  </style>
</head>
<body>
  <div class="container">
    <div class="box">
      Responsive Design
    </div>
  </div>
</body>
</html>
```

Explanation of the Code

The HTML file starts with the standard `<!DOCTYPE html>` declaration, followed by the `<html>` tag.

In the `<head>` section, we have a `<title>` tag that sets the page title to "Responsive Design Example."

Inside the `<style>` section, we define the following CSS classes:

`.container`: This class is applied to the parent container that holds the `<div>` element with the text. It uses `display: flex;`, `justify-content: center;`, and `align-items: center;` to center the content both horizontally and vertically.

`.box`: This class is applied to the `<div>` element that contains the text. It sets the width and height to 200 pixels, the background color to blue (#007bff), the text color to white (#fff), and the font size to 24 pixels. It also uses `display: flex;`, `justify-content: center;`, and `align-items: center;` to center the text within the `<div>`.

`@media` (max-width: 768px): This is a media query that applies the styles inside the curly braces when the screen width is less than or equal to 768 pixels (a common breakpoint for mobile devices).

Inside the media query, we modified the styles for the `.box` class by reducing the width and height to 150 pixels and the font size to 18 pixels.

In the `<body>` section, we have a `<div>` element with the `class="container"` attribute, which holds the `<div>` element with the text.

The inner `<div>` element has the `class="box"` attribute, which applies the styles defined in the CSS.

When you open this HTML file in a Web browser, you should see a centered `<div>` element with the text "Responsive Design." If you resize the browser window to a width of 768 pixels or less, the `<div>` element will automatically adjust its size and font size to maintain a responsive design. The media query @ media (max-width: 768px) is used to detect when the screen width is less than or equal to 768 pixels and apply the modified styles for the `.box` class. This allows the Web page to adapt its layout and appearance based on the user's device or screen size, providing a better user experience.

Now launch the Web page `perplex_css3_media_query.html` by navigating to the directory that contains this HTML Web page and then typing the following command:

```
open perplex_css3_media_query.html
```

After a few moments, you will see a green `<div>` element whose width equals the width of your browser session. Now resize the size of your browser and watch how the `<div>` elements adjust its width to match the width of the browser session.

KEYFRAME ANIMATION EFFECTS

The following prompt was supplied to Perplexity in order to generate an HTML Web page that contains CSS3 animation: "Please generate an HTML Web page with a 300 x 300 `<div>` that has keyframe animations, along with an explanation of the code."

Perplexity:

Here is an HTML Web page with a 300 x 300 `<div>` that has keyframe animations, along with an explanation of the code.

LISTING 5.7: perplex_css3_keyframe_animations1.html

```
<!DOCTYPE html>
<html>
<head>
  <title>Keyframe Animation Example</title>
  <style>
    .animated-box {
      width: 300px;
      height: 300px;
      background-color: #007bff;
      position: relative;
      animation: colorChange 5s infinite, moveBox 10s
        infinite;
    }

    @keyframes colorChange {
```

```
      0% {
        background-color: #007bff;
      }
      50% {
        background-color: #ff6b6b;
      }
      100% {
        background-color: #007bff;
      }
    }

    @keyframes moveBox {
      0% {
        left: 0;
        top: 0;
      }
      25% {
        left: calc(100% - 300px);
        top: 0;
      }
      50% {
        left: calc(100% - 300px);
        top: calc(100% - 300px);
      }
      75% {
        left: 0;
        top: calc(100% - 300px);
      }
      100% {
        left: 0;
        top: 0;
      }
    }
  </style>
</head>
<body>
  <div class="animated-box"></div>
```

<p>This HTML page contains a 300x300 pixel '<div>' element that has two keyframe animations applied to it:</p>

<h2>Color Change Animation</h2>
<p>The first animation, 'colorChange', changes the background color of the '<div>' from blue ('#007bff') to red ('#ff6b6b') and back to blue over a 5-second cycle. The '@keyframes' rule defines the color changes at different percentage points in the animation.</p>

<h2>Box Movement Animation</h2>
<p>The second animation, 'moveBox', moves the '<div>' element around the page, starting at the top-left corner, then moving to the top-right, bottom-right, and bottom-left corners, before returning to the top-left corner. This animation takes 10 seconds to complete one full cycle. The '@keyframes' rule defines the position of the '<div>' at different percentage points in the animation.</p>

```
<p>The 'animation' property on the '.animated-box' class
applies both the 'colorChange' and 'moveBox' animations to
the '<div>' element, with the 'infinite' value causing the
animations to repeat indefinitely.</p>
</body>
</html>
```

Explanation of the Code

The HTML file starts with the standard `<!DOCTYPE html>` declaration, followed by the `<html>` tag.

In the `<head>` section, we have a `<title>` tag that sets the page title to "Keyframe Animation Example."

Inside the `<style>` section, we define the following CSS:

`.animated-box`: This class is applied to the `<div>` element that will be animated. It sets the width and height to 300 pixels, the background color to blue (#007bff), and the position property to relative to allow the animations to move the `<div>` element.

`@keyframes colorChange`: This `@keyframes` rule defines the color change animation. It starts with a blue background (#007bff), changes to a red background (#ff6b6b) at the 50% mark, and then returns to the blue background by the end of the animation.

`@keyframes moveBox`: This `@keyframes` rule defines the box movement animation. It starts with the `<div>` element at the top-left corner, then moves it to the top-right, bottom-right, and bottom-left corners, before returning it to the top-left corner.

The animation property on the `.animated-box` class applies both the `colorChange` and `moveBox` animations to the `<div>` element, with the infinite value causing the animations to repeat indefinitely.

In the `<body>` section, we have a `<div>` element with the `class="animated-box"` attribute, which applies the animations defined in the CSS.

When you open this HTML file in a Web browser, you should see a 300 x 300 pixel `<div>` element that continuously changes color and moves around the page, creating a dynamic and visually interesting effect. The keyframe animations defined in the CSS allow you to precisely control the changes in the `<div>` element's appearance and position over time. This is a powerful technique for creating engaging and responsive user interfaces in Web applications.

Now launch the Web page `perplex_css3_keyframe_animations1.html` by navigating to the directory that contains this HTML Web page and then typing the following command:

```
open perplex_css3_keyframe_animation1.html
```

After a few moments, you will see the Web page in Figure 5.6 that displays a snapshot of CSS3-based animation.

FIGURE 5.6: A rectangle with CSS3-based animation

CSS3 ANIMATION EFFECTS

The following prompt was supplied to Perplexity to generate an HTML Web page that contains CSS3 animation: "Please generate an HTML Web page that contains an animated text string with linear gradient shading."

Perplexity:

Here is an HTML Web page with CSS3 animation effects as well as linear gradient shading.

LISTING 5.8:   perplex_css3_animated.html

```
<!DOCTYPE html>
<html>
<head>
    <title>Animated Gradient Text</title>
    <style>
        @keyframes gradient-animation {
            0% { background-position: 0% 50%; }
            50% { background-position: 100% 50%; }
            100% { background-position: 0% 50%; }
        }

        .animated-gradient-text {
            font-size: 40px;
            font-weight: bold;
            background: linear-gradient(45deg, blue, red,
                                       green, yellow);
            background-size: 200% 200%;
            color: transparent;
            background-clip: text;
            -webkit-background-clip: text;
```

```
        -webkit-text-fill-color: transparent;
        animation: gradient-animation 5s ease infinite;
    }
    </style>
</head>
<body>
    <div class="animated-gradient-text">Animated Gradient
Text</div>
</body>
</html>
```

Now launch the Web page `perplex_css3_animated.html` by navigating to the directory that contains this HTML Web page and then typing the following command:

```
open perplex_css3_animated.html
```

After a few moments you will see the image in Figure 5.7 that displays a snapshot of text that is rendered with CSS3-based animation.

Animated Gradient Text

FIGURE 5.7: Text with a CSS3-based animation

A CAROUSEL EFFECT WITH CSS3

The following prompt was supplied to Perplexity: "Please generate an HTML Web page that contains a horizontal carousel effect with multiple PNGs."

Perplexity:

Here is an HTML Web page that contains a horizontal carousel effect with multiple PNGs.

Listing 5.9 displays the contents of `perplex_css3_carousel.html` that show the code that Perplexity generated in order to display a carousel effect with multiple PNGs.

LISTING 5.9: *perplex_css3_carousel1.html*

```
<!DOCTYPE html>
<html>
<head>
  <title>Horizontal Carousel Example</title>
  <style>
    .carousel-container {
      width: 100%;
      height: 300px;
      overflow-x: scroll;
      white-space: nowrap;
      scrollbar-width: none; /* Hide scrollbar for Firefox */
```

```
          -ms-overflow-style: none; /* Hide scrollbar for IE and
Edge */
    }

    .carousel-container::-webkit-scrollbar {
      display: none; /* Hide scrollbar for Chrome, Safari,
                      and Opera */
    }

    .carousel-item {
      display: inline-block;
      width: 300px;
      height: 300px;
      margin-right: 20px;
    }

    .carousel-item img {
      width: 100%;
      height: 100%;
      object-fit: contain;
    }
  </style>
</head>
<body>
  <div class="carousel-container">
    <div class="carousel-item">
      <img src="image1.png" alt="Image 1">
    </div>
    <div class="carousel-item">
      <img src="image2.png" alt="Image 2">
    </div>
    <div class="carousel-item">
      <img src="image3.png" alt="Image 3">
    </div>
    <div class="carousel-item">
      <img src="image4.png" alt="Image 4">
    </div>
    <div class="carousel-item">
      <img src="image5.png" alt="Image 5">
    </div>
  </div>

  <p>This HTML page contains a horizontal carousel
effect that displays multiple PNG images. The carousel
is implemented using a container '<div>' with the class
'carousel-container', which has the following styles:</p>


    <li>'width: 100%;' and 'height: 300px;' to set the size
of the carousel container.</li>
    <li>'overflow-x: scroll;' to enable horizontal
scrolling.</li>
    <li>'white-space: nowrap;' to ensure the carousel items
are displayed in a single line.</li>
```

```
<li>'scrollbar-width: none;', '-ms-overflow-style:
none;', and '::-webkit-scrollbar { display: none; }' to hide
the scrollbar.</li>
```

```
<p>Inside the carousel container, there are multiple
'<div>' elements with the class 'carousel-item', each
containing an '<img>' element that displays a PNG image. The
'display: inline-block;' and 'margin-right: 20px;' styles are
used to position the carousel items side by side.</p>
```

```
<p>To use this carousel, you will need to replace the
'image1.png', 'image2.png', 'image3.png', 'image4.png', and
'image5.png' file names with the actual PNG images you want
to display.</p>
</body>
</html>
```

Explanation of the Code

The HTML file starts with the standard `<!DOCTYPE html>` declaration, followed by the `<html>` tag.

In the `<head>` section, we have a `<title>` tag that sets the page title to "Horizontal Carousel Example."

Inside the `<style>` section, we define the following CSS classes:

`.carousel-container`: This class is applied to the container `<div>` that holds the carousel items. It sets the width to 100%, the height to 300 pixels, enables horizontal scrolling with `overflow-x: scroll;`, and sets `white-space: nowrap;` to display the items in a single line. The `scrollbar-width: none;`, `-ms-overflow-style: none;`, and `::-webkit-scrollbar { display: none; }` styles are used to hide the scrollbar.

`.carousel-item`: This class is applied to each individual carousel item `<div>`. It sets the display to inline-block and adds a right margin of 20 pixels to create spacing between the items.

`.carousel-item img`: This style targets the `<img>` elements inside the carousel items. It sets the width and height to 100% and uses `object-fit: contain;` to ensure the images are displayed within the 300 x 300 pixel container.

In the `<body>` section, we have a `<div>` element with the `class="carousel-container"` attribute, which holds the carousel items.

Inside the carousel container, there are multiple `<div>` elements with the `class="carousel-item"` attribute, each containing an `<img>` element with the `src` attribute set to the corresponding PNG image file.

When you open this HTML file in a Web browser, you should see a horizontal carousel that displays the five PNG images. Users can scroll through the carousel by dragging or swiping horizontally. The key aspects of this implementation are the use of the `overflow-x: scroll;` and `white-space: nowrap;` styles to create the horizontal scrolling effect, and the `display: inline-block;` and `margin-right: 20px;` styles to position the carousel items side by side. The `object-fit: contain;` property ensures that the images are displayed within the 300 x 300 pixel container without distortion.

Now launch the Web page `perplex_css3_carousel1.html` by navigating to the directory that contains this HTML Web page and then typing the following command:

```
open perplex_css3_carousel1.html
```

After a few moments, you will see a set of PNG files displayed horizontally in a Web page. Now hover over any image and press the left arrow key or the right arrow key and you will see the row of images shift to the left or to the right, respectively, as shown in Figure 5.8.

FIGURE 5.8: A Web page with a carousel effect

CSS3 AND 2D TRANSFORMS

The following prompt was supplied to Perplexity: "`Please generate an HTML Web page that contains CSS3-based 2D transform effects on three HTML <div> elements, along with an explanation of the code.`"

Perplexity:

Here is an HTML Web page that contains CSS3-based 2D transform effects on three HTML <div> elements, along with an explanation of the code.

Listing 5.10 displays the contents of `perplex_css3_2d_transforms.html` that show the code that Perplexity generated in order to display a Web page that contains an SVG rectangle with linear gradient shading, an SVG polygon with radial gradient shading, and an SVG circle with radial gradient shading.

LISTING 5.10: *perplex_css3_2d_transforms.html*

```
<!DOCTYPE html>
<html>
<head>
  <title>CSS3 2D Transform Effects</title>
  <style>
    .transform-container {
      display: flex;
      justify-content: center;
      align-items: center;
```

```
      height: 100vh;
      gap: 20px;
    }

    .transform-box {
      width: 200px;
      height: 200px;
      background-color: #007bff;
      color: #fff;
      font-size: 24px;
      display: flex;
      justify-content: center;
      align-items: center;
      transition: all 0.5s ease;
    }

    .transform-box:hover {
      transform: scale(1.2) rotate(45deg);
    }

    .skew-box {
      width: 200px;
      height: 200px;
      background-color: #ff6b6b;
      color: #fff;
      font-size: 24px;
      display: flex;
      justify-content: center;
      align-items: center;
      transition: all 0.5s ease;
    }

    .skew-box:hover {
      transform: skewX(30deg) skewY(-20deg);
    }

    .translate-box {
      width: 200px;
      height: 200px;
      background-color: #ffa500;
      color: #fff;
      font-size: 24px;
      display: flex;
      justify-content: center;
      align-items: center;
      transition: all 0.5s ease;
    }

    .translate-box:hover {
      transform: translateX(50px) translateY(30px);
    }
  </style>
</head>
<body>
  <div class="transform-container">
    <div class="transform-box">
```

```
      Scale & Rotate
    </div>
    <div class="skew-box">
      Skew
    </div>
    <div class="translate-box">
      Translate
    </div>
  </div>
```

```
  <p>This HTML page contains three '<div>' elements with
different CSS3-based 2D transform effects:</p>
```

```
  <h2>Scale and Rotate</h2>
  <p>The first '<div>' element with the class 'transform-
box' has a hover effect that scales the element by 1.2
times its original size and rotates it by 45 degrees. The
'transform: scale(1.2) rotate(45deg);' property is used to
achieve this effect.</p>
```

```
  <h2>Skew</h2>
  <p>The second '<div>' element with the class 'skew-box'
has a hover effect that skews the element horizontally by
30 degrees and vertically by -20 degrees. The 'transform:
skewX(30deg) skewY(-20deg);' property is used to achieve
this effect.</p>
```

```
  <h2>Translate</h2>
  <p>The third '<div>' element with the class 'translate-
box' has a hover effect that moves the element 50
pixels to the right and 30 pixels down. The 'transform:
translateX(50px) translateY(30px);' property is used to
achieve this effect.</p>
```

```
  <p>All the '<div>' elements have a transition effect
with a duration of 0.5 seconds, which makes the transform
animations smooth and visually appealing.</p>
  </body>
  </html>
```

Explanation of the Code

The HTML file starts with the standard <!DOCTYPE html> declaration, followed by the <html> tag.

In the <head> section, we have a <title> tag that sets the page title to "CSS3 2D Transform Effects."

Inside the <style> section, we define the following CSS classes:

.transform-container: This class is applied to the parent container that holds the three <div> elements. It uses display: flex;, justify-content: center;, and align-items: center; to center the elements both horizontally and vertically. The height: 100vh; and gap: 20px; properties are used to fill the entire viewport height and add spacing between the elements.

`.transform-box`, `.skew-box`, and `.translate-box`: These classes are applied to the individual `<div>` elements. They set the width and height to 200 pixels, the background color, the text color and size, and use `display: flex;`, `justify-content: center;`, and `align-items: center;` to center the text within the `<div>` elements.

The `:hover` pseudo-class is used to define the transform effects that are applied when the user hovers over each `<div>` element:

`.transform-box:hover`: Scales the element by 1.2 times its original size and rotates it by 45 degrees.

`.skew-box:hover`: Skews the element horizontally by 30 degrees and vertically by -20 degrees.

`.translate-box:hover`: Moves the element 50 pixels to the right and 30 pixels down.

All the `<div>` elements have a transition: all 0.5s ease; property, which adds a smooth animation effect to the transform changes.

In the `<body>` section, we have a `<div>` element with the `class="transform-container"` attribute, which holds the three `<div>` elements with the transform effects.

Inside the container, we have three `<div>` elements with the classes transform-box, skew-box, and translate-box, which apply the respective transform effects.

When you open this HTML file in a Web browser, you should see three `<div>` elements side-by-side. Hovering over each `<div>` element will trigger the corresponding 2D transform effect, such as scaling, skewing, or translating the element. The CSS3 transform properties used in this example (`scale()`, `rotate()`, `skewX()`, `skewY()`, `translateX()`, and `translateY()`) allow you to easily apply various 2D transformations to HTML elements, creating dynamic and visually engaging user interfaces.

Now launch the Web page `perplex_css3_2d_transforms.html` by navigating to the directory that contains this HTML Web page and then typing the following command:

```
open perplex_css3_2d_transforms.html
```

After a few moments, you will see a Web page that displays three green HTML `<div>` elements that contain the text "Rotate," "Scale," and "Skew," respectively. Now hover over each of these `<div>` elements and you will see a corresponding 2D transform effect that is shown in Figure 5.9, Figure 5.10, and Figure 5.11, respectively.

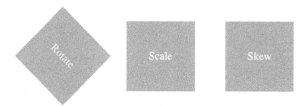

FIGURE 5.9: A Web page with a CSS3-based rotation effect

FIGURE 5.10: A Web page with a CSS3-based scaling effect

FIGURE 5.11: A Web page with a CSS3-based skew effect

CSS3 FILTERS

Filter effects in HTML Web pages can greatly enhance the visual experience. CSS3 supports the following filter types:

- blur
- drop-shadow
- brightness
- contrast
- grayscale
- hue-rotate
- invert
- opacity
- saturate
- sepia
- url

Note that SVG supports a larger set of filter effects, some of which you will see in the next chapter. Now let's take a look at some examples of CSS3 filter effects, which are shown in the following sections.

CSS3 BLUR FILTER

The following prompt was supplied to Perplexity to generate an HTML Web page that contains an HTML `<div>` element that is rendered with a CSS3 blur filter: "Please generate an HTML Web page that contains a <div> element of width 400 and height 200, with a box-shadow attribute with value inset 15px 12px 30px #000; that is displayed with a CSS3 blur filter."

Perplexity:

Here's an HTML Web page that contains a `<div>` element with a width of 400 pixels and a height of 200 pixels, with a box-shadow attribute and a CSS3 blur filter.

Listing 5.11 displays the contents of `perplex_css3_blur_filter.html` that show the code that Perplexity generated in order to display a Web page that contains an artistic pattern of cubic Bezier curves with random radial gradients.

LISTING 5.11: perplex_css3_blur_filter.html

```
<!DOCTYPE html>
<html>
<head>
  <title>Blurred Box-Shadow Effect</title>
  <style>
    body {
      display: flex;
      justify-content: center;
      align-items: center;
      height: 100vh;
      margin: 0;
      background-color: #f0f0f0;
    }

    .blurred-box {
      width: 400px;
      height: 200px;
      background-color: #fff;
      box-shadow: inset 15px 12px 30px #000;
      filter: blur(10px);
    }
  </style>
</head>
<body>
  <div class="blurred-box"></div>
</body>
</html>
```

Explanation of the Code
The HTML file starts with the standard `<!DOCTYPE html>` declaration, followed by the `<html>` tag.

In the `<head>` section, we have a `<title>` tag that sets the page title to "Blurred Box-Shadow Effect."

Inside the `<style>` section, we define the following CSS:

`body`: This rule sets the display to flex, centers the content both horizontally and vertically, sets the height to 100vh (viewport height), removes the margin, and sets the background color to a light gray (#f0f0f0).

`.blurred-box`: This class is applied to the `<div>` element that will display the blurred box-shadow effect. It sets the width to 400 pixels, the height to 200 pixels, the background color to white (#fff), and applies the box-shadow and blur filter.

The box-shadow property adds an inset shadow with a value of inset 15px 12px 30px #000, creating a dark, recessed effect.

The `filter: blur(10px);` property applies a CSS3 blur filter to the `<div>` element, creating a soft, blurred appearance.

In the `<body>` section, we have a `<div>` element with the `class="blurred-box"` attribute, which applies the styles defined in the CSS.

When you open this HTML file in a Web browser, you should see a centered `<div>` element with a width of 400 pixels and a height of 200 pixels, displaying a blurred box-shadow effect. The combination of the box-shadow and the blur filter creates a visually interesting and artistic effect, which can be used as a design element or to draw attention to specific content on the page.

Now launch the Web page `perplex_css3_blur_filter.html` by navigating to the directory that contains this HTML Web page and then typing the following command:

```
open perplex_css3_blur_filter.html
```

After a few moments, you will see the image in Figure 5.12 that displays a CSS3 blur filter effect.

FIGURE 5.12 CSS3 blur filter effect

CSS3 DROP SHADOW

The following prompt was supplied to Perplexity to generate an HTML Web page that contains an HTML <div> element that is rendered with a CSS3 drop shadow effect:

"Please generate an HTML Web page that contains a <div> element of width 400 and height 200, with a box-shadow attribute with value inset 15px 12px 30px #000; that is displayed with a CSS3 blur filter."

Perplexity:

Here's an HTML Web page that contains a <div> element with a width of 400 pixels and a height of 200 pixels, with a box-shadow attribute and a CSS3 blur filter.

Listing 5.12 displays the contents of perplex_css3_drop_shadow.html that show the code that Perplexity generated in order to display a Web page that contains an artistic pattern of cubic Bezier curves with random radial gradients.

LISTING 5.12: perplex_css3_drop_shadow.html

```
<!DOCTYPE html>
<html>
<head>
  <title>Blurred Box-Shadow Effect</title>
  <style>
    body {
      display: flex;
      justify-content: center;
      align-items: center;
      height: 100vh;
      margin: 0;
      background-color: #f0f0f0;
    }

    .blurred-box {
      width: 400px;
      height: 200px;
      background-color: #fff;
      box-shadow: inset 15px 12px 30px #000;
      filter: blur(10px);
    }
  </style>
</head>
<body>
  <div class="blurred-box"></div>
</body>
</html>
```

Explanation of the Code
The HTML file starts with the standard <!DOCTYPE html> declaration, followed by the <html> tag.

In the `<head>` section, we have a `<title>` tag that sets the page title to "Blurred Box-Shadow Effect."

Inside the `<style>` section, we define the following CSS:

`body`: This rule sets the display to `flex`, centers the content both horizontally and vertically, sets the height to 100vh (viewport height), removes the margin, and sets the background color to a light gray (#f0f0f0).

`.blurred-box`: This class is applied to the `<div>` element that will display the blurred box-shadow effect. It sets the width to 400 pixels, the height to 200 pixels, the background color to white (#fff), and applies the box-shadow and blur filter.

The box-shadow property adds an inset shadow with a value of inset 15px 12px 30px #000, creating a dark, recessed effect.

The `filter: blur(10px);` property applies a CSS3 blur filter to the `<div>` element, creating a soft, blurred appearance.

In the `<body>` section, we have a `<div>` element with the `class="blurred-box"` attribute, which applies the styles defined in the CSS.

When you open this HTML file in a Web browser, you should see a centered `<div>` element with a width of 400 pixels and a height of 200 pixels, displaying a blurred box-shadow effect. The combination of the box-shadow and the blur filter creates a visually interesting and artistic effect, which can be used as a design element or to draw attention to specific content on the page.

Now launch the Web page `perplex_css3_drop-shadow.html` by navigating to the directory that contains this HTML Web page and then typing the following command:

```
open perplex_css3_drop_shadow.html
```

After a few moments, you will see the image in Figure 5.13 that displays a CSS3 drop shadow effect.

FIGURE 5.13: CSS3 drop shadow effect

SUMMARY

This chapter started with a brief description of the strengths and weaknesses of HTML, as well as popular use cases for HTML. Then you saw a Perplexity-generated HTML Web page that contains a drop-down list with the days of the week.

Next, you learned about the strengths and weaknesses of CSS3, as well as use cases and potential security issues with CSS3. In addition, you saw code samples of CSS3 linear gradients, CSS3 radial gradients, rounded rectangles, diagonal gradients, and multi gradients.

In addition, you learned how to create CSS3 animation effects, keyframe animation effects, and a carousel with CSS3. Furthermore, you learned how to use CSS3 2D transforms, quadratic Bezier curves, and cubic Bezier curves.

Finally, you saw examples of CSS3 filters, such as blur filters and drop shadow filter effects.

CHAPTER 6

INTRODUCTION TO SVG

This chapter gives an overview of scalable vector graphics (SVG) as well as numerous SVG-based code samples, along with examples of how to reference SVG documents in CSS3 selectors. The CSS3 examples in this book are for WebKit-based browsers, but the code can be inserted for other browsers by using browser-specific prefixes, which were discussed briefly in Chapter 3.

OVERVIEW OF SVG

This section contains various examples that illustrate some of the 2D shapes and effects that can be created with SVG. This section gives an overview, and to learn more about SVG, perform an Internet search for details about books and many online tutorials.

SVG is an XML-based technology for rendering 2D shapes. SVG supports linear gradients, radial gradients, filter effects, transforms (translate, scale, skew, and rotate), and animation effects using an XML-based syntax. Although SVG does not support 3D effects, SVG provides functionality that is unavailable in CSS3, such as support for arbitrary polygons, elliptic arcs, quadratic and cubic Bezier curves, and filters.

Fortunately, SVG documents can be referenced in CSS selectors via the CSS url() function, and the third part of this chapter contains examples of combining CSS3 and SVG in an HTML page. Moreover, the combination of CSS3 and SVG gives a powerful mechanism for leveraging the functionality of SVG in CSS3 selectors. With the information learned in this chapter, Claude 3 can be used to generate SVG documents. More can be learned about SVG by performing an Internet search and then choosing from the many online tutorials that provide SVG code samples.

Basic 2D Shapes in SVG

SVG supports a `<line>` element for rendering line segments, and its syntax looks like this:

```
<line x1="20" y1="20" x2="100" y2="150".../>
```

SVG `<line>` elements render line segments that connect the two points `(x1,y1)` and `(x2,y2)`.

SVG also supports a `<rect>` element for rendering rectangles, and its syntax looks like this:

```
<rect width="200" height="50" x="20" y="50".../>
```

The SVG `<rect>` element renders a rectangle whose width and height are specified in the width and height attributes. The upper-left vertex of the rectangle is specified by the point with coordinates (x,y). Listing 6.1 displays the contents of `BasicShapes1.svg`, which illustrates how to render line segments and rectangles.

LISTING 6.1:   BasicShapes1.svg

```
<?xml version="1.0" encoding="iso-8859-1"?>
<!DOCTYPE svg PUBLIC "-//W3C//DTD SVG 20001102//EN"
"http://www.w3.org/TR/2000/CR-SVG-20001102/DTD/svg-
20001102.dtd">

<svg xmlns="http://www.w3.org/2000/svg"
     xmlns:xlink="http://www.w3.org/1999/xlink"
     width="100%" height="100%">
<g>
<!-- left-side figures -->
<line x1="20" y1="20" x2="220" y2="20"
        stroke="blue" stroke-width="4"/>

<line x1="20" y1="40" x2="220" y2="40"
        stroke="red" stroke-width="10"/>

<rect width="200" height="50" x="20" y="70"
        fill="red" stroke="black" stroke-width="4"/>

<path d="M20,150 1200,0 10,50 1-200,0 z"
        fill="blue" stroke="red" stroke-width="4"/>

<!-- right-side figures -->
<path d="M250,20 1200,0 1-100,50 z"
        fill="blue" stroke="red" stroke-width="4"/>

<path d="M300,100 1100,0 150,50 1-50,50 1-100,0 1-50,-50 z"
        fill="yellow" stroke="red" stroke-width="4"/>
</g>
</svg>
```

The first SVG <line> element in Listing 6.1 specifies the color blue and a stroke-width (i.e., line width) of 4, whereas the second SVG <line> element specifies the color red and a stroke-width of 10.

Notice that the first SVG <rect> element renders a rectangle that looks the same (except for the color) as the second SVG <line> element, which shows that more than one SVG element can be used to render a rectangle (or a line segment).

The SVG <path> element is probably the most flexible and powerful element because it can be used to create arbitrarily complex shapes based on a concatenation of other SVG elements. Later in this chapter, an example of how to render multiple Bezier curves in an SVG <path> element will be given.

An SVG <path> element contains a d attribute that specifies the points in the desired path. For example, the first SVG <path> element in Listing 6.1 contains the following d attribute:

```
d="M20,150 l200,0 10,50 l-200,0 z"
```

This is how to interpret the contents of the d attribute:

- move to the absolute point (20, 150)
- draw a horizontal line segment 200 pixels to the right
- draw a line segment 10 pixels to the right and 50 pixels down
- draw a horizontal line segment 200 pixels toward the left
- draw a line segment to the initial point (z)

Similar comments apply to the other two SVG <path> elements in Listing 6.1. One thing to keep in mind is that uppercase letters (C, L, M, and Q) refer to absolute positions, whereas lowercase letters (c, l, m, and q) refer to relative positions with respect to the element that is to the immediate left. Experiment with the code in Listing 6.1 by using combinations of lowercase and uppercase letters to gain a better understanding of how to create different visual effects. Figure 6.1 displays the result of rendering the SVG document BasicShapes1.svg.

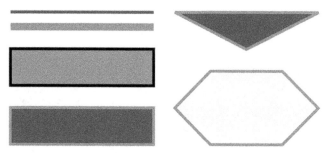

FIGURE 6.1: SVG line segments and rectangles

SVG Gradients

SVG supports linear gradients as well as radial gradients that can be applied to 2D shapes. For example, the SVG <path> element can be used to define elliptic arcs (using the d attribute) and then specify gradient effects. Note that SVG supports the stroke-dasharray attribute and the <polygon> element, neither of which is available in HTML5 Canvas. Listing 6.2 displays the contents of BasicShapesLRG1.svg, which illustrates how to render 2D shapes with linear gradients and with radial gradients.

LISTING 6.2: BasicShapesLRG1.svg

```
<?xml version="1.0" encoding="iso-8859-1"?>
<!DOCTYPE svg PUBLIC "-//W3C//DTD SVG 20001102//EN"
 "http://www.w3.org/TR/2000/CR-SVG-20001102/DTD/svg-
20001102.dtd">

<svg xmlns="http://www.w3.org/2000/svg"
    xmlns:xlink="http://www.w3.org/1999/xlink"
    width="100%" height="100%">
<defs>
<linearGradient id="pattern1"
                    x1="0%" y1="100%" x2="100%" y2="0%">
<stop offset="0%"    stop-color="yellow"/>
<stop offset="40%"   stop-color="red"/>
<stop offset="80%"   stop-color="blue"/>
</linearGradient>

<radialGradient id="pattern2">
<stop offset="0%"    stop-color="yellow"/>
<stop offset="40%"   stop-color="red"/>
<stop offset="80%"   stop-color="blue"/>
</radialGradient>
</defs>

<g>
<ellipse cx="120" cy="80" rx="100" ry="50"
            fill="url(#pattern1)"/>

<ellipse cx="120" cy="200" rx="100" ry="50"
            fill="url(#pattern2)"/>

<ellipse cx="320" cy="80" rx="50" ry="50"
            fill="url(#pattern2)"/>

<path d="M 505,145 v -100 a 250,100 0 0,1 -200,100"
        fill="black"/>

<path d="M 500,140 v -100 a 250,100 0 0,1 -200,100"
        fill="url(#pattern1)"
        stroke="black" stroke-thickness="8"/>

<path d="M 305,165 v  100 a 250,100 0 0,1  200,-100"
        fill="black"/>

<path d="M 300,160 v  100 a 250,100 0 0,1  200,-100"
        fill="url(#pattern1)"
        stroke="black" stroke-thickness="8"/>
```

```
<ellipse cx="450" cy="240" rx="50" ry="50"
         fill="url(#pattern1)"/>
</g>
</svg>
```

Listing 6.2 contains an SVG `<defs>` element that specifies a `<linearGradi-
ent>` element (whose `id` attribute has the value `pattern1`) with three stop
values using an XML-based syntax, followed by a `<radialGradient>` element with three `<stop>` elements and an `id` attribute whose value is `pat-
tern2`.

The SVG `<g>` element contains four `<ellipse>` elements, the first of
which specifies the point `(120, 80)` as its center `(cx, cy)`, with a major radius
of `100`, a minor radius of `50`, filled with the linear gradient `pattern1`, as
shown here:

```
<ellipse cx="120" cy="80" rx="100" ry="50"
         fill="url(#pattern1)"/>
```

Similar comments apply to the other three SVG `<ellipse>` elements.

The SVG `<g>` element also contains four `<path>` elements that render
elliptic arcs. The first `<path>` element specifies a black background for the
elliptic arc defined with the following `d` attribute:

```
d="M 505,145 v -100 a 250,100 0 0,1 -200,100"
```

Unfortunately, the SVG syntax for elliptic arcs is nonintuitive, and it is based
on the notion of major arcs and minor arcs that connect two points on an ellipse. This example is only for illustrative purposes, so it is not necessary to
delve into a detailed explanation of elliptic arcs work in SVG. To learn the details, perform an Internet search and read the information found at the various
links (be prepared to spend some time experimenting with how to generate
various types of elliptic arcs).

The second SVG `<path>` element renders the same elliptic arc with a slight
offset, using the linear gradient `pattern1`, which creates a shadow effect.
Similar comments apply to the other pair of SVG `<path>` elements, which
render an elliptic arc with the radial gradient `pattern2` (also with a shadow
effect). Figure 6.2 displays the result of rendering `BasicShapesLRG1.svg`.

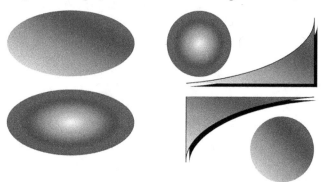

FIGURE 6.2: SVG elliptic arcs with linear and radial gradients

SVG `<polygon>` Element

The SVG `<polygon>` element contains a polygon attribute in which points can be specified that represent the vertices of a polygon. The SVG `<polygon>` element is most useful when creating polygons with an arbitrary number of sides, but this element can also be used to render line segments and rectangles. Listing 6.3 displays the contents of SVGCube1.svg, which illustrates how to render a cube in SVG.

LISTING 6.3:   SvgCube1.svg

```
<?xml version="1.0" encoding="iso-8859-1"?>
<!DOCTYPE svg PUBLIC "-//W3C//DTD SVG 20001102//EN"
 "http://www.w3.org/TR/2000/CR-SVG-20001102/DTD/
                                     svg-20001102.dtd">

<svg xmlns="http://www.w3.org/2000/svg"
     xmlns:xlink="http://www.w3.org/1999/xlink"
     width="100%" height="100%">
<defs>
  <linearGradient id="pattern1">
    <stop offset="0%"   stop-color="yellow"/>
    <stop offset="40%"  stop-color="red"/>
    <stop offset="80%"  stop-color="blue"/>
  </linearGradient>

  <radialGradient id="pattern2">
    <stop offset="0%"   stop-color="yellow"/>
    <stop offset="40%"  stop-color="red"/>
    <stop offset="80%"  stop-color="blue"/>
  </radialGradient>

  <radialGradient id="pattern3">
    <stop offset="0%"   stop-color="red"/>
    <stop offset="30%"  stop-color="yellow"/>
    <stop offset="60%"  stop-color="white"/>
    <stop offset="90%"  stop-color="blue"/>
  </radialGradient>
</defs>

<!-- top face (counter clockwise) -->
<polygon fill="url(#pattern1)"
            points="50,50 200,50 240,30 90,30"/>

<!-- front face -->
<rect width="150" height="150" x="50" y="50"
                            fill="url(#pattern2)"/>
```

```
<!-- right face (counter clockwise) -->
<polygon fill="url(#pattern3)"
         points="200,50 200,200 240,180 240,30"/>
</svg>
```

Listing 6.3 contains an SVG `<defs>` element that defines a linear gradient and two radial gradients. Next, the SVG `<g>` element contains the three faces of a cube: an SVG `<polygon>` element renders the top face (which is a parallelogram), an SVG `<rect>` element renders the front face, and another SVG `<polygon>` element renders the right face (which is also a parallelogram). The three faces of the cube are rendered with the linear gradient, and the two radial gradients defined in the SVG `<defs>` element at the beginning of Listing 6.3. Figure 6.3 displays the result of rendering the SVG document `SVGCube1. svg`.

FIGURE 6.3: An SVG cube with gradient shading

Bezier Curves

SVG supports quadratic and cubic Bezier curves that can be rendered with linear gradients or radial gradients. Multiple Bezier curves can also be concatenated using an SVG `<path>` element. Listing 6.4 displays the contents of `BezierCurves1.svg`, which illustrates how to render various Bezier curves.

LISTING 6.4: *BezierCurves1.svg*

```
<?xml version="1.0" encoding="iso-8859-1"?>
<!DOCTYPE svg PUBLIC "-//W3C//DTD SVG 20001102//EN"
 "http://www.w3.org/TR/2000/CR-SVG-20001102/DTD/svg-
20001102.dtd">

<svg xmlns="http://www.w3.org/2000/svg"
     xmlns:xlink="http://www.w3.org/1999/xlink"
     width="100%" height="100%">
<defs>
```

```
<linearGradient id="pattern1"
                x1="0%" y1="100%" x2="100%" y2="0%">
<stop offset="0%"   stop-color="yellow"/>
<stop offset="40%"  stop-color="red"/>
<stop offset="80%"  stop-color="blue"/>
</linearGradient>

<linearGradient id="pattern2"
                gradientTransform="rotate(90)">
<stop offset="0%"   stop-color="#C0C040"/>
<stop offset="30%"  stop-color="#303000"/>
<stop offset="60%"  stop-color="#FF0F0F"/>
<stop offset="90%"  stop-color="#101000"/>
</linearGradient>
</defs>

<g transform="scale(1.5,0.5)">
<path d="m 0,50 C 400,200 200,-150 100,350"
        stroke="black" stroke-width="4"
        fill="url(#pattern1)"/>
</g>

<g transform="translate(50,50)">
<g transform="scale(0.5,1)">
<path d="m 50,50 C 400,100 200,200 100,20"
        fill="red" stroke="black" stroke-width="4"/>
</g>

<g transform="scale(1,1)">
<path d="m 50,50 C 400,100 200,200 100,20"
        fill="yellow" stroke="black" stroke-width="4"/>
</g>
</g>

<g transform="translate(-50,50)">
<g transform="scale(1,2)">
<path d="M 50,50 C 400,100 200,200 100,20"
        fill="blue" stroke="black" stroke-width="4"/>
</g>
</g>

<g transform="translate(-50,50)">
<g transform="scale(0.5, 0.5) translate(195,345)">
<path d="m20,20 C20,50 20,450 300,200 s-150,-250 200,100"
        fill="blue" style="stroke:#880088;
        stroke-width:4;"/>
</g>

<g transform="scale(0.5, 0.5) translate(185,335)">
<path d="m20,20 C20,50 20,450 300,200 s-150,-250 200,100"
        fill="url(#pattern2)"
style="stroke:#880088;stroke-width:4;"/>
</g>

<g transform="scale(0.5, 0.5) translate(180,330)">
```

```
<path d="m20,20 C20,50 20,450 300,200 s-150,-250 200,100"
    fill="blue" style="stroke:#880088;stroke-width:4;"/>
</g>

<g transform="scale(0.5, 0.5) translate(170,320)">
<path d="m20,20 C20,50 20,450 300,200 s-150,-250 200,100"
        fill="url(#pattern2)" style="stroke:black;
            stroke-width:4;"/>
</g>
</g>

<g transform="scale(0.8,1) translate(380,120)">
<path d="M0,0 C200,150 400,300 20,250"
        fill="url(#pattern2)" style="stroke:blue;
            stroke-width:4;"/>
</g>

<g transform="scale(2.0,2.5) translate(150,-80)">
<path d="M200,150 C0,0 400,300 20,250"
        fill="url(#pattern2)" style="stroke:blue;
            stroke-width:4;"/>
</g>
</svg>
```

Listing 6.4 contains an SVG <defs> element that defines two linear gradients, followed by 10 SVG <path> elements, each of which renders a cubic Bezier curve. The SVG <path> elements are enclosed in SVG <g> elements, whose transform attributes contain the SVG scale() function or the SVG translate() function (or both).

The first SVG <g> element invokes the SVG scale() function to scale the cubic Bezier curve that is specified in an SVG <path> element, as shown here:

```
<g transform="scale(1.5,0.5)">
<path d="m 0,50 C 400,200 200,-150 100,350"
        stroke="black" stroke-width="4"
        fill="url(#pattern1)"/>
</g>
```

The cubic Bezier curve has an initial point (0,50), with control points (400,200) and (200,-150), followed by the second control point (100,350). The Bezier curve is black, with a width of 4, and its fill color is defined in the <linearGradient> element (whose id attribute is pattern1) that is contained in the SVG <defs> element. The remaining SVG <path> elements are similar to the first SVG <path> element, so they will not be described. Figure 6.4 displays the result of rendering the Bezier curves that are defined in the SVG document BezierCurves1.svg.

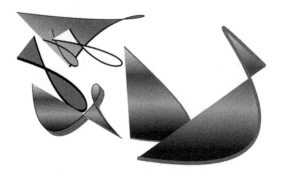

FIGURE 6.4: SVG Bezier curves

SVG FILTERS, SHADOW EFFECTS, AND TEXT PATHS

Filter effects can be created to apply to 2D shapes and also to text strings; this section contains three SVG-based examples of creating such effects. Listing 6.5, Listing 6.6, and Listing 6.7 display the contents of the three SVG documents `BlurFilterText1.svg`, `ShadowFilterText1.svg`, and `TextOn-QBezierPath1.svg`, respectively.

LISTING 6.5: *BlurFilterText1.svg*

```
<?xml version="1.0" encoding="iso-8859-1"?>
<!DOCTYPE svg PUBLIC "-//W3C//DTD SVG 20001102//EN"
  "http://www.w3.org/TR/2000/CR-SVG-20001102/DTD/
    svg-20001102.dtd">

<svg xmlns="http://www.w3.org/2000/svg"
     xmlns:xlink="http://www.w3.org/1999/xlink"
     width="100%" height="100%">
<defs>
<filter
     id="blurFilter1"
     filterUnits="objectBoundingBox"
     x="0" y="0"
     width="100%" height="100%">
     <feGaussianBlur stdDeviation="4"/>
</filter>
</defs>

<g transform="translate(50,100)">
<text id="normalText" x="0" y="0"
      fill="red" stroke="black" stroke-width="4"
      font-size="72">
    Normal Text
</text>

<text id="horizontalText" x="0" y="100"
      filter="url(#blurFilter1)"
      fill="red" stroke="black" stroke-width="4"
```

```
        font-size="72">
      Blurred Text
</text>
</g>
</svg>
```

The SVG <defs> element in Listing 6.5 contains an SVG <filter> element that specifies a Gaussian blur with the following line:

```
<feGaussianBlur stdDeviation="4"/>
```

Larger values can be specified for the stdDeviation attribute for creating more-diffuse filter effects.

The first SVG <text> element that is contained in the SVG <g> element renders a normal text string, whereas the second SVG <text> element contains a filter attribute that references the filter (defined in the SVG <defs> element) to render the same text string, as shown here:

```
filter="url(#blurFilter1)"
```

Figure 6.5 displays the result of rendering BlurFilterText1.svg, which creates a filter effect.

Normal Text

FIGURE 6.5: SVG filter effect

LISTING 6.6: *ShadowFilterText1.svg*

```
<?xml version="1.0" encoding="iso-8859-1"?>
<!DOCTYPE svg PUBLIC "-//W3C//DTD SVG 20001102//EN"
  "http://www.w3.org/TR/2000/CR-SVG-20001102/DTD/
    svg-20001102.dtd">

<svg xmlns="http://www.w3.org/2000/svg"
     xmlns:xlink="http://www.w3.org/1999/xlink"
     width="100%" height="100%">
<defs>
<filter
     id="blurFilter1"
     filterUnits="objectBoundingBox"
     x="0" y="0"
     width="100%" height="100%">
<feGaussianBlur stdDeviation="4"/>
</filter>
</defs>
```

```
<g transform="translate(50,150)">
<text id="horizontalText" x="15" y="15"
      filter="url(#blurFilter1)"
      fill="red" stroke="black" stroke-width="2"
      font-size="72">
    Shadow Text
</text>

<text id="horizontalText" x="0" y="0"
      fill="red" stroke="black" stroke-width="4"
      font-size="72">
    Shadow Text
</text>
</g>
</svg>
```

Listing 6.6 is very similar to the code in Listing 6.5, except that the relative offset for the second SVG `<text>` element is slightly different, thereby creating a shadow effect. Figure 6.6 displays the result of rendering `ShadowFilterText1.svg`, which creates a shadow effect.

FIGURE 6.6: SVG text with a shadow effect

LISTING 6.7: *TextOnQBezierPath1.svg*

```
<?xml version="1.0" encoding="iso-8859-1"?>
<!DOCTYPE svg PUBLIC "-//W3C//DTD SVG 20001102//EN"
 "http://www.w3.org/TR/2000/CR-SVG-20001102/DTD/
   svg-20001102.dtd">

<svg xmlns="http://www.w3.org/2000/svg"
     xmlns:xlink="http://www.w3.org/1999/xlink"
     width="100%" height="100%">
<defs>
<path id="pathDefinition"
      d="m0,0 Q100,0 200,200 T300,200 z"/>
</defs>

<g transform="translate(100,100)">
<text id="textStyle" fill="red"
      stroke="blue" stroke-width="2"
      font-size="24">

<textPath xlink:href="#pathDefinition">
      Sample Text that follows a path specified by a
         Quadratic Bezier curve
</textPath>
</text>
</g>
</svg>
```

The SVG <defs> element in Listing 6.7 contains an SVG <path> element that defines a quadratic Bezier curve (note the Q in the d attribute). This SVG <path> element has an id attribute whose value is pathDefinition, which is referenced later in this code sample.

The SVG <g> element contains an SVG <text> element that specifies a text string to render, as well as an SVG <textPath> element that specifies the path along which the text is rendered, as shown here:

```
<textPath xlink:href="#pathDefinition">
        Sample Text that follows a path specified by a
        Quadratic Bezier curve
</textPath>
```

Notice that the SVG <textPath> element contains the attribute xlink:href whose value is pathDefinition, which is also the id of the SVG <path> element that is defined in the SVG <defs> element. As a result, the text string is rendered along the path of a quadratic Bezier curve instead of rendering the text string horizontally (which is the default behavior). Figure 6.7 displays the result of rendering TextOnQBezierPath1.svg, which renders a text string along the path of a quadratic Bezier curve.

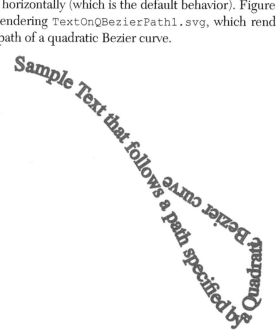

FIGURE 6.7: SVG text on a quadratic Bezier curve

SVG TRANSFORMS

Earlier in this chapter were some examples of SVG transform effects. In addition to the SVG functions scale(), translate(), and rotate(), SVG provides the skew() function to create skew effects. Listing 6.8 displays the contents of TransformEffects1.svg, which illustrates how to apply transforms to rectangles and circles in SVG.

LISTING 6.8:   TransformEffects1.svg

```
<?xml version="1.0" encoding="iso-8859-1"?>
<!DOCTYPE svg PUBLIC "-//W3C//DTD SVG 20001102//EN"
 "http://www.w3.org/TR/2000/CR-SVG-20001102/DTD/
    svg-20001102.dtd">

<svg xmlns="http://www.w3.org/2000/svg"
     xmlns:xlink="http://www.w3.org/1999/xlink"
     width="100%" height="100%">
<defs>
<linearGradient id="gradientDefinition1"
     x1="0" y1="0" x2="200" y2="0"
     gradientUnits="userSpaceOnUse">
<stop offset="0%"   style="stop-color:#FF0000"/>
<stop offset="100%" style="stop-color:#440000"/>
</linearGradient>

<pattern id="dotPattern" width="8" height="8"
         patternUnits="userSpaceOnUse">

<circle id="circle1" cx="2" cy="2" r="2"
        style="fill:red;"/>
</pattern>
</defs>

<!-- full cylinder -->
<g id="largeCylinder" transform="translate(100,20)">
<ellipse cx="0"  cy="50" rx="20" ry="50"
            stroke="blue" stroke-width="4"
            style="fill:url(#gradientDefinition1)"/>

<rect x="0" y="0" width="300" height="100"
        style="fill:url(#gradientDefinition1)"/>

<rect x="0" y="0" width="300" height="100"
        style="fill:url(#dotPattern)"/>

<ellipse cx="300" cy="50" rx="20"  ry="50"
            stroke="blue" stroke-width="4"
            style="fill:yellow;"/>
</g>

<!-- half-sized cylinder -->
<g transform="translate(100,100) scale(.5)">
<use xlink:href="#largeCylinder" x="0" y="0"/>
</g>

<!-- skewed cylinder -->
<g transform="translate(100,100) skewX(40) skewY(20)">
<use xlink:href="#largeCylinder" x="0" y="0"/>
</g>

<!-- rotated cylinder -->
<g transform="translate(100,100) rotate(40)">
<use xlink:href="#largeCylinder" x="0" y="0"/>
```

```
</g>
</svg>
```

The SVG <defs> element in Listing 6.8 contains a <linearGradient> element that defines a linear gradient, followed by an SVG <pattern> element that defines a custom pattern, which is shown here:

```
<pattern id="dotPattern" width="8" height="8"
        patternUnits="userSpaceOnUse">

<circle id="circle1" cx="2" cy="2" r="2"
        style="fill:red;"/>
</pattern>
```

The SVG <pattern> element contains an SVG <circle> element that is repeated in a grid-like fashion inside an 8 x 8 rectangle (note the values of the width attribute and the height attribute). The SVG <pattern> element has an id attribute whose value is dotPattern because, as will become apparent, this element creates a "dotted" effect.

Listing 6.8 contains four SVG <g> elements, each of which renders a cylinder that references the SVG <pattern> element that is defined in the SVG <defs> element. The first SVG <g> element in Listing 6.8 contains two SVG <ellipse> elements and two SVG <rect> elements. The first <ellipse> element renders the left-side "cover" of the cylinder with the linear gradient that is defined in the SVG <defs> element. The first <rect> element renders the "body" of the cylinder with a linear gradient, and the second <rect> element renders the "dot pattern" on the body of the cylinder. Finally, the second <ellipse> element renders the right-side "cover" of the ellipse.

The other three cylinders are easy to create: they simply reference the first cylinder and apply a transformation to change the size, shape, and orientation. Specifically, these three cylinders reference the first cylinder with the following code:

```
<use xlink:href="#largeCylinder" x="0" y="0"/>
```

and then they apply scale, skew, and rotate functions in order to render scaled, skewed, and rotated cylinders. Figure 6.8 displays the result of rendering TransformEffects1.svg.

FIGURE 6.8 : SVG transform effects

SVG ANIMATION

SVG supports animation effects that can be specified as part of the declaration of SVG elements. Listing 6.9 displays the contents of the SVG document AnimateMultiRect1.svg, which illustrates how to create an animation effect with four rectangles.

LISTING 6.9:   AnimateMultiRect1.svg

```
<?xml version="1.0" encoding="iso-8859-1"?>
<!DOCTYPE svg PUBLIC "-//W3C//DTD SVG 20010904//EN"
  "http://www.w3.org/TR/2001/REC-SVG-20010904/DTD/svg10.dtd">

<svg xmlns="http://www.w3.org/2000/svg"
     xmlns:xlink="http://www.w3.org/1999/xlink"
     width="100%" height="100%">
<defs>
<rect id="rect1" width="100" height="100"
        stroke-width="1" stroke="blue"/>
</defs>

<g transform="translate(10,10)">
<rect width="500" height="400"
        fill="none" stroke-width="4" stroke="black"/>
</g>

<g transform="translate(10,10)">
<use xlink:href="#rect1" x="0" y="0" fill="red">
<animate attributeName="x" attributeType="XML"
                begin="0s" dur="4s"
                fill="freeze" from="0" to="400"/>
</use>

<use xlink:href="#rect1" x="400" y="0" fill="green">
<animate attributeName="y" attributeType="XML"
                begin="0s" dur="4s"
                fill="freeze" from="0" to="300"/>
</use>

<use xlink:href="#rect1" x="400" y="300" fill="blue">
<animate attributeName="x" attributeType="XML"
                begin="0s" dur="4s"
                fill="freeze" from="400" to="0"/>
</use>

<use xlink:href="#rect1" x="0" y="300" fill="yellow">
<animate attributeName="y" attributeType="XML"
                begin="0s" dur="4s"
                fill="freeze" from="300" to="0"/>
</use>
</g>
</svg>
```

The SVG <defs> element in Listing 6.9 contains an SVG <rect> element that defines a blue rectangle, followed by an SVG <g> element that renders the border of a large rectangle that "contains" the animation effect, which involves the movement of four rectangles in a clockwise fashion along the perimeter of an outer rectangle.

The second SVG <g> element contains four <use> elements that perform a parallel animation effect on four rectangles. The first <use> element references the rectangle defined in the SVG <defs> element and then animates the x attribute during a four-second interval as shown here:

```
<use xlink:href="#rect1" x="0" y="0" fill="red">
<animate attributeName="x" attributeType="XML"
                begin="0s" dur="4s"
                fill="freeze" from="0" to="400"/>
</use>
```

Notice that the x attribute varies from 0 to 400, which moves the rectangle horizontally from left to right. The second SVG <use> element also references the rectangle defined in the SVG <defs> element, except that the animation involves changing the y attribute from 0 to 300 in order to move the rectangle downward, as shown here:

```
<use xlink:href="#rect1" x="400" y="0" fill="green">
<animate attributeName="y" attributeType="XML"
                begin="0s" dur="4s"
                fill="freeze" from="0" to="300"/>
</use>
```

In a similar fashion, the third SVG <use> element moves the referenced rectangle horizontally from right to left, and the fourth SVG <use> element moves the referenced rectangle vertically and upward.

To create a sequential animation effect (or a combination of sequential and parallel), then the values of the begin attribute (and possibly the dur attribute) need to be modified to achieve the desired animation effect. Figure 6.9 displays the result of rendering AnimateMultiRect1.svg.

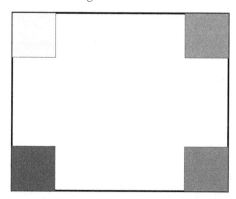

FIGURE 6.9: SVG animation effect with four rectangles

Listing 6.10 displays the contents of the SVG AnimateText1.svg, which illustrates how to animate a text string.

LISTING 6.10:   AnimateText1.svg

```
<?xml version="1.0" encoding="iso-8859-1"?>
<!DOCTYPE svg PUBLIC "-//W3C//DTD SVG 20010904//EN"
  "http://www.w3.org/TR/2001/REC-SVG-20010904/DTD/svg10.dtd">

<svg xmlns="http://www.w3.org/2000/svg"
     xmlns:xlink="http://www.w3.org/1999/xlink"
     width="100%" height="100%">

<g transform="translate(100,100)">
<text x="0" y="0" font-size="48" visibility="hidden"
         stroke="black" stroke-width="2">
      Animating Text in SVG
<set attributeName="visibility"
             attributeType="CSS" to="visible"
             begin="2s" dur="5s" fill="freeze"/>

<animateMotion path="M0,0 L50,150"
             begin="2s" dur="5s" fill="freeze"/>

<animateColor attributeName="fill"
             attributeType="CSS"
             from="yellow" to="red"
             begin="2s" dur="8s" fill="freeze"/>

<animateTransform attributeName="transform"
             attributeType="XML"
             type="rotate" from="-90" to="0"
             begin="2s" dur="5s" fill="freeze"/>

<animateTransform attributeName="transform"
             attributeType="XML"
             type="scale" from=".5" to="1.5" additive="sum"
             begin="2s" dur="5s" fill="freeze"/>
</text>
</g>
</svg>
```

Listing 6.10 contains an SVG `<text>` element that specifies four different effects. The `<set>` element specifies the visibility of the text string for a five-second interval with an initial offset of two seconds.

The SVG `<animateMotion>` element shifts the upper-left corner of the text string from the point (0,0) to the point (50,150) in a linear fashion. This effect is combined with two other motion effects: rotation and scaling.

The SVG `<animateColor>` element changes the text color from yellow to red, and because the dur attribute has value 8s, this effect lasts three seconds longer than the other animation effects, whose dur attributes have the values 5s. Note that all the animation effects start at the same time.

The first SVG `<animateTransform>` element performs a clockwise rotation of 90 degrees from vertical to horizontal. The second SVG `<animate-Transform>` element performs a scaling effect that occurs in parallel with the first SVG `<animateTransform>` element because they have the same values for the `begin` attribute and the `dur` attribute. Figure 6.10 displays the result of rendering `AnimateText1.svg`.

Animating Text in SVG

FIGURE 6.10 : SVG text animation effect

SVG AND JAVASCRIPT

SVG allows the user to embed JavaScript in a CDATA section, which means that SVG elements can be programmatically created. Listing 6.11 displays the contents of the SVG document `ArchEllipses1.svg`, which illustrates how to render a set of ellipses that follow the path of an Archimedean spiral.

LISTING 6.11: ArchEllipses1.svg

```
<?xml version="1.0" standalone="no"?>
<!DOCTYPE svg PUBLIC "-//W3C//DTD SVG 20010904//EN"
   "http://www.w3.org/TR/2001/REC-SVG-20010904/DTD/svg10.dtd">

<svg xmlns="http://www.w3.org/2000/svg"
     xmlns:xlink="http://www.w3.org/1999/xlink"
     onload="init(evt)"
     width="100%" height="100%">

<script type="text/ecmascript">
<![CDATA[
    var basePointX    = 250;
    var basePointY    = 200;
    var currentX      = 0;
    var currentY      = 0;
    var offsetX       = 0;
    var offsetY       = 0;
    var radius        = 0;
    var minorAxis     = 60;
    var majorAxis     = 30;
    var spiralCount   = 4;
    var Constant      = 0.25;
    var angle         = 0;
    var maxAngle      = 720;
    var angleDelta    = 2;
    var strokeWidth   = 1;
    var redColor      = "rgb(255,0,0)";

    var ellipseNode   = null;
    var svgDocument   = null;
    var target        = null;
    var gcNode        = null;

    var svgNS         = „http://www.w3.org/2000/svg";

    function init(event)
    {
        svgDocument = event.target.ownerDocument;
```

```
        gcNode = svgDocument.getElementById("gc");

        drawSpiral(event);
    ]

    function drawSpiral(event)
    {
        for(angle=0; angle<maxAngle; angle+=angleDelta)
        {
            radius    = Constant*angle;
            offsetX  = radius*Math.cos(angle*Math.PI/180);
            offsetY  = radius*Math.sin(angle*Math.PI/180);
            currentX = basePointX+offsetX;
            currentY = basePointY-offsetY;

            ellipseNode =
                    svgDocument.createElementNS(svgNS,
                                            "ellipse");

            ellipseNode.setAttribute("fill", redColor);
            ellipseNode.setAttribute("stroke-width",
                                    strokeWidth);

            if( angle % 3 == 0 ) {
                ellipseNode.setAttribute("stroke", "yellow");
            ] else {
                ellipseNode.setAttribute("stroke", "green");
            ]

            ellipseNode.setAttribute("cx", currentX);
            ellipseNode.setAttribute("cy", currentY);
            ellipseNode.setAttribute("rx", majorAxis);
            ellipseNode.setAttribute("ry", minorAxis);

            gcNode.appendChild(ellipseNode);
        ]
    ] // drawSpiral
  ]]></script>
<!-- =========================== -->
<g id="gc" transform="translate(10,10)">
<rect x="0" y="0"
        width="800" height="500"
        fill="none" stroke="none"/>
</g>
</svg>
```

Notice that the SVG <svg> element in Listing 6.11 contains an onload attribute that references the JavaScript function init(), and as may be surmised, the init() function is executed when this SVG document is launched in a browser. In this example, the purpose of the init() function is to reference the graphics context that is defined in the SVG <g> element at the bottom of Listing 6.11, and then to invoke the drawSpiral() function.

To include JavaScript in an SVG document, place the JavaScript code inside a CDATA section that is embedded in a <script> element. The CDATA section in Listing 6.11 initializes some variables, along with the definition of the `init()` function and the `drawSpiral()` function.

The code in the `drawSpiral()` function consists of a loop that renders a set of dynamically created SVG `<ellipse>` elements. Each SVG `<ellipse>` element is created in the SVG namespace that is specified in the variable `svgNS`, after which values are assigned to the required attributes of an ellipse, as shown here:

```
ellipseNode = svgDocument.createElementNS(svgNS,
"ellipse");
ellipseNode.setAttribute("fill", redColor);
ellipseNode.setAttribute("stroke-width", strokeWidth);

// conditional logic omitted
ellipseNode.setAttribute("cx", currentX);
ellipseNode.setAttribute("cy", currentY);
ellipseNode.setAttribute("rx", majorAxis);
ellipseNode.setAttribute("ry", minorAxis);
```

After each SVG `<ellipse>` element is dynamically created, the element is appended to the DOM with one line of code, as shown here:

```
gcNode.appendChild(ellipseNode);
```

Finally, the SVG `<g>` element at the bottom of Listing 6.11 acts as a canvas on which the dynamically generated ellipses are rendered. Figure 6.11 displays the result of rendering `ArchEllipses1.svg`.

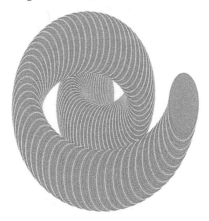

FIGURE 6.11: Dynamically generated SVG `<ellipse>` elements

CSS3 AND SVG BAR CHARTS

Now that it has been explained how to reference SVG documents in CSS3 selectors, an example will be presented of referencing an SVG-based bar chart in a CSS3 selector. Listing 6.12 displays the contents of the HTML Web page `CSS3SVGBarChart1.html`, Listing 6.13 displays the contents of the CSS3 stylesheet `CSS3SVGBarChart1.css` (whose selectors are applied to the contents of Listing 6.13), and Listing 6.14 displays the contents of the SVG document CSS3SVGBarChart1.svg (referenced in a selector in Listing 6.13), which contains the SVG code for rendering a bar chart.

LISTING 6.12: CSS3SVGBarChart1.html

```
<!doctype html>
<html en>
<head>
<title>CSS Multi Column Text and SVG Bar Chart</title>
<meta charset="utf-8" />
<link href="CSS3SVGBarChart1.css" rel="stylesheet"
                                  type="text/css">
</head>

<body>
<div id="outer">
<article>
<p id="line1">.</p>
<div id="columns">
<p>
CSS enables you to define so-called "selectors" that
specify the style or the manner in which you want to render
elements in an HTML page.  CSS helps you modularize your
HTML content and since you can place your CSS definitions
in a separate file, you can also re-use the same CSS
definitions in multiple HTML files.</p>
<p>
Moreover, CSS also enables you to simplify the updates that
you need to make to elements in HTML pages.  For example,
suppose that multiple HTML table elements use a CSS rule
that specifies the color red.  If you later need to change
the color to blue, you can effect such a change simply by
making one change (i.e., changing red to blue) in one CSS
rule.</p>
<p>
Without a CSS rule, you would be forced to manually update
the color attribute in every HTML table element that
is affected, which is error-prone, time-consuming, and
extremely inefficient.</p>
<p>
As you can see, it's very easy to reference an SVG document
in CSS selectors, and in this example, an SVG-based bar
chart is rendered on the left-side of the screen.</p>
</div>

<p id="line1">.</p>
</article>
</div>
<div id="chart1">
</div>
</body>
</html>
```

Chapter 4 showed an example of rendering multicolumn text, and the contents of Listing 6.12 are essentially the same as the contents of that example. There is an additional HTML <div> element (whose id attribute has value chart1), however, that is used for rendering an SVG bar chart via a CSS selector in Listing 6.13.

LISTING 6.13: *CSS3SVGBarChart1.css*

```
#columns {
-webkit-column-count : 4;
-webkit-column-gap : 40px;
-webkit-column-rule : 1px solid rgb(255,255,255);
column-count : 3;
column-gap : 40px;
column-rule : 1px solid rgb(255,255,255);
]

#line1 {
color: red;
font-size: 24px;
background-image: -webkit-gradient(linear, 0% 0%, 0% 100%,
  from(#fff), to(#f00));
background-image: -gradient(linear, 0% 0%, 0% 100%,
  from(#fff), to(#f00));
-webkit-border-radius: 4px;
border-radius: 4px;
]

#chart1 {
opacity: 0.5;
color: red;
width: 800px;
height: 50%;
position: absolute; top: 20px; left: 20px;
font-size: 24px;
-webkit-border-radius: 4px;
-moz-border-radius: 4px;
border-radius: 4px;
border-radius: 4px;
-webkit-background: url(CSS3SVGBarChart1.svg) top right;
-moz-background: url(CSS3SVGBarChart1.svg) top right;
background: url(CSS3SVGBarChart1.svg) top right;
]
```

The #chart selector contains various attributes, along with a reference to an SVG document that renders an actual bar chart, as shown here:

```
-webkit-background: url(CSS3SVGBarChart1.svg) top right;
-moz-background: url(CSS3SVGBarChart1.svg) top right;
background: url(CSS3SVGBarChart1.svg) top right;
```

Now that the contents of the HTML Web page and the selectors in the CSS stylesheet have been shown, the following is the SVG document that renders the bar chart.

LISTING 6.14: CSS3SVGBarChart1.svg

```
<?xml version="1.0" encoding="iso-8859-1"?>
<!DOCTYPE svg PUBLIC "-//W3C//DTD SVG 20001102//EN"
 "http://www.w3.org/TR/2000/CR-SVG-20001102/DTD/
    svg-20001102.dtd">

<svg xmlns="http://www.w3.org/2000/svg"
     xmlns:xlink="http://www.w3.org/1999/xlink"
     width="100%" height="100%">
<defs>
<linearGradient id="pattern1">
<stop offset="0%"   stop-color="yellow"/>
<stop offset="40%"  stop-color="red"/>
<stop offset="80%"  stop-color="blue"/>
</linearGradient>

<radialGradient id="pattern2">
<stop offset="0%"   stop-color="yellow"/>
<stop offset="40%"  stop-color="red"/>
<stop offset="80%"  stop-color="blue"/>
</radialGradient>

<radialGradient id="pattern3">
<stop offset="0%"   stop-color="red"/>
<stop offset="30%"  stop-color="yellow"/>
<stop offset="60%"  stop-color="white"/>
<stop offset="90%"  stop-color="blue"/>
</radialGradient>
</defs>

<g id="chart1" transform="translate(0,0) scale(1,1)">
<rect width="30" height="235" x="15"  y="15"
fill="black"/>
<rect width="30" height="240" x="10"  y="10"
 fill="url(#pattern1)"/>

<rect width="30" height="145" x="45"  y="105"
   fill="black"/>
<rect width="30" height="150" x="40"  y="100"
   fill="url(#pattern2)"/>

<rect width="30" height="195" x="75"  y="55"
   fill="black"/>
<rect width="30" height="200" x="70"  y="50"
   fill="url(#pattern1)"/>

<rect width="30" height="185" x="105" y="65"
   fill="black"/>
<rect width="30" height="190" x="100" y="60"
   fill="url(#pattern3)"/>

<rect width="30" height="145" x="135" y="105"
   fill="black"/>
<rect width="30" height="150" x="130" y="100"
   fill="url(#pattern1)"/>
```

```
<rect width="30" height="225" x="165" y="25"
  fill="black"/>
<rect width="30" height="230" x="160" y="20"
fill="url(#pattern2)"/>

<rect width="30" height="145" x="195" y="105"
  fill="black"/>
<rect width="30" height="150" x="190" y="100"
fill="url(#pattern1)"/>

<rect width="30" height="175" x="225" y="75"
  fill="black"/>
<rect width="30" height="180" x="220" y="70"
  fill="url(#pattern3)"/>
</g>

<g id="chart2" transform="translate(250,125) scale(1,0.5)"
               width="100%" height="100%">
<use xlink:href="#chart1"/>
</g>
</svg>
```

Listing 6.14 contains an SVG <defs> element in which three gradients are defined (one linear gradient and two radial gradients), whose id attribute has values pattern1, pattern2, and pattern3, respectively. These gradients are referenced by their id in the SVG <g> element that renders a set of rectangular bars for a bar chart. The second SVG <g> element (whose id attribute has value chart2) performs a transform involving the SVG translate() and scale() functions, and then renders the actual bar chart, as shown in this code:

```
<g id="chart2" transform="translate(250,125) scale(1,0.5)"
               width="100%" height="100%">
<use xlink:href="#chart1"/>
</g>
```

Figure 6.12 displays the result of applying CSS3SVGBarChart1.css to the elements in the HTML page CSS3SVGBarChart1.html.

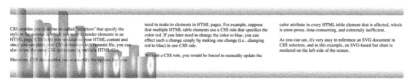

FIGURE 6.12: CSS3 with SVG applied to an HTML page

SUMMARY

This chapter gave an introduction to SVG and presented several code samples that illustrated the graphics capabilities of SVG. We also discussed how to render 2D shapes and how to combine the functionality of SVG with CSS3. You learned how to do the following:

- create SVG linear gradients and radial gradients
- apply SVG gradients to ellipses and elliptic arcs
- render quadratic Bezier curves and cubic Bezier curves in SVG
- reference SVG documents in CSS3 selectors

CSS3 and SVG support additional features for creating sophisticated effects, and an Internet search can be performed to find links that discuss those features.

SVG AND PERPLEXITY

This chapter provides an assortment of SVG-based code samples that are generated by Perplexity based on prompts. Some of the code samples will be familiar: the difference is that almost all the code samples in this chapter are all generated by Perplexity.

The first portion of this chapter contains descriptions of the strengths and weaknesses of SVG, followed by its use cases, accessibility, and potential security issues. The second portion of this chapter contains examples of Perplexity generating linear gradients, radial gradients, and various SVG 2D shapes and gradients. You will also see how to render a bar chart in SVG. The third section shows you how to render quadratic Bezier curves and cubic Bezier curves, as well as how to add animation effects for Bezier curves. In addition, you will learn how to create hover effects. The fourth section compares SVG with CSS3 and also compares SVG with PNGs. Then you will learn how to work with SVG filters, such as blur filters and turbulence filters. The fifth section contains code samples that combine SVG and CSS3 in an HTML Web page, as well as combining SVG and JavaScript in an HTML Web page. You will learn how to create other effects that involve JavaScript and SVG, such as rendering elliptic arts, checkerboard patterns, and a master-detail HTML Web page that involves SVG.

One more detail to keep in mind: the SVG code samples involving Bezier curves (toward the end of the chapter) are created by Python code that is generated by Perplexity. Many laptops have Python already installed, and if need be, you can search online with the keywords "install Python Windows" to find links where you can download Python onto your laptop (and also replace "Windows" with your operating system).

WORKING WITH SVG

The following prompt was supplied to Perplexity: "`Please provide a de-scription of the features of SVG, along with its strengths and weaknesses.`"

`Perplexity:`

Based on the information provided in the search results, here is a description of the features of SVG, along with its strengths and weaknesses: Features of SVG:

- SVG is a vector-based image format that uses XML to describe 2D graphics.
- SVG images are composed of mathematical equations and instructions rather than a grid of pixels, making them scalable without loss of quality.
- SVG supports various graphic primitives such as lines, rectangles, circles, ellipses, polygons, and paths.
- SVG can be manipulated and animated using JavaScript, allowing for dynamic and interactive graphics.
- SVG is an open standard maintained by the W3C, ensuring consistent behavior across different browsers and platforms.

Strengths of SVG:

- *Scalability*: SVG images can be resized without losing quality, making them ideal for responsive Web design and high-resolution displays.
- *Small file size:* SVG files are typically smaller in size compared to raster-based formats like PNG, especially for simple graphics, improving Web site performance.
- *Editability*: SVG code can be directly edited using a text editor, allowing for fine-tuning and customization.
- *Accessibility*: SVG graphics can be made accessible to screen readers and other assistive technologies.
- *Interactivity*: SVG's integration with JavaScript enables the creation of dynamic and interactive graphics.

Weaknesses of SVG:

- *Complexity*: SVG may not be suitable for highly detailed or complex graphics, as the file size can become large and potentially impact performance.
- *Browser support*: While SVG is widely supported, older browsers may not have full support for all SVG features.
- *Editing limitations*: SVG files are primarily editable with vector graphics software like Adobe Illustrator, which may not be accessible to all users.
- *Lack of support for certain features*: SVG may not be able to replicate all the features and effects available in raster-based formats like PNG, such as advanced transparency and blending modes.

In summary, SVG is a powerful vector-based image format that offers scalability, small file size, editability, and interactivity, making it a valuable tool for Web design and development. However, it may not be the best choice for highly complex graphics or in cases where full browser support is not guaranteed.

USE CASES FOR SVG

The following prompt was supplied to Perplexity in order to describe use cases for SVG in HTML Web pages: "Please describe significant use cases that involve SVG in HTML Web pages, along with an explanation of the use cases."

Perplexity:

Based on the information provided in the search results, here are some significant use cases for SVG in HTML Web pages, along with an explanation of each:

1. Icons

   Explanation: One of the most common use cases for SVG is as icons for Web sites and applications. SVG icons can be easily scaled to any size without losing quality, making them ideal for responsive design. They can also be easily customized and animated using CSS and JavaScript.

2. Logos

   Explanation: Similar to icons, logos are another common use case for SVG. SVG format allows logos to be scaled up or down depending on the context in which they're being used, ensuring that they always look sharp and professional.

3. Charts and Graphs

   Explanation: SVG is an excellent choice for creating charts and graphs, as it allows for precise control over the appearance and layout of data visualizations. Additionally, SVG charts can be made interactive and dynamic using JavaScript, allowing them to update in real-time based on user input or data changes.

4. Illustrations and Artwork

   Explanation: For more complex illustrations and artwork, the SVG format offers a level of detail and flexibility that is unmatched by other image formats. SVG supports features like gradients, patterns, and advanced graphical effects, enabling the creation of stunning visuals that can be scaled without losing quality.

5. Responsive Design

   Explanation: One of the key advantages of using SVG in Web pages is its ability to scale without losing quality. This makes SVG particularly well-suited for responsive Web design, as it ensures that graphics will always look crisp and clear, regardless of the device or screen size.

6. Performance Optimization

   Explanation: Embedding SVG files directly into HTML documents can help reduce the number of HTTP requests a Web site needs to make, resulting in faster page load times and improved overall performance. Additionally, SVG files can be compressed to further optimize their file size.

7. Interactivity and Animation

   Explanation: SVG's integration with JavaScript allows for the creation of interactive and animated graphics that can enhance the user experience. Developers can use JavaScript to manipulate SVG elements, respond to user input, and dynamically modify the appearance of SVG graphics.

8. Accessibility and SEO

   Explanation: The text-based nature of SVG files means that they can be easily indexed by search engines and read by screen readers, improving the accessibility and searchability of Web content. This can help improve a Web site's search engine rankings and make it more accessible to users with disabilities.

By leveraging these use cases, Web developers can take advantage of the unique features and benefits of SVG to create visually stunning, responsive, and high-performance Web experiences.

ACCESSIBILITY AND SVG

The following prompt was supplied to Perplexity: `"Please provide a de-tailed description of the level of support for accessibility in SVG."`

`Perplexity:`

Based on the information provided in the search results, here is a detailed description of the level of support for accessibility in SVG:

1. Accessibility Support in SVG

   The SVG specification includes built-in accessibility features, such as the `<title>` and `<desc>` elements, which are intended to provide short and long text descriptions for SVG graphics. The `<title>` element is meant to provide a short, concise description of the SVG graphic, while the `<desc>` element can be used to provide a more detailed, longer description. These accessibility-related elements are designed to be exposed through the browser's accessibility API, allowing screen readers and other assistive technologies to access and convey the information to users.

2. Browser Support for SVG Accessibility

   Browser support for properly exposing the `<title>` and `<desc>` elements through the accessibility API is inconsistent across different browsers and platforms. According to the research cited in the search results, Internet Explorer 10 and later on Windows is the only browser that correctly exposes both the `<title>` and `<desc>` elements, as well as the role of the SVG element, through the accessibility API. Other browsers, such as Firefox, Chrome, Safari, and Android Chrome, either do not expose the information correctly or fail to expose it altogether.

3. Screen Reader Support for SVG Accessibility

   Screen reader support for the accessibility information provided in SVG graphics is largely dependent on how the information is exposed through the browser's accessibility API. The search results indicate that screen readers, such as JAWS, NVDA, VoiceOver, and TalkBack, can provide varying levels of support for accessing the `<title>` and `<desc>` elements, depending on the browser and platform. In some cases, screen readers may not correctly interpret the accessibility information or may present it in a way that is not intuitive for users.

4. Enhancing SVG Accessibility with ARIA

   To address the inconsistent browser and screen reader support for the built-in SVG accessibility features, the search results suggest using ARIA (Accessible Rich Internet Applications) to enhance the accessibility of SVG graphics. By adding ARIA attributes, such as `aria-labelled` by and `role="graphic"` or `role="image"`, the accessibility information can be more reliably exposed through the browser's accessibility API and interpreted by screen readers. The search results indicate that using ARIA to enhance SVG accessibility can improve the support and consistency across different browsers and screen readers.

In summary, the accessibility support for SVG graphics is currently limited and inconsistent across different browsers and screen readers. While the SVG specification includes built-in accessibility features, their implementation and exposure through the accessibility API is not yet fully reliable. Using ARIA to enhance SVG accessibility can help improve the situation, but the overall support for accessible SVG graphics remains an area that requires further development and standardization.

SECURITY ISSUES WITH SVG

The following prompt was supplied to Perplexity: `"Please provide a detailed description of potential security issues involving SVG."`

Perplexity:

Based on the search results provided, the key potential security issues involving SVG files are:

1. **Cross-Site Scripting (XSS) Attacks**

   SVG files can contain embedded scripts, which can be exploited to inject malicious code into a Web site. An attacker can upload an SVG file with malicious JavaScript code, and when a user views the Web page containing the SVG, the embedded script executes, potentially leading to unauthorized access to user data or other malicious actions.

2. **Mitigating XSS Risks in SVGs**

   Thoroughly vet and sanitize any SVG files uploaded to your Web site, ensuring they do not contain potentially harmful scripts. Disable script execution within SVG by setting your Web site's Content-Security-Policy (CSP) header, which restricts the types of content that can be loaded and executed.

3. **Performance Issues with SVGs**

   SVGs can be resource-intensive to render, particularly on older devices or slow connections, resulting in slow-loading Web sites or even crashes. Animations and JavaScript manipulations within SVGs can further strain performance, especially on mobile devices or older computers with limited processing power.

4. **Optimizing SVG Performance**

   Simplify SVG files by removing unnecessary elements, optimizing complex paths, and reducing the number of nodes. Consider using alternative formats or techniques for complex animations, such as CSS animations or video files, which may be more efficient and less resource intensive.

5. **Browser Compatibility**

   Older browsers may not display SVG correctly, leading to compatibility issues and degraded user experience.

It is important to test your Web site on various browsers and devices to identify compatibility issues and address them accordingly. In summary, the key potential security issues with SVGs are the risk of XSS attacks due to embedded scripts, as well as performance and compatibility concerns. Mitigating these risks requires careful vetting, sanitization, and optimization of SVG files, along with appropriate security measures and browser compatibility testing.

SVG LINEAR GRADIENTS

The following prompt was supplied to Perplexity to generate an HTML Web page that contains an SVG rectangle with a linear gradient:

```
"Please generate an HTML Web page containing an SVG rec-
tangle of width 500 and height 300 that is rendered with an
SVG linear gradient, along with an explanation of the code."
```

Perplexity:

Listing 7.1 displays the contents of `perplex_svg_linear_gradient.html` that show the code that Perplexity generated in order to display a Web page that contains an SVG rectangle with linear gradient shading, an SVG polygon with radial gradient shading, and an SVG circle with radial gradient shading.

Here's an HTML Web page containing an SVG rectangle of width 500 and height 300 that is rendered with an SVG linear gradient, along with an explanation of the code.

LISTING 7.1: *perplex_svg_linear_gradient.html*

```
<!DOCTYPE html>
<html>
<head>
  <title>SVG Linear Gradient Example</title>
</head>
<body>
  <svg width="500" height="300">
    <defs>
      <linearGradient id="myGradient" x1="0%" y1="0%"
                                      x2="100%" y2="100%">
        <stop offset="0%" style="stop-color:#ff6b6b;stop-
                                               opacity:1" />
        <stop offset="25%" style="stop-color:#ffa500;
                                          stop-opacity:1" />
        <stop offset="50%" style="stop-color:#ffff00;
                                          stop-opacity:1" />
        <stop offset="75%" style="stop-color:#00ff00;
                                          stop-opacity:1" />
        <stop offset="100%" style="stop-color:#00ffff;
                                          stop-opacity:1" />
      </linearGradient>
    </defs>
    <rect x="0" y="0" width="500" height="300"
                          fill="url(#myGradient)" />
  </svg>

  <p>This HTML page contains an SVG element with a width of
500 pixels and a height of 300 pixels.</p>

  <p>Inside the SVG element, there are two main parts:</p>

  <ol>
   <li>
     <strong>Definitions ('<defs>'):</strong> This section
defines a linear gradient with the ID "myGradient". The
gradient starts with a red color ('#ff6b6b') at the 0%
offset, transitions to orange ('#ffa500') at 25%, yellow
('#ffff00') at 50%, green ('#00ff00') at 75%, and finally
reaches cyan ('#00ffff') at the 100% offset.
   </li>
   <li>
```

```
      <strong>Rectangle ('<rect>'):</strong> This element
creates a rectangle with the same dimensions as the SVG
container (500x300 pixels). The 'fill' attribute is set
to 'url(#myGradient)', which applies the linear gradient
defined earlier to the rectangle.
    </li>
  </ol>

  <p>When you open this HTML file in a Web browser, you
should see a rectangular area filled with a smooth,
multicolored linear gradient.</p>
</body>
</html>
```

Explanation of the Code

The HTML file starts with the standard `<!DOCTYPE html>` declaration, followed by the `<html>` tag. In the `<head>` section, we have a `<title>` tag that sets the page title to "SVG Linear Gradient Example." In the `<body>` section, we have an `<svg>` element with a width of 500 pixels and a height of 300 pixels.

Inside the `<svg>` element, there are two main parts:

`<defs>`: This section is used to define reusable elements, in this case, a linear gradient.

The `<linearGradient>` element defines the gradient, with the id attribute set to `myGradient`. The x1, y1, x2, and y2 attributes specify the start and end points of the gradient, in this case, from the top-left to the bottom-right corner.

The `<stop>` elements define the color stops along the gradient, with the offset attribute specifying the position (0% to 100%) and the style attribute setting the color and opacity.

`<rect>`: This element creates a rectangle with the same dimensions as the SVG container (500 x 300 pixels). The fill attribute is set to `url(#myGradient)`, which applies the linear gradient defined earlier to the rectangle.

Below the SVG element, there are several `<p>` elements that provide an explanation of the code.

When you open this HTML file in a Web browser, you should see a rectangular area filled with a smooth, multicolored linear gradient, as defined by the SVG code. The key aspects of this implementation are the use of the `<defs>` section to define the reusable linear gradient, and the `<rect>` element to apply the gradient to a rectangular shape within the SVG container. This allows for the creation of dynamic and visually appealing graphics using SVG.

Now launch the Web page `perplex_svg_rect_poly.html` by navigating to the directory that contains this HTML Web page and then typing the following command:

```
open perplex_svg_linear_gradient.html
```

After a few moments, you will see the image in Figure 7.1 that displays a snapshot of SVG-based rectangle with a linear gradient.

FIGURE 7.1: An SVG-based rectangle with a linear gradient

SVG RADIAL GRADIENTS

The following prompt was supplied to Perplexity to generate an HTML Web page that contains an SVG rectangle with a radial gradient:

"Please generate an HTML Web page containing an SVG rectangle of width 500 and height 300 that is rendered with an SVG radial gradient, along with an explanation of the code."

Perplexity:

Listing 7.2 displays the contents of perplex_svg_radial_gradient.html that show the code that Perplexity generated in order to display a Web page that contains an SVG rectangle with radial gradient shading.

LISTING 7.2: *perplex_svg_radial_gradient.html*

```
<!DOCTYPE html>
<html>
<head>
  <title>SVG Radial Gradient Example</title>
</head>
<body>
  <svg width="500" height="300">
    <defs>
      <radialGradient id="myGradient" cx="50%" cy="50%"
                              r="50%" fx="50%" fy="50%">
        <stop offset="0%" style="stop-color:#ff6b6b;
                              stop-opacity:1" />
        <stop offset="25%" style="stop-color:#ffa500;
                              stop-opacity:1" />
        <stop offset="50%" style="stop-color:#ffff00;
                              stop-opacity:1" />
        <stop offset="75%" style="stop-color:#00ff00;
                              stop-opacity:1" />
```

```
            <stop offset="100%" style="stop-color:#00ffff;
                                stop-opacity:1" />
        </radialGradient>
      </defs>
      <rect x="0" y="0" width="500" height="300"
                                fill="url(#myGradient)" />
    </svg>

    <p>This HTML page contains an SVG element with a width of
500 pixels and a height of 300 pixels.</p>

    <p>Inside the SVG element, there are two main parts:</p>

    <ol>
      <li>
        <strong>Definitions ('<defs>'):</strong> This section
defines a radial gradient with the ID "myGradient". The
gradient starts with a red color ('#ff6b6b') at the 0%
offset, transitions to orange ('#ffa500') at 25%, yellow
('#ffff00') at 50%, green ('#00ff00') at 75%, and finally
reaches cyan ('#00ffff') at the 100% offset.

        <li>The 'cx', 'cy', and 'r' attributes define the
center and radius of the gradient, respectively.</li>
        <li>The 'fx' and 'fy' attributes define the focal
point of the gradient, which is the same as the center in
this case.</li>

      </li>
      <li>
        <strong>Rectangle ('<rect>'):</strong> This element
creates a rectangle with the same dimensions as the SVG
container (500x300 pixels). The 'fill' attribute is set
to 'url(#myGradient)', which applies the radial gradient
defined earlier to the rectangle.
      </li>
    </ol>

    <p>When you open this HTML file in a Web browser, you
should see a rectangular area filled with a smooth,
multicolored radial gradient.</p>
  </body>
</html>
```

Explanation of the Code

The HTML file starts with the standard `<!DOCTYPE html>` declaration, followed by the `<html>` tag. In the `<head>` section, we have a `<title>` tag that sets the page title to "SVG Radial Gradient Example." In the `<body>` section, we have an `<svg>` element with a width of 500 pixels and a height of 300 pixels.

Inside the `<svg>` element, there are two main parts:

`<defs>`: This section is used to define reusable elements, in this case, a radial gradient.

The <radialGradient> element defines the gradient, with the id attribute set to myGradient. The cx, cy, and r attributes specify the center and radius of the gradient, respectively. The fx and fy attributes define the focal point of the gradient, which is the same as the center in this case.

The <stop> elements define the color stops along the gradient, with the offset attribute specifying the position (0% to 100%) and the style attribute setting the color and opacity.

<rect>: This element creates a rectangle with the same dimensions as the SVG container (500 x 300 pixels). The fill attribute is set to url(#myGradient), which applies the radial gradient defined earlier to the rectangle.

Below the SVG element, there are several <p> elements that provide an explanation of the code.

When you open this HTML file in a Web browser, you should see a rectangular area filled with a smooth, multicolored radial gradient, as defined by the SVG code. The key aspects of this implementation are the use of the <defs> section to define the reusable radial gradient, and the <rect> element to apply the gradient to a rectangular shape within the SVG container. The cx, cy, r, fx, and fy attributes of the <radialGradient> element allow you to control the appearance and positioning of the radial gradient. This example demonstrates how SVG can be used to create dynamic and visually appealing graphics with advanced gradient effects, which can be useful for a variety of Web design and development applications.

Now launch the Web page perplex_svg_radial_gradient.html by navigating to the directory that contains this HTML Web page and then typing the following command:

```
open perplex_svg_radial_gradient.html
```

After a few moments you will see the image in Figure 7.2 that displays a rectangle rendered with a radial gradient.

FIGURE 7.2: A SVG-based rectangle with a radial gradient

A TRIANGLE WITH A RADIAL GRADIENT

The following prompt was supplied to Perplexity to generate SVG code for a triangle that is rendered with a radial gradient in an HTML Web page:

"Please generate an HTML Web page containing a triangle with width 200 and height 400 that is rendered with a radial gradient and a drop shadow, along with an explanation of the code."

Perplexity:

LISTING 7.3: triangleRG1.html

```
<!DOCTYPE html>
<html>
<head>
  <title>SVG Triangle with Radial Gradient and Drop
Shadow</title>
  <style>
    .triangle-container {
      display: flex;
      justify-content: center;
      align-items: center;
      height: 100vh;
    }

    .triangle {
      width: 0;
      height: 0;
      border-top: 200px solid transparent;
      border-right: 200px solid transparent;
      border-bottom: 400px solid transparent;
      border-left: 200px solid transparent;
      filter: drop-shadow(0 0 20px rgba(0, 0, 0, 0.5));
      position: relative;
    }

    .triangle:before {
      content: "";
      position: absolute;
      top: 0;
      left: 0;
      width: 100%;
      height: 100%;
      background: radial-gradient(circle at 50% 50%,
                  #ff6b6b, #ffa500, #ffff00, #00ff00,
                  #00ffff, #0000ff, #ff00ff);
      opacity: 0.5;
      z-index: -1;
    }
  </style>
</head>
<body>
  <div class="triangle-container">
```

```
      <div class="triangle"></div>
    </div>
```

```
    <p>This HTML page contains a triangle with a width of 200
pixels and a height of 400 pixels, rendered using CSS.</p>
```

```
    <p>The key aspects of the code are:</p>
```

```
    <ol>
      <li>
        <strong>Triangle Shape:</strong> The triangle
is created using CSS border properties. The 'border-
top', 'border-right', 'border-bottom', and 'border-
left' properties are set to different values to form the
triangular shape.
      </li>
      <li>
        <strong>Radial Gradient:</strong> The triangle is
rendered with a radial gradient background, which is
applied using the '::before' pseudo-element. The gradient
starts with a red color ('#ff6b6b') at the center and
transitions to other colors, including orange, yellow,
green, cyan, blue, and purple.
      </li>
      <li>
        <strong>Drop Shadow:</strong> The triangle has a drop
shadow effect applied using the 'filter: drop-shadow()'
property. This adds a soft, blurred shadow around the
triangle, creating a more visually appealing and three-
dimensional effect.
      </li>
      <li>
        <strong>Centering the Triangle:</strong> The triangle
is centered both horizontally and vertically within
the page using the 'display: flex;', 'justify-content:
center;', and 'align-items: center;' properties on the
parent container.
      </li>
    </ol>
```

```
    <p>When you open this HTML file in a web browser, you
should see a large, triangular shape with a radial gradient
background and a drop shadow effect, centered on the
page.</p>
  </body>
</html>
```

Explanation of the Code

The HTML file starts with the standard `<!DOCTYPE html>` declaration, followed by the `<html>` tag. In the `<head>` section, we have a `<title>` tag that sets the page title to "SVG Triangle with Radial Gradient and Drop Shadow."

Inside the `<style>` section, we define the following CSS:

`.triangle-container`: This class is applied to the parent container that holds the triangle. It uses `display: flex;`, `justify-content: center;`, and `align-items:   center;` to center the triangle both horizontally and vertically.

`.triangle`: This class is applied to the triangle element. It uses CSS border properties to create the triangular shape:

`border-top`, `border-right`, `border-bottom`, and `border-left` are set to different values to form the triangle.

`filter: drop-shadow(0 0 20px rgba(0, 0, 0, 0.5));` applies a drop shadow effect to the triangle.

`position:   relative;` is used to position the `::before` pseudo-element.

`.triangle:before`: This pseudo-element is used to apply the radial gradient background to the triangle. It covers the entire area of the triangle and has an opacity of 0.5 to create a semi-transparent effect.

In the `<body>` section, we have a `<div>` element with the `class="triangle-container"` attribute, which holds the triangle. Inside the container, there is a `<div>` element with the `class="triangle"` attribute, which represents the triangle.

When you open this HTML file in a Web browser, you should see a large, triangular shape with a radial gradient background and a drop shadow effect, centered on the page. The key aspects of this implementation are the use of CSS border properties to create the triangular shape, the application of a radial gradient background using the `::before` pseudo-element, and the addition of a drop shadow effect using the `filter:   drop-shadow()` property. The centering of the triangle is achieved through the use of `flexbox` layout. This example demonstrates how SVG-like effects can be achieved using CSS, which can be useful for creating dynamic and visually appealing graphics without the need for external image files.

Now launch the Web page `perplex_triangleRG1.html` by navigating to the directory that contains this HTML Web page and then typing the following command:

`open triangleRG1.html`

After a few moments, you will see the image in Figure 7.3 that displays a triangle with a radial gradient.

FIGURE 7.3: An SVG triangle with a radial gradient

SVG 2D SHAPES AND GRADIENTS

The following prompt was supplied to Perplexity to generate an HTML Web page that contains several SVG-based elements:

"Please generate an HTML Web page that contains an SVG triangle, SVG circle, SVG ellipse, and an 8-sided SVG polygon that are rendered with either a linear gradient or a radial gradient, along with an explanation of the code."

Perplexity:

Here is an HTML Web page that contains various SVG shapes rendered with linear and radial gradients, along with an explanation of the code:

Listing 7.4 displays the contents of perplex_svg_2d_shapes.html that show the code that Perplexity generated in order to display a Web page that contains an SVG rectangle with linear gradient shading, an SVG polygon with radial gradient shading, and an SVG circle with radial gradient shading.

LISTING 7.4: perplex_svg_2d_shapes.html

```
<!DOCTYPE html>
<html lang="en">
<head>
  <meta charset="UTF-8">
  <meta name="viewport" content="width=device-width,
                             initial-scale=1.0">
  <title>SVG Shapes with Gradients</title>
  <style>
    body {
      display: flex;
      justify-content: center;
      align-items: center;
      height: 100vh;
      margin: 0;
      background-color: #f0f0f0;
    }

    .container {
      display: grid;
      grid-template-columns: repeat(2, 1fr);
      grid-gap: 20px;
    }

    .shape {
      width: 200px;
      height: 200px;
      display: flex;
      justify-content: center;
      align-items: center;
    }
  </style>
</head>
<body>
```

```
<div class="container">
  <!-- Triangle with Linear Gradient -->
  <div class="shape">
    <svg viewBox="0 0 100 100">
      <defs>
        <linearGradient id="triangleGradient" x1="0%"
                        y1="0%" x2="100%" y2="100%">
          <stop offset="0%" stop-color="#ff6b6b" />
          <stop offset="100%" stop-color="#ffa500" />
        </linearGradient>
      </defs>
      <polygon points="50,10 10,90 90,90"
                        fill="url(#triangleGradient)" />
    </svg>
  </div>

  <!-- Circle with Radial Gradient -->
  <div class="shape">
    <svg viewBox="0 0 100 100">
      <defs>
        <radialGradient id="circleGradient" cx="50%"
                        cy="50%" r="50%" fx="50%" fy="50%">
          <stop offset="0%" stop-color="#9b59b6" />
          <stop offset="100%" stop-color="#8e44ad" />
        </radialGradient>
      </defs>
      <circle cx="50" cy="50" r="40"
                        fill="url(#circleGradient)" />
    </svg>
  </div>

  <!-- Ellipse with Linear Gradient -->
  <div class="shape">
    <svg viewBox="0 0 100 100">
      <defs>
        <linearGradient id="ellipseGradient" x1="0%"
                        y1="0%" x2="100%" y2="0%">
          <stop offset="0%" stop-color="#2980b9" />
          <stop offset="100%" stop-color="#3498db" />
        </linearGradient>
      </defs>
      <ellipse cx="50" cy="50" rx="40" ry="30"
                        fill="url(#ellipseGradient)" />
    </svg>
  </div>

  <!-- Polygon with Radial Gradient -->
  <div class="shape">
    <svg viewBox="0 0 100 100">
      <defs>
        <radialGradient id="polygonGradient" cx="50%"
                        cy="50%" r="50%" fx="50%" fy="50%">
          <stop offset="0%" stop-color="#16a085" />
          <stop offset="100%" stop-color="#1abc9c" />
        </radialGradient>
      </defs>
```

```
        <polygon points="50,10 75,50 50,90 25,90 0,50
                     25,10" fill="url(#polygonGradient)" />
      </svg>
    </div>
  </div>
</body>
</html>
```

Explanation of the Code:

The HTML page includes a `<style>` section that sets up the layout and positioning of the SVG shapes using CSS. Inside the `<body>`, there is a `<div>` with the class `container` that holds the four SVG shapes. Each SVG shape is wrapped in a `<div>` with the class `shape` to ensure proper centering and sizing. The `<svg>` element defines the SVG viewport and contains the specific shapes. The `<defs>` section defines the gradient definitions that will be used to fill the shapes. For the triangle and ellipse, a linear gradient is used, with the gradient direction specified by the `x1`, `y1`, `x2`, and `y2` attributes. For the circle and polygon, a radial gradient is used, with the gradient center and radius specified by the `cx`, `cy`, and `r` attributes.

The gradient stops are defined using the `<stop>` elements, specifying the color and offset (0% to 100%) of the gradient. The specific shapes are then defined using SVG elements like `<polygon>`, `<circle>`, `<ellipse>`, and `<polygon>`, with the fill attribute set to the corresponding gradient id.

This code will render the four SVG shapes (triangle, circle, ellipse, and 8-sided polygon) with the specified linear and radial gradients, creating a visually appealing and interactive display on the Web page.

Now launch the Web page `perplex_svg_2d_shapes.html` in Listing 7.4 by navigating to the directory that contains this HTML Web page and then typing the following command:

```
open perplex_svg_2d_shapes.html
```

After a few moments, you will see the image in Figure 7.4 that displays a triangle, circle, ellipse, and polygon with gradient shading.

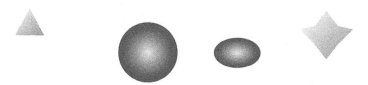

FIGURE 7.4: SVG-based 2D shapes

A BAR CHART IN SVG

Before you read this section, note that the Perplexity-generated code in Listing 7.5 is *incorrect*, whereas Listing 7.6 contains a manually modified of Listing 7.5 that does display an SVG-based bar chart.

The following prompt was supplied to Perplexity to generate SVG code for a bar chart in an HTML Web page:

"Please generate an HTML Web page with synthetic data that is used for rendering an SVG bar chart in an HTML Web page, along with an explanation of the code."

Perplexity:

The generated synthetic data for the SVG bar chart is as follows:

```
Category A: 18
Category B: 13
Category C: 98
Category D: 11
Category E: 55
```

Now, let's create an SVG bar chart in an HTML page using this data. Listing 7.5 contains the SVG and HTML code.

LISTING 7.5:   *perplex_svg_barchart.html*

```
<!DOCTYPE html>
<html>
<head>
  <title>SVG Bar Chart</title>
  <style>
    .bar {
      fill: #007bff;
    }

    .bar:hover {
      fill: #0056b3;
    }

    .axis path,
    .axis line {
      fill: none;
      stroke: #000;
      shape-rendering: crispEdges;
    }

    .axis text {
      font-family: sans-serif;
      font-size: 11px;
    }
  </style>
</head>
<body>
  <svg id="chart" width="600" height="400"></svg>

  <script>
    // Generate synthetic data
    const data = [
      { label: 'Category 1', value: 80 },
```

```
      { label: 'Category 2', value: 60 },
      { label: 'Category 3', value: 90 },
      { label: 'Category 4', value: 40 },
      { label: 'Category 5', value: 70 },
   ];

   // Set up the chart dimensions
   const width = 600;
   const height = 400;
   const margin = { top: 20, right: 20, bottom: 30, left:
                    40 };

   // Create the SVG container
   const svg = d3.select('#chart')
     .attr('width', width)
     .attr('height', height);

   // Create the scales
   const x = d3.scaleBand()
     .range([margin.left, width - margin.right])
     .padding(0.1);
   const y = d3.scaleLinear()
     .range([height - margin.bottom, margin.top]);

   // Set the domains for the scales
   x.domain(data.map(d => d.label));
   y.domain([0, d3.max(data, d => d.value)]);

   // Create the bars
   svg.selectAll('.bar')
     .data(data)
     .enter().append('rect')
     .attr('class', 'bar')
     .attr('x', d => x(d.label))
     .attr('width', x.bandwidth())
     .attr('y', d => y(d.value))
     .attr('height', d => height - margin.bottom -
                           y(d. value));

   // Create the axes
   const xAxis = d3.axisBottom(x);
   const yAxis = d3.axisLeft(y);

   svg.append('g')
     .attr('transform', 'translate(0,${height - margin.
                                   bottom})')
     .call(xAxis);

   svg.append('g')
     .attr('transform', 'translate(${margin.left},0)')
     .call(yAxis);
  </script>
</body>
</html>
```

Explanation of the Code

The HTML file starts with the standard `<!DOCTYPE html>` declaration, followed by the `<html>` tag.

In the `<head>` section, we have a `<title>` tag that sets the page title to "SVG Bar Chart." Inside the `<style>` section, we define the following CSS styles:

`.bar`: This class is applied to the bar elements in the chart. It sets the initial fill color to blue (#007bff) and changes the color to a darker blue (#0056b3) on hover.

`.axis path`, `.axis line`: These styles are applied to the axis lines and ticks, setting the stroke color to black and ensuring crisp rendering.

`.axis text`: This style sets the font family and size for the axis labels.

In the `<body>` section, we have an `<svg>` element whose id value equals chart and a width of 600 pixels and a height of 400 pixels.

Inside the `<script>` section, we have the following code:

1. Generate Synthetic Data: We create an array of objects, each with a label and a value property, to represent the data for the bar chart.

2. Set up the Chart Dimensions: We define the overall width and height of the chart, as well as the margins for the axes.

3. Create the SVG Container: We select the `<svg>` element whose id value equals chart and set its width and height.

4. Create the Scales: We create two scales: x for the horizontal axis (using `d3.scaleBand()`) and y for the vertical axis (using `d3.scaleLinear()`). These scales map the data values to the appropriate positions within the SVG container.

5. Set the Domains for the Scales: We set the domains for the x and y scales based on the data. The x scale uses the labels, and the y scale uses the maximum value in the data.

6. Create the Bars: We select all the `.bar` elements, bind the data to them, and append `<rect>` elements to represent the bars. We set the x, width, y, and height attributes of the rectangles based on the scales.

7. Create the Axes: We create the xAxis and yAxis using `d3.axisBottom()` and `d3.axisLeft()`, respectively, and append them to the SVG container.

When you open this HTML file in a Web browser, you should see an SVG bar chart with five bars, each representing a category from the synthetic data. The key aspects of this implementation are the use of the D3.js library to create the scales, generate the bar elements, and append the axes. The synthetic data is generated within the JavaScript code, but in a real-world scenario, this data would typically come from an external source, such as an API or a database. This example demonstrates how SVG can be used to create dynamic and interactive data visualizations, such as bar charts, within an HTML Web page.

As noted in the beginning this section, the code in Listing 7.5 is incorrect, so let us ask Perplexity to fix the code: "The code that you generated is incorrect. Please generate a corrected version of this code."

Perplexity:

Listing 7.6 displayed a modified version of Listing 7.5 that correctly displays an SVG-based bar chart.

LISTING 7.6: perplex_svg_barchart2.html

```
<!DOCTYPE html>
<html>
<head>
  <title>SVG Bar Chart</title>
  <script src="https://d3js.org/d3.v6.min.js"></script>
  <style>
    .bar {
      fill: #007bff;
    }

    .bar:hover {
      fill: #0056b3;
    }

    .axis path,
    .axis line {
      fill: none;
      stroke: #000;
      shape-rendering: crispEdges;
    }

    .axis text {
      font-family: sans-serif;
      font-size: 11px;
    }
  </style>
</head>
<body>
  <svg id="chart" width="600" height="400"></svg>

  <script>
    // Generate synthetic data
    const data = [
      { label: 'Category 1', value: 80 },
      { label: 'Category 2', value: 60 },
      { label: 'Category 3', value: 90 },
      { label: 'Category 4', value: 40 },
      { label: 'Category 5', value: 70 },
    ];

    // Set up the chart dimensions
    const width = 600;
    const height = 400;
```

```
      const margin = { top: 20, right: 20, bottom: 30, left:
                           40 };

      // Create the SVG container
      const svg = d3.select('#chart')
        .attr('width', width)
        .attr('height', height);

      // Create the scales
      const x = d3.scaleBand()
        .range([margin.left, width - margin.right])
        .padding(0.1);
      const y = d3.scaleLinear()
        .range([height - margin.bottom, margin.top]);

      // Set the domains for the scales
      x.domain(data.map(d => d.label));
      y.domain([0, d3.max(data, d => d.value)]);

      // Create the bars
      svg.selectAll('.bar')
        .data(data)
        .enter().append('rect')
        .attr('class', 'bar')
        .attr('x', d => x(d.label))
        .attr('width', x.bandwidth())
        .attr('y', d => y(d.value))
        .attr('height', d => height - margin.bottom -
                                     y(d.value));

      // Create the axes
      const xAxis = d3.axisBottom(x);
      const yAxis = d3.axisLeft(y);

      svg.append('g')
        .attr('transform', 'translate(0,${height -
                                     margin.bottom})')
        .call(xAxis);

      svg.append('g')
        .attr('transform', 'translate(${margin.left},0)')
        .call(yAxis);
  </script>
</body>
</html>
```

Explanation of the Corrected Code

The main changes in the corrected code are [as follows]:

- added the `<script src="https://d3js.org/d3.v6.min.js"></script>` line in the `<head>` section to include the D3.js library
- moved the `<script>` section to the end of the `<body>` element, as it is a common practice to load JavaScript at the end of the HTML document to improve page load performance

- corrected the `y` scale range to use `height - margin.bottom` as the minimum value and `margin.top` as the maximum value, to ensure the bars are displayed correctly
- corrected the height calculation for the bars to use `height - margin.bottom - y(d.value)` instead of just `height - margin.bottom`, to ensure the bars are displayed at the correct height

The rest of the code remains the same as the previous version, with the generation of synthetic data, the creation of the SVG container, the setup of the scales, the rendering of the bars, and the addition of the axes. When you open this HTML file in a Web browser, you should see an SVG bar chart with five bars, each representing a category from the synthetic data. The key aspects of this implementation are the use of the `D3.js` library to create the scales, generate the bar elements, and append the axes. The synthetic data is generated within the JavaScript code, but in a real-world scenario, this data would typically come from an external source, such as an API or a database. This example demonstrates how SVG can be used to create dynamic and interactive data visualizations, such as bar charts, within an HTML Web page.

Now launch the Web page `perplex_svg_barchart2.html` by navigating to the directory that contains this HTML Web page and then typing the following command:

```
open perplex_svg_barchart2.html
```

After a few moments, you will see the image displayed in Figure 7.5 that shows an SVG-based bar chart.

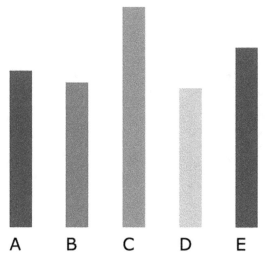

FIGURE 7.5: An SVG-based bar chart

SVG QUADRATIC BEZIER CURVES

The following prompt was supplied to Perplexity in order to create an HTML Web page that contains 50 random SVG quadratic Bezier curves:

"Please generate an HTML Web page containing a set of 50 random SVG quadratic Bezier curves with a fill pattern alternating between two different radial gradients, with a maximum width of 600 and a maximum height of 400, along with an explanation of the code."

Perplexity:

Listing 7.7 displays the contents of the HTML Web page `perplex_svg_random_quadratic_bezier_curves.html` that generate an SVG document that contains randomly generated quadratic Bezier curves.

Here's an HTML Web page that contains a set of 50 random SVG quadratic Bezier curves with a fill pattern alternating between two different radial gradients, with a maximum width of 600 and a maximum height of 400, along with an explanation of the code.

LISTING 7.7: perplex_svg_random_quadratic_bezier_curves.html

```
<!DOCTYPE html>
<html>
<head>
  <title>Random Quadratic Bezier Curves</title>
  <style>
    body {
      margin: 0;
      padding: 0;
      background-color: #f0f0f0;
    }

    .bezier-container {
      width: 100%;
      height: 100vh;
      display: flex;
      justify-content: center;
      align-items: center;
    }

    .bezier-curve {
      position: absolute;
      max-width: 600px;
      max-height: 400px;
    }
  </style>
</head>
<body>
  <div class="bezier-container">
    <svg class="bezier-curve"></svg>
  </div>
```

```
<script>
  const container = document.querySelector
                              ('.bezier-container');
  const svg = document.querySelector('.bezier-curve');

  // Generate 50 random quadratic Bezier curves
  for (let i = 0; i < 50; i++) {
    const curve = document.createElementNS
                  ('http://www.w3.org/2000/svg', 'path');
    curve.setAttribute('d', generateRandomBezierPath());
    curve.setAttribute('fill', i % 2 === 0 ?
                  'url(#gradient1)' : 'url(#gradient2)');
    svg.appendChild(curve);
  }

  // Define the two radial gradients
  const defs = document.createElementNS
                  ('http://www.w3.org/2000/svg', 'defs');
  const gradient1 = document.createElementNS
        ('http://www.w3.org/2000/svg', 'radialGradient');
  gradient1.setAttribute('id', 'gradient1');
  gradient1.setAttribute('cx', '50%');
  gradient1.setAttribute('cy', '50%');
  gradient1.setAttribute('r', '50%');
  gradient1.setAttribute('fx', '50%');
  gradient1.setAttribute('fy', '50%');
  const stop1 = document.createElementNS
                  ('http://www.w3.org/2000/svg', 'stop');
  stop1.setAttribute('offset', '0%');
  stop1.setAttribute('style', 'stop-color:#ff6b6b;
                              stop-opacity:1');
  const stop2 = document.createElementNS
                  ('http://www.w3.org/2000/svg', 'stop');
  stop2.setAttribute('offset', '100%');
  stop2.setAttribute('style', 'stop-color:#ffa500;
                              stop-opacity:1');
  gradient1.appendChild(stop1);
  gradient1.appendChild(stop2);

  const gradient2 = document.createElementNS
        ('http://www.w3.org/2000/svg', 'radialGradient');
  gradient2.setAttribute('id', 'gradient2');
  gradient2.setAttribute('cx', '50%');
  gradient2.setAttribute('cy', '50%');
  gradient2.setAttribute('r', '50%');
  gradient2.setAttribute('fx', '50%');
  gradient2.setAttribute('fy', '50%');
  const stop3 = document.createElementNS
                  ('http://www.w3.org/2000/svg', 'stop');
  stop3.setAttribute('offset', '0%');
  stop3.setAttribute('style', 'stop-color:#00ff00;
                              stop-opacity:1');
  const stop4 = document.createElementNS
                  ('http://www.w3.org/2000/svg', 'stop');
  stop4.setAttribute('offset', '100%');
  stop4.setAttribute('style', 'stop-color:#00ffff;
                              stop-opacity:1');
```

```
        gradient2.appendChild(stop3);
        gradient2.appendChild(stop4);

        defs.appendChild(gradient1);
        defs.appendChild(gradient2);
        svg.appendChild(defs);

        // Helper function to generate random quadratic Bezier
        // paths
        function generateRandomBezierPath() {
          const x1 = Math.floor(Math.random() * 600);
          const y1 = Math.floor(Math.random() * 400);
          const x2 = Math.floor(Math.random() * 600);
          const y2 = Math.floor(Math.random() * 400);
          const x3 = Math.floor(Math.random() * 600);
          const y3 = Math.floor(Math.random() * 400);
          return 'M${x1},${y1} Q${x2},${y2} ${x3},${y3}';
        }
    </script>
</body>
</html>
```

Explanation of the Code
The HTML file starts with the standard `<!DOCTYPE html>` declaration, followed by the `<html>` tag. In the `<head>` section, we have a `<title>` tag that sets the page title to "Random Quadratic Bezier Curves."

Inside the `<style>` section, we define the following CSS:

`body`: Sets the margin and padding to 0, and the background color to a light gray (#f0f0f0).

`.bezier-container`: This class is applied to the container that holds the SVG element. It sets the width to 100%, the height to 100vh (viewport height), and centers the content both horizontally and vertically using `display: flex;`, `justify-content: center;`, and `align-items: center;`.

`.bezier-curve`: This class is applied to the SVG element that will contain the Bezier curves. It sets the position to absolute and the max-width and max-height to 600 and 400 pixels, respectively.

In the `<body>` section, we have a `<div>` element with the `class="bezier-container"` attribute, which holds the SVG element. Inside the container, we have an `<svg>` element with the `class="bezier-curve"` attribute.

In the portion of the code that starts with the HTML `<script>` element we proceed as follows.

We select the `.bezier-container` and `.bezier-curve` elements using `document.querySelector()`.

We generate 50 random quadratic Bezier curves and append them to the SVG element.

We create a new `<path>` element using `document.createElementNS()`.

We set the `d` attribute of the path to a randomly generated Bezier path using the `generateRandomBezierPath()` function.

We set the fill attribute of the path to either `url(#gradient1)` or `url(#gradient2)`, alternating between the two gradients. We append the path to the SVG element.

We define two radial gradients, `gradient1` and `gradient2`, using the `<radialGradient>` element. These gradients are used to fill the Bezier curves.

We append the gradient definitions to the `<defs>` section of the SVG element.

The `generateRandomBezierPath()` function generates a random quadratic Bezier path with coordinates within the 600 x 400 pixel range.

When you open this HTML file in a Web browser, you should see a set of 50 random quadratic Bezier curves, with the fill pattern alternating between the two radial gradients defined in the code. The key aspects of this implementation are the use of JavaScript to dynamically generate and append the Bezier curves to the SVG element, and the definition of the two radial gradients within the `<defs>` section to provide the fill pattern for the curves. This example demonstrates how SVG can be used to create dynamic and visually interesting graphics, with the ability to customize the appearance and behavior of the elements using a combination of HTML, CSS, and JavaScript.

Launch the HTML Web page from the command line as follows:

```
open perplex_svg_random_quadratic_bezier_curves.html
```

After a few moments, you will see the image (or something similar) that is displayed in Figure 7.6.

FIGURE 7.6: SVG-based quadratic Bezier curves

SVG CUBIC BEZIER CURVES

The following prompt was supplied to Perplexity in order to create an HTML Web page that contains 50 random SVG cubic Bezier curves.

"Please generate an HTML Web page containing a set of 50 random SVG cubic Bezier curves with a fill pattern alternating between two different radial gradients, with a maximum width of 600 and a maximum height of 400, along with an explanation of the code."

Perplexity:

Bezier curves with a fill pattern alternating between two different radial gradients, with a maximum width of 600 and a maximum height of 400, along with an explanation of the code.

LISTING 7.8:   perplex_svg_random_cubic_bezier_curves.html

```
Here's an HTML Web page that contains a set of 50 random
SVG cubic
<!DOCTYPE html>
<html>
<head>
  <title>Random Cubic Bezier Curves</title>
  <style>
    body {
      margin: 0;
      padding: 0;
      background-color: #f0f0f0;
    }

    .bezier-container {
      width: 100%;
      height: 100vh;
      display: flex;
      justify-content: center;
      align-items: center;
    }

    .bezier-curve {
      position: absolute;
      max-width: 600px;
      max-height: 400px;
    }
  </style>
</head>
<body>
  <div class="bezier-container">
    <svg class="bezier-curve"></svg>
  </div>

  <script>
    const container = document.querySelector
                                ('.bezier-container');
    const svg = document.querySelector('.bezier-curve');

    // Generate 50 random cubic Bezier curves
    for (let i = 0; i < 50; i++) {
      const curve = document.createElementNS
                    ('http://www.w3.org/2000/svg', 'path');
      curve.setAttribute('d', generateRandomBezierPath());
```

```
        curve.setAttribute('fill', i % 2 === 0 ?
'url(#gradient1)' : 'url(#gradient2)');
        svg.appendChild(curve);
    }

    // Define the two radial gradients
    const defs = document.createElementNS
                    ('http://www.w3.org/2000/svg', 'defs');
    const gradient1 = document.createElementNS
            ('http://www.w3.org/2000/svg', 'radialGradient');
    gradient1.setAttribute('id', 'gradient1');
    gradient1.setAttribute('cx', '50%');
    gradient1.setAttribute('cy', '50%');
    gradient1.setAttribute('r', '50%');
    gradient1.setAttribute('fx', '50%');
    gradient1.setAttribute('fy', '50%');
    const stop1 = document.createElementNS
                    ('http://www.w3.org/2000/svg', 'stop');
    stop1.setAttribute('offset', '0%');
    stop1.setAttribute('style',
                    'stop-color:#ff6b6b;stop-opacity:1');
    const stop2 = document.createElementNS
                    ('http://www.w3.org/2000/svg', 'stop');
    stop2.setAttribute('offset', '100%');
    stop2.setAttribute('style', 'stop-color:#ffa500;
                                stop-opacity:1');
    gradient1.appendChild(stop1);
    gradient1.appendChild(stop2);

    const gradient2 = document.createElementNS
            ('http://www.w3.org/2000/svg', 'radialGradient');
    gradient2.setAttribute('id', 'gradient2');
    gradient2.setAttribute('cx', '50%');
    gradient2.setAttribute('cy', '50%');
    gradient2.setAttribute('r', '50%');
    gradient2.setAttribute('fx', '50%');
    gradient2.setAttribute('fy', '50%');
    const stop3 = document.createElementNS
                    ('http://www.w3.org/2000/svg', 'stop');
    stop3.setAttribute('offset', '0%');
    stop3.setAttribute('style', 'stop-color:#00ff00;
                                    stop-opacity:1');
    const stop4 = document.createElementNS
                    ('http://www.w3.org/2000/svg', 'stop');
    stop4.setAttribute('offset', '100%');
    stop4.setAttribute('style',
                    'stop-color:#00ffff;stop-opacity:1');
    gradient2.appendChild(stop3);
    gradient2.appendChild(stop4);

    defs.appendChild(gradient1);
    defs.appendChild(gradient2);
    svg.appendChild(defs);

    // Helper function to generate random cubic Bezier
    // paths
```

```
    function generateRandomBezierPath() {
      const x1 = Math.floor(Math.random() * 600);
      const y1 = Math.floor(Math.random() * 400);
      const x2 = Math.floor(Math.random() * 600);
      const y2 = Math.floor(Math.random() * 400);
      const x3 = Math.floor(Math.random() * 600);
      const y3 = Math.floor(Math.random() * 400);
      const x4 = Math.floor(Math.random() * 600);
      const y4 = Math.floor(Math.random() * 400);
      return 'M${x1},${y1} C${x2},${y2} ${x3},${y3}
             ${x4},${y4}';
    }
  </script>
</body>
</html>
```

Explanation of the Code

The code is very similar to the previous example, with the main difference being the use of cubic Bezier curves instead of quadratic Bezier curves. The HTML file starts with the standard `<!DOCTYPE html>` declaration, followed by the `<html>` tag. In the `<head>` section, we have a `<title>` tag that sets the page title to "Random Cubic Bezier Curves."

Inside the `<style>` section, we define the following CSS:

`body`: Sets the margin and padding to 0, and the background color to a light gray (#f0f0f0).

`.bezier-container`: This class is applied to the container that holds the SVG element. It sets the width to 100%, the height to 100vh (viewport height), and centers the content both horizontally and vertically using `display: flex;`, `justify-content: center;`, and `align-items: center;`.

`.bezier-curve`: This class is applied to the SVG element that will contain the Bezier curves. It sets the position to absolute and the max-width and max-height to 600 and 400 pixels, respectively.

In the `<body>` section, we have a `<div>` element with the `class="bezier-container"` attribute, which holds the SVG element.

Inside the container, we have an `<svg>` element with the `class="bezier-curve"` attribute.

In the `<script>` section, we have the following code:

We select the `.bezier-container` and `.bezier-curve` elements using `document.querySelector()`.

We generate 50 random cubic Bezier curves and append them to the SVG element:

We create a new `<path>` element using `document.createElementNS()`.

We set the `d` attribute of the path to a randomly generated Bezier path using the `generateRandomBezierPath()` function.

We set the fill attribute of the path to either `url(#gradient1)` or `url(#gradient2)`, alternating between the two gradients.

We append the path to the SVG element.

We define two radial gradients, `gradient1` and `gradient2`, using the `<radialGradient>` element. These gradients are used to fill the Bezier curves. We append the gradient definitions to the `<defs>` section of the SVG element.

The `generateRandomBezierPath()` function generates a random cubic Bezier path with coordinates within the 600 x 400 pixel range.

When you open this HTML file in a Web browser, you should see a set of 50 random cubic Bezier curves, with the fill pattern alternating between the two radial gradients defined in the code. The key aspects of this implementation are the use of JavaScript to dynamically generate and append the Bezier curves to the SVG element, and the definition of the two radial gradients within the `<defs>` section to provide the fill pattern for the curves. This example demonstrates how SVG can be used to create dynamic and visually interesting graphics, with the ability to customize the appearance and behavior of the elements using a combination of HTML, CSS, and JavaScript. The main difference between this example and the previous one is the use of cubic Bezier curves instead of quadratic Bezier curves. Cubic Bezier curves have four control points, which allows for more complex and varied curve shapes compared to quadratic Bezier curves, which have only three control points.

Launch the HTML Web page in Listing 7.8 from the command line as follows:

```
open perplex_svg_random_cubic_bezier_curves.html
```

After a few moments, you will see the image (or something similar) that is displayed in Figure 7.7.

FIGURE 7.7: SVG-based cubic Bezier curves

SVG AND 2D TRANSFORMS

The following prompt was supplied to Perplexity to generate SVG-based 2D transformation effects:

"Please generate an HTML Web page that contains an SVG-based rectangle with animated rotation, an SVG triangle with an animated skew effect, an SVG polygon with animated scaling effect, and an SVG-based ellipse with an animated rotation and also an animated scaling effect, along with an explanation of the SVG code."

Perplexity:

Here's an HTML Web page that contains an SVG-based rectangle with animated rotation, an SVG triangle with an animated skew effect, an SVG polygon with an animated scaling effect, and an SVG-based ellipse with an animated rotation and scaling effect, along with an explanation of the SVG code.

Listing 7.9 displays the contents of perplex_svg_2d_transforms.html that contains Perplexity-generated SVG code that performs 2D transform-based animation effects on four 2D shapes.

LISTING 7.9: perplex_svg_2d_transforms.html

```
<!DOCTYPE html>
<html>
<head>
  <title>SVG Animations</title>
  <style>
    body {
      margin: 0;
      padding: 0;
      background-color: #f0f0f0;
      display: flex;
      justify-content: center;
      align-items: center;
      height: 100vh;
    }

    .svg-container {
      width: 600px;
      height: 400px;
      display: grid;
      grid-template-columns: repeat(2, 1fr);
      grid-template-rows: repeat(2, 1fr);
      grid-gap: 20px;
    }
  </style>
</head>
<body>
  <div class="svg-container">
    <!-- Animated Rectangle -->
    <svg viewBox="0 0 100 100">
      <rect x="20" y="20" width="60" height="60"
                                fill="#007bff">
        <animateTransform
          attributeName="transform"
          type="rotate"
          from="0 50 50"
```

```
            to="360 50 50"
            dur="5s"
            repeatCount="indefinite" />
      </rect>
    </svg>

    <!-- Animated Triangle -->
    <svg viewBox="0 0 100 100">
      <polygon points="50,20 20,80 80,80" fill="#ff6b6b">
        <animateTransform
          attributeName="transform"
          type="skewX"
          from="0"
          to="45"
          dur="3s"
          repeatCount="indefinite" />
      </polygon>
    </svg>

    <!-- Animated Polygon -->
    <svg viewBox="0 0 100 100">
      <polygon points="50,20 30,80 70,80 90,20"
                                   fill="#ffa500">
        <animateTransform
          attributeName="transform"
          type="scale"
          from="1"
          to="1.5"
          dur="4s"
          repeatCount="indefinite" />
      </polygon>
    </svg>

    <!-- Animated Ellipse -->
    <svg viewBox="0 0 100 100">
      <ellipse cx="50" cy="50" rx="30" ry="20"
                                   fill="#00ff00">
        <animateTransform
          attributeName="transform"
          type="rotate"
          from="0 50 50"
          to="360 50 50"
          dur="6s"
          repeatCount="indefinite" />
        <animateTransform
          attributeName="transform"
          type="scale"
          from="1"
          to="1.5"
          dur="3s"
          repeatCount="indefinite" />
      </ellipse>
    </svg>
  </div>
</body>
</html>
```

Explanation of the SVG Code

The HTML file starts with the standard `<!DOCTYPE html>` declaration, followed by the `<html>` tag. In the `<head>` section, we have a `<title>` tag that sets the page title to "SVG Animations."

Inside the `<style>` section, we define the following CSS:

`body`: Sets the margin and padding to 0, the background color to a light gray (#f0f0f0), and centers the content both horizontally and vertically using `display: flex;`, `justify-content: center;`, and `align-items: center;`.

`.svg-container`: This class is applied to the container that holds the SVG elements. It sets the width to 600 pixels, the height to 400 pixels, and arranges the SVG elements in a 2 x 2 grid using CSS Grid.

In the `<body>` section, we have a `<div>` element with the `class="svg-container"` attribute, which holds the SVG elements.

Inside the container, we have four SVG elements:

1. Animated Rectangle

   The `<rect>` element creates a blue (#007bff) rectangle with a width of 60 pixels and a height of 60 pixels, positioned at (20, 20).

   The `<animateTransform>` element animates the rotation of the rectangle. The `attributeName="transform"` attribute specifies that the transformation should be animated, the `type="rotate"` attribute sets the animation to be a rotation, the `from="0 50 50"` and `to="360 50 50"` attributes define the starting and ending rotation angles, the `dur="5s"` attribute sets the duration of the animation to 5 seconds, and the `repeatCount="indefinite"` attribute makes the animation loop continuously.

2. Animated Triangle

   The `<polygon>` element creates a red (#ff6b6b) triangle with vertices at (50, 20), (20, 80), and (80, 80).

   The `<animateTransform>` element animates the skew of the triangle. The `attributeName="transform"` attribute specifies that the transformation should be animated, the `type="skewX"` attribute sets the animation to be a horizontal skew, the `from="0"` and `to="45"` attributes define the starting and ending skew angles, the `dur="3s"` attribute sets the duration of the animation to 3 seconds, and the `repeatCount="indefinite"` attribute makes the animation loop continuously.

3. Animated Polygon

   The `<polygon>` element creates an orange (#ffa500) polygon with vertices at (50, 20), (30, 80), (70, 80), and (90, 20).

   The `<animateTransform>` element animates the scaling of the polygon. The `attributeName="transform"` attribute specifies that the transformation should be animated, the `type="scale"` attribute sets the animation to be a scaling transformation, the `from="1"` and `to="1.5"` attributes define the starting and ending scale factors, the `dur="4s"` attribute sets the duration of the animation to 4 seconds, and the `repeatCount="indefinite"` attribute makes the animation loop continuously.

4. Animated Ellipse

The `<ellipse>` element creates a green (#00ff00) ellipse with a center at (50, 50), a horizontal radius of 30 pixels, and a vertical radius of 20 pixels.

The first `<animateTransform>` element animates the rotation of the ellipse. The `attributeName="transform"` attribute specifies that the transformation should be animated, the `type="rotate"` attribute sets the animation to be a rotation, the `from="0 50 50"` and `to="360 50 50"` attributes define the starting and ending rotation angles, the `dur="6s"` attribute sets the duration of the animation to 6 seconds, and the `repeatCount="indefinite"` attribute makes the animation loop continuously.

The second `<animateTransform>` element animates the scaling of the ellipse. The `attributeName="transform"` attribute specifies that the transformation should be animated, the `type="scale"` attribute sets the animation to be a scaling transformation, the `from="1"` and `to="1.5"` attributes define the starting and ending scale factors, the `dur="3s"` attribute sets the duration of the animation to 3 seconds, and the `repeatCount="indefinite"` attribute makes the animation loop continuously.

When you open this HTML file in a Web browser, you should see the four SVG elements (rectangle, triangle, polygon, and ellipse) with their respective animated transformations. The key aspects of this implementation are the use of SVG elements to create the shapes and the `<animateTransform>` elements to define the animations. The `attributeName="transform"` attribute specifies that the transformation should be animated, and the `type` attribute sets the type of transformation (e.g., rotate, skew, or scale). The `from` and `to` attributes define the starting and ending values of the transformation, and the `dur` attribute sets the duration of the animation. The `repeatCount="indefinite"` attribute makes the animations loop continuously. This example demonstrates how SVG can be used to create dynamic and visually engaging graphics with various animated transformations, which can be useful for creating interactive user interfaces, data visualizations, and other Web-based applications.

Now launch the Web page `perplex_svg_2d_transforms.html` by navigating to the directory that contains Listing 7.9 and then typing the following command:

```
open perplex_svg_2d_transforms.html
```

After a few moments, you will see the image in Figure 7.8 that displays a snapshot of SVG-based animation of various polygonal shapes.

FIGURE 7.8: SVG-based animation with polygonal shapes

ANIMATED SVG CUBIC BEZIER CURVES

The following prompt was supplied to Perplexity to generate animated cubic Bezier curves: "Please generate an HTML Web page that contains 50 random cubic SVG-based Bezier curves with random radial gradients."

Perplexity:

Here's an HTML Web page that contains 50 random cubic SVG-based Bezier curves with random radial gradients.

Listing 7.10 displays the contents of the HTML Web page perplex_svg_ animated_cubic_bezier_curves.html that generate an SVG document that contains randomly generated quadratic Bezier curves.

LISTING 7.10: perplex_svg_animated_cubic_bezier_curves.html

```
<!DOCTYPE html>
<html>
<head>
  <title>Random Cubic Bezier Curves with Radial Gradients
                                                   </title>
  <style>
    body {
      margin: 0;
      padding: 0;
      background-color: #f0f0f0;
      display: flex;
      justify-content: center;
      align-items: center;
      height: 100vh;
    }

    .svg-container {
      width: 100%;
      height: 100%;
      position: relative;
      overflow: hidden;
    }

    .bezier-curve {
      position: absolute;
      width: 100%;
      height: 100%;
      opacity: 0.5;
      animation: bezier-animation 20s infinite linear;
```

```
}

@keyframes bezier-animation {
  0% {
    d: path("M0,100 C25,0 75,0 100,100");
  }
  5% {
    d: path("M0,0 C25,100 75,100 100,0");
  }
  10% {
    d: path("M0,50 C25,50 75,50 100,50");
  }
  15% {
    d: path("M0,0 C25,100 75,0 100,100");
  }
  20% {
    d: path("M0,100 C25,0 75,100 100,0");
  }
  25% {
    d: path("M0,50 C25,100 75,100 100,50");
  }
  30% {
    d: path("M0,0 C25,0 75,100 100,100");
  }
  35% {
    d: path("M0,100 C25,100 75,0 100,0");
  }
  40% {
    d: path("M0,50 C25,0 75,100 100,100");
  }
  45% {
    d: path("M0,0 C25,50 75,0 100,0");
  }
  50% {
    d: path("M0,100 C25,100 75,100 100,100");
  }
  55% {
    d: path("M0,0 C25,0 75,0 100,0");
  }
  60% {
    d: path("M0,50 C25,100 75,50 100,50");
  }
  65% {
    d: path("M0,100 C25,50 75,100 100,100");
  }
  70% {
    d: path("M0,0 C25,100 75,100 100,100");
  }
  75% {
    d: path("M0,50 C25,0 75,0 100,0");
  }
  80% {
    d: path("M0,100 C25,100 75,50 100,50");
  }
  85% {
    d: path("M0,0 C25,50 75,100 100,100");
  }
```

```
      90% {
        d: path("M0,50 C25,0 75,0 100,0");
      }
      95% {
        d: path("M0,100 C25,100 75,100 100,100");
      }
      100% {
        d: path("M0,0 C25,0 75,0 100,0");
      }
    }

    .bezier-curve:before {
      content: "";
      position: absolute;
      top: 0;
      left: 0;
      width: 100%;
      height: 100%;
      background: radial-gradient(circle at random,
                  #ff6b6b, #ffa500, #ffff00, #00ff00,
                  #00ffff, #0000ff, #ff00ff);
      opacity: 0.5;
      z-index: -1;
    }
  </style>
</head>
<body>
  <div class="svg-container">
    <svg class="bezier-curve"></svg>
  </div>

  <script>
    const container = document.querySelector('.svg-
                                               container');
    const svg = document.querySelector('.bezier-curve');

    // Generate 50 random cubic Bezier curves
    for (let i = 0; i < 50; i++) {
      const curve = document.createElementNS
                    ('http://www.w3.org/2000/svg', 'path');
      curve.setAttribute('d', generateRandomBezierPath());
      svg.appendChild(curve);
    }
  </script>
</body>
</html>
```

Explanation of the Code

The HTML file starts with the standard `<!DOCTYPE html>` declaration, followed by the `<html>` tag. In the `<head>` section, we have a `<title>` tag that sets the page title to "Random Cubic Bezier Curves with Radial Gradients."

Inside the `<style>` section, we define the following CSS:

`body`: Sets the margin and padding to 0, the background color to a light gray (#f0f0f0), and centers the content both horizontally and vertically using `display: flex;`, `justify-content: center;`, and `align-items: center;`.

`.svg-container`: This class is applied to the container that holds the SVG element. It sets the width and height to 100%, the `position` to `relative`, and the `overflow` to `hidden`.

`.bezier-curve`: This class is applied to the SVG element that will contain the Bezier curves. It sets the position to absolute, the width and height to 100%, the opacity to 0.5, and adds an animation using the `@keyframes bezier-animation` rule.

`@keyframes bezier-animation`: This rule defines the animation for the Bezier curves. It uses the d property to set the path of the curves, which is a cubic Bezier curve. The path coordinates are randomly generated within the 0-100 range for both the x and y axes.

`.bezier-curve:before`: This pseudo-element is used to add a random radial gradient background to each Bezier curve. The `radial-gradient()` function is used to create a gradient that radiates outward from a random point within the curve's area. The gradient colors are set to a random selection of colors.

In the `<body>` section, we have a `<div>` element with the `class="svg-container"` attribute, which holds the SVG element.

Inside the container, we have an `<svg>` element with the `class="bezier-curve"` attribute. In the `<script>` section, we have the following code:

We select the `.svg-container` and `.bezier-curve` elements using `document.querySelector()`.

We generate 50 random cubic Bezier curves and append them to the SVG element:

We create a new `<path>` element using `document.createElementNS()`. We set the d attribute of the path to a randomly generated Bezier path using the `generateRandomBezierPath()` function. We append the path to the SVG element. The `generateRandomBezierPath()` function generates a random cubic Bezier path with coordinates within the 0-100 range for both the x and y axes.

When you open this HTML file in a Web browser, you should see 50 random cubic Bezier curves with random radial gradient backgrounds, continuously animating within the SVG container. The key aspects of this implementation are the use of JavaScript to dynamically generate and append the Bezier curves to the SVG element, and the use of CSS to define the animation and the random radial gradient backgrounds for the curves. This example demonstrates how SVG can be used to create dynamic and visually interesting graphics, with the ability to customize the appearance and behavior of the elements using a combination of HTML, CSS, and JavaScript.

Launch the HTML Web page in Listing 7.10 from the command line as follows:

```
open perplex_svg_animated_cubic_bezier_curves.html
```

After a few moments, you will see the image (or something similar) that is displayed in Figure 7.9.

FIGURE 7.9: Animation with cubic Bezier curves

HOVER EFFECTS

The following prompt was supplied to Perplexity to generate an HTML Web page that contains SVG and a hover animation effect: "Please generate an HTML Web page with a 300 x 300 SVG rectangle that has a rotating animation effect on a hover event."

Perplexity:

Here's an HTML Web page that contains a 300x300 SVG rectangle with a rotating animation effect on a hover event.

LISTING 7.11:   perplex_svg_hover.html

```
<!DOCTYPE html>
<html>
<head>
  <title>Rotating SVG Rectangle</title>
  <style>
    body {
      margin: 0;
      padding: 0;
      display: flex;
      justify-content: center;
      align-items: center;
      height: 100vh;
      background-color: #f0f0f0;
    }

    .svg-container {
      width: 300px;
      height: 300px;
      position: relative;
      overflow: hidden;
    }

    .svg-container:hover .rect {
      animation: rotate 2s linear infinite;
```

```
      }

    @keyframes rotate {
      0% {
        transform: rotate(0deg);
      }
      100% {
        transform: rotate(360deg);
      }
    }
  </style>
</head>
<body>
  <div class="svg-container">
    <svg viewBox="0 0 300 300">
      <rect class="rect" x="0" y="0" width="300"
                         height="300" fill="#007bff" />
    </svg>
  </div>
</body>
</html>
```

Explanation of the Code

The HTML file starts with the standard <!DOCTYPE html> declaration, followed by the <html> tag. In the <head> section, we have a <title> tag that sets the page title to "Rotating SVG Rectangle."

Inside the <style> section, we define the following CSS:
body: Sets the margin and padding to 0, centers the content both horizontally and vertically using display: flex;, justify-content: center;, and align-items: center;, and sets the background color to a light gray (#f0f0f0).

.svg-container: This class is applied to the container that holds the SVG element. It sets the width and height to 300 pixels, the position to relative, and the overflow to hidden.

.svg-container:hover .rect: This rule applies the rotate animation to the rectangle element when the .svg-container is hovered over.

@keyframes rotate: This rule defines the rotate animation. It starts with a rotation of 0 degrees and ends with a rotation of 360 degrees, creating a full rotation effect.

In the <body> section, we have a <div> element with the class="svg-container" attribute, which holds the SVG element. Inside the container, we have an <svg> element with a viewBox of "0 0 300 300," which sets the SVG viewport to 300 x 300 pixels.

Inside the SVG element, we have a <rect> element with the class rect. This rectangle has a width and height of 300 pixels, and a blue (#007bff) fill color.

When you open this HTML file in a Web browser and hover over the SVG container, the rectangle inside will start rotating continuously, creating a dynamic and visually interesting effect. The key aspects of this implementation are

- the use of the `<svg>` element to create the rectangle
- the application of the rotate animation to the rectangle element using the `:hover` pseudo-class on the parent container
- the definition of the rotate animation using the `@keyframes` rule, which transitions the rotation from 0 degrees to 360 degrees

This example demonstrates how SVG can be used to create simple yet visually engaging animations, and how CSS can be used to apply those animations based on user interactions, such as a hover event.

Now launch the Web page `Perplex_svg_hover.html` by navigating to the directory that contains this HTML Web page and then typing the following command:

```
open perplex_svg_hover.html
```

After a few moments, you will see the image in Figure 7.10 that displays a snapshot of an SVG-based hover effect.

FIGURE 7.10: SVG-based hover effect

HOVER ANIMATION EFFECTS

The following prompt was supplied to Perplexity to generate an HTML Web page that contains SVG and a hover animation effect: "`Please generate an HTML Web page with a 300 x 300 SVG rectangle that has a rotating animation effect on a hover event.`"

`Perplexity:`

Here's an HTML web page that contains a 300x300 SVG rectangle with a rotating animation effect on a hover event.

LISTING 7.12: perplex_svg_hover_rotate.html

```
<!DOCTYPE html>
<html>
<head>
  <title>Rotating SVG Rectangle</title>
```

```
<style>
  body {
    margin: 0;
    padding: 0;
    display: flex;
    justify-content: center;
    align-items: center;
    height: 100vh;
    background-color: #f0f0f0;
  }

  .svg-container {
    width: 300px;
    height: 300px;
    position: relative;
    overflow: hidden;
  }

  .svg-container:hover .rect {
    animation: rotate 2s linear infinite;
  }

  @keyframes rotate {
    0% {
      transform: rotate(0deg);
    }
    100% {
      transform: rotate(360deg);
    }
  }
</style>
</head>
<body>
  <div class="svg-container">
    <svg viewBox="0 0 300 300">
      <rect class="rect" x="0" y="0" width="300"
                         height="300" fill="#007bff" />
    </svg>
  </div>
</body>
</html>
```

Explanation of the Code

The HTML file starts with the standard <!DOCTYPE html> declaration, followed by the <html> tag.

In the <head> section, we have a <title> tag that sets the page title to "Rotating SVG Rectangle".

Inside the <style> section, we define the following CSS:

body: Sets the margin and padding to 0, centers the content both horizontally and vertically using display: flex;, justify-content: center;, and align-items: center;, and sets the background color to a light gray (#f0f0f0).

.svg-container: This class is applied to the container that holds the SVG element. It sets the width and height to 300 pixels, the position to relative, and the overflow to hidden.

.svg-container:hover .rect: This rule applies the rotate animation to the rectangle element when the .svg-container is hovered over.

@keyframes rotate: This rule defines the rotate animation. It starts with a rotation of 0 degrees and ends with a rotation of 360 degrees, creating a full rotation effect.

In the <body> section, we have a <div> element with the class="svg-container" attribute, which holds the SVG element.

Inside the container, we have an <svg> element with a viewBox of "0 0 300 300", which sets the SVG viewport to 300x300 pixels.

Inside the SVG element, we have a <rect> element with the class rect. This rectangle has a width and height of 300 pixels, and a blue (#007bff) fill color.

When you open this HTML file in a web browser and hover over the SVG container, the rectangle inside will start rotating continuously, creating a dynamic and visually interesting effect. The key aspects of this implementation are:

The use of the <svg> element to create the rectangle.

The application of the rotate animation to the rectangle element using the :hover pseudo-class on the parent container.

The definition of the rotate animation using the @keyframes rule, which transitions the rotation from 0 degrees to 360 degrees.

This example demonstrates how SVG can be used to create simple yet visually engaging animations, and how CSS can be used to apply those animations based on user interactions, such as a hover event.

Now launch the Web page `perplex_svg_hover_rotate.html` by navigating to the directory that contains this HTML Web page and then typing the following command:

```
open perplex_svg_hover_rotate.html
```

After a few moments, you will see the image in Figure 7.11 that displays a snapshot of SVG-based hover animation.

FIGURE 7.11: A Web page with SVG-based hover animation

SVG VERSUS CSS3: A COMPARISON

The following prompt was supplied to Perplexity: `"Please provide a detailed comparison of SVG and CSS3, along with scenarios where it's better to use SVG instead of CSS3, and scenarios where it's better to use CSS3 instead of SVG."`

`Perplexity:`

SVG vs. CSS3

Advantages of SVG:
- SVG is a vector-based format, which means it is resolution-independent and can be scaled without losing quality.
- SVG elements can be directly manipulated using CSS and JavaScript, allowing for advanced animations and interactivity.
- SVG is easier to get started with and can be more performant, especially for a smaller number of elements.
- SVG makes it easier to register user interactions and update the content.

Advantages of CSS3:
- CSS is generally faster and more performant than SVG, especially when dealing with a large number of objects (1,000+).
- CSS is better suited for simple UI/UX animations and effects, as it requires less code and is easier to manage.
- CSS is more widely supported and has better browser compatibility compared to some SVG features.
- CSS is better for creating responsive and adaptive designs, as it integrates seamlessly with the layout and structure of the Web page.

Scenarios for using SVG
Use SVG when
- you want to create complex animations and interactions that can be controlled using CSS and JavaScript
- you have a smaller number of elements and want to prioritize performance and ease of implementation
- you need to create accessible graphics that can be easily integrated into the DOM and interact with other page elements

Scenarios for using CSS3
Use CSS3 when
- you need to create simple UI/UX effects and animations, such as hover states, transitions, or small-scale movements
- you are dealing with a large number of elements (1,000+) and need to prioritize performance over advanced features. You want to create responsive and adaptive designs that seamlessly integrate with the layout and structure of the Web page.
- you need better browser compatibility and wider support for your design features

In summary, SVG is the better choice for vector-based graphics, complex animations, and interactive elements, while CSS3 excels at simple UI/UX effects, responsive design, and performance-critical scenarios with a large number of element.

SVG VERSUS PNG: A COMPARISON

The following prompt was supplied to Perplexity: "Please provide a detailed comparison of SVG and PNG, along with scenarios where it's better to use SVG instead of PNG, and scenarios where it's better to use PNG instead of SVG."

Perplexity provided the following sources:

https://www.fotor.com/blog/svg-vs-png/
https://kinsta.com/blog/svg-vs-png/
https://www.freepik.com/blog/know-the-difference-between-png-and-svg/
https://cloudinary.com/guides/image-formats/svg-vs-png-4-key-differences-and-how-to-choose

Perplexity:

Based on the information provided in the search results, here is a detailed comparison of SVG and PNG, along with scenarios where it's better to use each format.

SVG vs. PNG

Key Differences:

1. Image Quality and Scaling

   SVG is a vector-based format, allowing images to be scaled up or down without losing quality. PNG is a raster-based format, where images are made up of pixels, leading to quality degradation when scaled.

2. File Size

   SVG files are generally smaller in size compared to PNG files, especially for simple graphics and icons. PNG files can have larger file sizes, particularly for complex images with many colors and details.

3. Browser Support

   Both SVG and PNG are widely supported across modern Web browsers. However, some older browsers or platforms like email clients may not support one or both formats.

4. Manipulation and Animation

   SVG files can be easily manipulated using CSS and JavaScript, allowing for dynamic and interactive elements. PNG files are essentially static images and require image editing software for any modifications.

Scenarios for using SVG

Use SVG when

- you need vector-based graphics that need to be scalable and resolution-independent, such as icons, logos, or illustrations
- you want to create simple graphics, icons, or decorative elements that require animation or interactivity
- you need to optimize for performance and file size, especially for Web-based applications
- you want to create responsive and adaptive designs that can seamlessly scale across different screen sizes

Scenarios for using PNG

Use PNG when
- you have complex images, photographs, or graphics with a large number of colors and fine details
- you need to display images in older browsers or platforms that may not fully support SVG features
- you are working on projects where file size is not a critical concern, and image quality is the priority
- you do not require advanced manipulation or animation features, and the image can be treated as a static element

In summary, SVG is the better choice for vector-based graphics, simple animations, and responsive Web design, while PNG is more suitable for complex images, photographs, and scenarios where file size is not a primary concern.

SVG FILTERS

As you know from the previous chapter, filter effects can significantly enhance the visual experience of the contents of an HTML Web page. In Chapter 3, you learned about learned about CSS3 filters. In the following sections, you will learn about some of the SVG filters shown in this list:

- `<feBlend>` - filter for combining images
- `<feColorMatrix>` - filter for color transforms
- `<feComponentTransfer>`
- `<feComposite>`
- `<feConvolveMatrix>`
- `<feDiffuseLighting>`
- `<feDisplacementMap>`
- `<feFlood>`
- `<feGaussianBlur>`
- `<feTurbulence>`

SVG BLUR FILTER

The following prompt was supplied to Perplexity: "Please generate an HTML Web page that contains a rectangle that is rendered with an SVG blur filter, along with an explanation of the code."

Perplexity:

Here's an HTML Web page that contains a rectangle rendered with an SVG blur filter, along with an explanation of the code.

Listing 7.13 displays the contents of perplex_svg_blur_filter.html that contain Perplexity-generated SVG rectangle with a blur filter effect.

LISTING 7.13: perplex_svg_blur1.html

```
<!DOCTYPE html>
<html>
<head>
  <title>SVG Blur Filter</title>
  <style>
    body {
      margin: 0;
      padding: 0;
      display: flex;
      justify-content: center;
      align-items: center;
      height: 100vh;
      background-color: #f0f0f0;
    }

    .svg-container {
      width: 500px;
      height: 300px;
      position: relative;
      overflow: hidden;
    }
  </style>
</head>
<body>
  <div class="svg-container">
    <svg viewBox="0 0 500 300">
      <defs>
        <filter id="blur-filter">
          <feGaussianBlur in="SourceGraphic"
                                  stdDeviation="10" />
        </filter>
      </defs>
      <rect x="100" y="50" width="300" height="200"
            fill="#007bff" filter="url(#blur-filter)" />
    </svg>
  </div>

  <script>
    // No additional JavaScript code is needed for this
    // example
```

```
    </script>
</body>
</html>
```

Explanation of the Code

The HTML file starts with the standard `<!DOCTYPE html>` declaration, followed by the `<html>` tag. In the `<head>` section, we have a `<title>` tag that sets the page title to "SVG Blur Filter." Inside the `<style>` section, we define the following CSS:

`body`: Sets the margin and padding to 0, centers the content both horizontally and vertically using `display: flex;`, `justify-content: center;`, and `align-items: center;`, and sets the background color to a light gray (#f0f0f0).

`.svg-container`: This class is applied to the container that holds the SVG element. It sets the width to 500 pixels, the height to 300 pixels, the `position` to `relative`, and the `overflow` to `hidden`.

In the `<body>` section, we have a `<div>` element with the `class="svg-container"` attribute, which holds the SVG element. Inside the container, we have an `<svg>` element with a `viewBox` of "0 0 500 300," which sets the SVG viewport to 500 x 300 pixels.

Inside the SVG element, we have the following:

`<defs>`: This section is used to define reusable elements, in this case, a blur filter.

The `<filter>` element defines the blur filter with the `id` "blur-filter."

The `<feGaussianBlur>` element applies a Gaussian blur to the input, which is the `SourceGraphic` (the rectangle). The `stdDeviation` attribute sets the standard deviation of the Gaussian function, which determines the amount of blur.

`<rect>`: This element creates a blue (#007bff) rectangle with a width of 300 pixels, a height of 200 pixels, and positioned at (100, 50) within the SVG viewport.

The `filter="url(#blur-filter)"` attribute applies the blur filter defined earlier to the rectangle.

There is no additional JavaScript code in this example.

When you open this HTML file in a Web browser, you should see a blue rectangle with a blurred effect, centered within the SVG container. The key aspects of this implementation are:

- the use of the `<defs>` section to define the blur filter, which is then applied to the rectangle using the filter attribute
- the `<feGaussianBlur>` element, which applies the Gaussian blur to the input (the rectangle) with a standard deviation of 10 pixels, creating the blurred effect
- the use of the SVG container to center the blurred rectangle within the page

This example demonstrates how SVG can be used to apply various filters and effects to graphical elements, which can be useful for creating visually interesting and dynamic designs within Web pages.

Now launch the Web page `Perplex_svg_blur1.html` by navigating to the directory that contains this HTML Web page and then typing the following command:

```
open perplex_svg_blur1.html
```

After a few moments, you will see an SVG rectangle rendered with an SVG blur filter.

FIGURE 7.12: An SVG rectangle with a blur filter

SVG TURBULENCE FILTER

The following prompt was supplied to Perplexity: "Please generate an HTML Web page that contains a rectangle that is rendered with an SVG turbulence filter, along with an explanation of the code."

Perplexity:

Here's an HTML Web page that contains a rectangle rendered with an SVG turbulence filter, along with an explanation of the code.

Listing 7.14 displays the contents of `perplex_svg_turbulence1.html` that contain Perplexity-generated SVG rectangle with a blur filter effect.

LISTING 7.14: perplex_svg_turbulence1.html

```
<!DOCTYPE html> <!DOCTYPE html>
<html>
<head>
  <title>SVG Turbulence Filter</title>
  <style>
    body {
      margin: 0;
      padding: 0;
```

```
        display: flex;
        justify-content: center;
        align-items: center;
        height: 100vh;
        background-color: #f0f0f0;
    }

    .svg-container {
        width: 500px;
        height: 300px;
        position: relative;
        overflow: hidden;
    }
    </style>
</head>
<body>
    <div class="svg-container">
        <svg viewBox="0 0 500 300">
            <defs>
                <filter id="turbulence-filter">
                    <feTurbulence type="fractalNoise"
                        baseFrequency="0.05" numOctaves="2" seed="1" />
                    <feDisplacementMap in="SourceGraphic"
                                       in2="turbulence" scale="50" />
                </filter>
            </defs>
            <rect x="100" y="50" width="300" height="200"
                fill="#007bff" filter="url(#turbulence-filter)" />
        </svg>
    </div>

    <script>
        // No additional JavaScript code is needed for this
        // example
    </script>
</body>
</html>
```

Explanation of the Code

The HTML file starts with the standard `<!DOCTYPE html>` declaration, followed by the `<html>` tag. In the `<head>` section, we have a `<title>` tag that sets the page title to "SVG Turbulence Filter." Inside the `<style>` section, we define the following CSS:

`body`: Sets the margin and padding to 0, centers the content both horizontally and vertically using `display: flex;`, `justify-content: center;`, and `align-items: center;`, and sets the background color to a light gray (#f0f0f0).

`.svg-container`: This class is applied to the container that holds the SVG element. It sets the width to 500 pixels, the height to 300 pixels, the `position` to `relative`, and the `overflow` to `hidden`.

In the `<body>` section, we have a `<div>` element with the `class="svg-container"` attribute, which holds the SVG element. Inside the container, we have an `<svg>` element with a `viewBox` of "0 0 500 300," which sets the SVG viewport to 500 x 300 pixels. Inside the SVG element, we have the following:

`<defs>`: This section is used to define reusable elements, in this case, a turbulence filter.

The `<filter>` element defines the turbulence filter with the ID "turbulence-filter."

The `<feTurbulence>` element generates a turbulence pattern based on Perlin noise. The type attribute is set to `fractalNoise`, which creates a fractal-like pattern. The `baseFrequency` attribute sets the base frequency of the turbulence, `numOctaves` sets the number of octaves (levels of detail), and `seed` sets the random seed for the turbulence.

The `<feDisplacementMap>` element uses the turbulence pattern generated by `<feTurbulence>` to displace the input graphic (the rectangle). The `in` attribute specifies the input graphic, the `in2` attribute specifies the turbulence pattern, and the `scale` attribute sets the amount of displacement.

`<rect>`: This element creates a blue (#007bff) rectangle with a width of 300 pixels, a height of 200 pixels, and positioned at (100, 50) within the SVG viewport.

The `filter="url(#turbulence-filter)"` attribute applies the turbulence filter defined earlier to the rectangle.

There is no additional JavaScript code in this example.

When you open this HTML file in a Web browser, you should see a blue rectangle with a turbulent, distorted appearance, centered within the SVG container. The key aspects of this implementation are:

- the use of the `<defs>` section to define the turbulence filter, which is then applied to the rectangle using the filter attribute
- the `<feTurbulence>` element, which generates a fractal-like turbulence pattern based on Perlin noise
- the `<feDisplacementMap>` element, which uses the turbulence pattern to displace the input graphic (the rectangle), creating the distorted appearance
- the use of the SVG container to center the turbulent rectangle within the page

This example demonstrates how SVG can be used to apply various filters and effects to graphical elements, which can be useful for creating visually interesting and dynamic designs within Web pages. The turbulence filter can be used to create a wide range of distortion and displacement effects, which can be useful for creating abstract or surreal visual effects.

Now launch the Web page `perplex_svg_css3.html` by navigating to the directory that contains this HTML Web page and then typing the following command:

```
open perplex_svg_turbulence1.html
```

After a few moments, you will see an SVG rectangle rendered with an SVG turbulence filter, as shown in Figure 7.13.

FIGURE 7.13: An SVG rectangle with a turbulence filter

SVG AND CSS3 IN HTML WEB PAGES

The following prompt was supplied to Perplexity: "Please generate an HTML Web page that contains SVG-based 2D shapes and CSS3 effects, along with an explanation of the code."

Perplexity:

Here's an HTML Web page that contains SVG-based 2D shapes and CSS3 effects, along with an explanation of the code.

Listing 7.15 displays the contents of `perplex_svg_css3.html` that contains Perplexity-generated SVG code with CSS3 effects.

LISTING 7.15: perplex_svg_css3.html

```
<!DOCTYPE html>
<html>
<head>
  <title>SVG Shapes with CSS3 Effects</title>
  <style>
    body {
      margin: 0;
      padding: 0;
      display: flex;
      justify-content: center;
      align-items: center;
      height: 100vh;
      background-color: #f0f0f0;
    }
```

```css
.svg-container {
  width: 600px;
  height: 400px;
  position: relative;
  perspective: 1000px;
}

.shape {
  position: absolute;
  width: 150px;
  height: 150px;
  transition: transform 0.5s ease-in-out;
}

.shape:hover {
  transform: scale(1.2) rotate(45deg);
}

.circle {
  top: 50px;
  left: 50px;
  border-radius: 50%;
  background-color: #007bff;
  box-shadow: 0 0 20px rgba(0, 0, 0, 0.5);
}

.rectangle {
  top: 200px;
  left: 200px;
  background-color: #ff6b6b;
  transform-style: preserve-3d;
}

.rectangle:before {
  content: "";
  position: absolute;
  top: 0;
  left: 0;
  width: 100%;
  height: 100%;
  background-color: #ffa500;
  transform: translateZ(-20px);
}

.triangle {
  top: 50px;
  left: 400px;
  width: 0;
  height: 0;
  border-top: 75px solid transparent;
  border-right: 130px solid #00ff00;
  border-bottom: 75px solid transparent;
  filter: drop-shadow(0 0 10px rgba(0, 0, 0, 0.5));
}
    </style>
  </head>
```

```
<body>
  <div class="svg-container">
    <div class="shape circle"></div>
    <div class="shape rectangle"></div>
    <div class="shape triangle"></div>
  </div>
</body>
</html>
```

Explanation of the Code

The HTML file starts with the standard `<!DOCTYPE html>` declaration, followed by the `<html>` tag. In the `<head>` section, we have a `<title>` tag that sets the page title to "SVG Shapes with CSS3 Effects." Inside the `<style>` section, we define the following CSS:

`body`: Sets the margin and padding to 0, centers the content both horizontally and vertically using `display: flex;`, `justify-content: center;`, and `align-items: center;`, and sets the background color to a light gray (#f0f0f0).

`.svg-container`: This class is applied to the container that holds the SVG-based shapes. It sets the width to 600 pixels, the height to 400 pixels, the position to `relative`, and adds a 3D perspective using perspective: 1000px;.

`.shape`: This class is applied to each of the SVG-based shapes. It sets the position to absolute, the width and height to 150 pixels, and adds a transition effect for the `transform` property with a duration of 0.5 seconds and an ease-in-out timing function.

`.shape:hover`: This rule applies a scale and rotation transformation to the shapes when they are hovered over.

`.circle`: This class is applied to the circle shape. It sets the top and left positions to 50 pixels, the border radius to 50% to create a circle, the background color to blue (#007bff), and adds a drop shadow using the `box-shadow` property.

`.rectangle`: This class is applied to the rectangle shape. It sets the top and left positions to 200 pixels, the background color to red (#ff6b6b) and sets the `transform-style` to `preserve-3d` to enable 3D transformations.

`.rectangle:before`: This pseudo-element creates a second rectangle behind the main one, with a background color of orange (#ffa500) and a `transform` that translates it along the Z-axis by -20 pixels, creating a 3D effect.

`.triangle`: This class is applied to the triangle shape. It sets the top and left positions to 50 and 400 pixels, respectively, and uses CSS border properties to create a triangle with a green (#00ff00) fill. It also adds a drop shadow using the `filter` property.

In the `<body>` section, we have a `<div>` element with the `class="svg-container"` attribute, which holds the SVG-based shapes.

Inside the container, we have three `<div>` elements with the `class="shape"` attribute, representing the circle, rectangle, and triangle shapes.

When you open this HTML file in a Web browser, you should see a circle, a rectangle, and a triangle, all positioned within the SVG container. The shapes have various CSS3 effects applied to them, such as hover-based transformations, 3D effects, and drop shadows. The key aspects of this implementation are:

- the use of CSS to create and position the SVG-based shapes, rather than using the `<svg>` element directly
- the application of CSS3 effects, such as transformations, 3D properties, and filters, to enhance the visual appearance of the shapes
- the use of the `.svg-container` class to provide a 3D perspective and a consistent layout for the shapes
- the hover-based transformation effect, which adds a dynamic and interactive element to the shapes

This example demonstrates how SVG-based shapes can be combined with CSS3 effects to create visually interesting and interactive graphics within a Web page, without the need for complex SVG code or external image files.

Now launch the Web page `perplex_svg_css3.html` by navigating to the directory that contains this HTML Web page and then typing the following command:

```
open perplex_svg_css3.html
```

After a few moments, you will see an SVG green circle, an SVG yellow square, and an SVG red triangle.

FIGURE 7.14: Three SVG shapes

Hover over each of these three shapes and you will see the green circle turn blue; the border of the yellow rectangle changes from blue to red; and the red triangle becomes partially transparent.

SVG AND JAVASCRIPT IN HTML WEB PAGES

There are several ways to render SVG in an HTML Web page:

- "pure" SVG code
- SVG and CSS3 code
- SVG and JavaScript code

You have already seen examples of the first two techniques, and the remaining code samples in this chapter show you how to use the third technique. Specifically, you will see examples of combining SVG and JavaScript to perform the following tasks:

- render a set of SVG elliptic arcs with a radial gradient
- render an SVG checkerboard pattern
- render an SVG checkerboard pattern with an SVG filter
- render a master/detail HTML Web page
- quadratic Bezier curves
- cubic Bezier curves

Recall that you have already seen SVG Filters in a previous section in this chapter.

ELLIPTIC ARCS WITH A RADIAL GRADIENT

The following prompt was supplied to Perplexity: "Please generate a random set of 50 elliptic arcs in a screen of width 600 and height 400 where each elliptic arc has a fill pattern of a radial gradient and a drop shadow, along with an explanation of the code."

Perplexity:

Here's an HTML Web page that contains a random set of 50 elliptic arcs, each with a fill pattern of a radial gradient and a drop shadow, within a screen of width 600 and height 400, along with an explanation of the code.

LISTING 7.16:   perplex_svg_elliptic_arcs.html

```
<!DOCTYPE html>
<html>
<head>
  <title>Random Elliptic Arcs with Radial Gradients</title>
  <style>
    body {
      margin: 0;
      padding: 0;
      display: flex;
      justify-content: center;
      align-items: center;
      height: 100vh;
      background-color: #f0f0f0;
    }

    .svg-container {
      width: 600px;
      height: 400px;
      position: relative;
      overflow: hidden;
    }
```

```css
.arc {
  position: absolute;
  width: 100px;
  height: 100px;
  opacity: 0.7;
  filter: drop-shadow(0 0 10px rgba(0, 0, 0, 0.5));
  animation: arc-animation 20s infinite linear;
}

.arc:before {
  content: "";
  position: absolute;
  top: 0;
  left: 0;
  width: 100%;
  height: 100%;
  background: radial-gradient(circle at random,
    #ff6b6b, #ffa500, #ffff00, #00ff00, #00ffff,
    #0000ff, #ff00ff);
  opacity: 0.5;
  z-index: -1;
}

@keyframes arc-animation {
  0% {
    transform: translate(0, 0) rotate(0deg);
  }
  100% {
    transform: translate(random(500), random(300))
                                rotate(360deg);
  }
}
    </style>
  </head>
  <body>
    <div class="svg-container">
      <script>
        const container = document.querySelector
                                ('.svg-container');

        // Generate 50 random elliptic arcs
        for (let i = 0; i < 50; i++) {
          const arc = document.createElement('div');
          arc.classList.add('arc');
          arc.style.left = '${random(600)}px';
          arc.style.top = '${random(400)}px';
          arc.style.width = '${random(50, 150)}px';
          arc.style.height = '${random(50, 150)}px';
          arc.style.borderRadius = '${random(50, 100)}%
                            ${random(50, 100)}%';
          container.appendChild(arc);
        }

        // Helper function to generate random numbers
        function random(min, max) {
          if (min === undefined && max === undefined) {
```

```
            return Math.floor(Math.random() * 600);
        } else if (max === undefined) {
            return Math.floor(Math.random() * min);
        } else {
            return Math.floor(Math.random() *
                                    (max - min + 1)) + min;
        }
    }
    </script>
  </div>
</body>
</html>
```

Explanation of the Code

The HTML file starts with the standard `<!DOCTYPE html>` declaration, followed by the `<html>` tag. In the `<head>` section, we have a `<title>` tag that sets the page title to "Random Elliptic Arcs with Radial Gradients." Inside the `<style>` section, we define the following CSS:

`body`: Sets the margin and padding to 0, centers the content both horizontally and vertically using `display: flex;`, `justify-content: center;`, and `align-items: center;`, and sets the background color to a light gray (#f0f0f0).

`.svg-container`: This class is applied to the container that holds the elliptic arcs. It sets the width to 600 pixels, the height to 400 pixels, the `position` to `relative`, and the `overflow` to `hidden`.

`.arc`: This class is applied to each of the elliptic arcs. It sets the `position` to `absolute`, the width and height to 100 pixels, the `opacity` to 0.7, and adds a drop shadow using the `filter` property. It also applies an animation called `arc-animation` that lasts 20 seconds and loops infinitely.

`.arc:before`: This pseudo-element creates a radial gradient background for each elliptic arc. The gradient colors are randomly selected from a predefined set, and the gradient's center point is also randomly positioned within the arc's area.

`@keyframes arc-animation`: This rule defines the `arc-animation` that is applied to the elliptic arcs. It starts with the arcs positioned at (0, 0) and rotated 0 degrees, and ends with the arcs positioned at random coordinates within the 600 x 400 pixel container and rotated 360 degrees.

In the `<body>` section, we have a `<div>` element with the `class="svg-container"` attribute, which holds the elliptic arcs. Inside the container, we have the following JavaScript code:

We select the `.svg-container` element using `document.querySelector()`.

We generate 50 random elliptic arcs and append them to the container:
We create a new `<div>` element and add the `arc` class to it.

We set the left, top, width, height, and border-radius styles of the arc using random values. We append the arc to the container.

The `random()` function is a helper function that generates random numbers within a specified range (or a default range of 0 to 600 if no range is provided).

When you open this HTML file in a Web browser, you should see a set of 50 randomly positioned and rotating elliptic arcs, each with a radial gradient fill and a drop shadow effect. The key aspects of this implementation are:

- the use of CSS to create and position the elliptic arcs, rather than using the `<svg>` element directly
- the application of a radial gradient fill and a drop shadow effect to each arc using CSS
- the use of the `.svg-container` class to provide a consistent layout and overflow handling for the arcs
- the animation of the arcs using the `@keyframes` rule, which moves and rotates them within the container
- the use of JavaScript to dynamically generate and append the elliptic arcs to the container

This example demonstrates how CSS can be used to create dynamic and visually interesting graphics, even without the use of SVG or other vector-based formats. The combination of CSS effects and JavaScript-driven animation creates a unique and engaging visual experience.

Now launch the Web page `perplex_svg_elliptic_arcs.html` by navigating to the directory that contains this HTML Web page and then typing the following command:

```
open perplex_svg_elliptic_arcs.html
```

After a few moments, you will see the image in Figure 7.15 that displays a set of elliptic arcs.

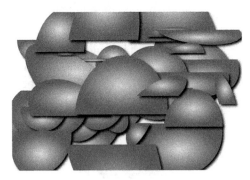

FIGURE 7.15: SVG elliptic arcs

AN SVG CHECKERBOARD PATTERN

The following prompt was supplied to Perplexity in order to generate SVG-based 2D transformation effects:

"Please generate an HTML Web page that contains an 8 x 8 checkerboard pattern of red and yellow rectangles whose width is 60 and whose height is 60 that are rendered with an SVG drop shadow, along with an explanation of the code."

Perplexity:

Here's an HTML Web page that contains an 8x8 checkerboard pattern of red and yellow rectangles, each with a width of 60 pixels and a height of 60 pixels, rendered with an SVG drop shadow.

Listing 7.17 displays the contents of perplex_svg_checkerboard1. html that contains Perplexity-generated SVG code that performs 2D transform-based animation effects on four 2D shapes.

LISTING 7.17: *perplex_svg_checkerboard1.html*

```
<!DOCTYPE html>
<!DOCTYPE html>
<html>
<head>
  <title>Checkerboard with SVG Drop Shadow</title>
  <style>
    body {
      margin: 0;
      padding: 0;
      display: flex;
      justify-content: center;
      align-items: center;
      height: 100vh;
      background-color: #f0f0f0;
    }

    .checkerboard {
      width: 480px;
      height: 480px;
      display: grid;
      grid-template-columns: repeat(8, 1fr);
      grid-template-rows: repeat(8, 1fr);
      position: relative;
    }

    .square {
      width: 60px;
      height: 60px;
      position: relative;
    }

    .square:before {
      content: "";
```

```
        position: absolute;
        top: 0;
        left: 0;
        width: 100%;
        height: 100%;
        filter: drop-shadow(0 0 10px rgba(0, 0, 0, 0.5));
      }

      .red {
        background-color: #ff6b6b;
      }

      .yellow {
        background-color: #ffff00;
      }
    </style>
  </head>
  <body>
    <div class="checkerboard">
      <script>
        const checkerboard = document.querySelector('.
                                           checkerboard');

        for (let i = 0; i < 8; i++) {
          for (let j = 0; j < 8; j++) {
            const square = document.createElement('div');
            square.classList.add('square');
            if ((i + j) % 2 === 0) {
              square.classList.add('red');
            } else {
              square.classList.add('yellow');
            }
            checkerboard.appendChild(square);
          }
        }
      </script>
    </div>
  </body>
</html>
```

Explanation of the Code

The HTML file starts with the standard `<!DOCTYPE html>` declaration, followed by the `<html>` tag. In the `<head>` section, we have a `<title>` tag that sets the page title to "Checkerboard with SVG Drop Shadow." Inside the `<style>` section, we define the following CSS:

`body`: Sets the margin and padding to 0, centers the content both horizontally and vertically using `display: flex;`, `justify-content: center;`, and `align-items: center;`, and sets the background color to a light gray (#f0f0f0).

`.checkerboard`: This class is applied to the container that holds the checkerboard pattern. It sets the width and height to 480 pixels, creates an 8 x 8 grid using CSS `Grid`, and sets the `position` to `relative`.

`.square`: This class is applied to each square in the checkerboard pattern. It sets the width and height to 60 pixels, and the `position` to `relative`.

`.square:before`: This pseudo-element creates an SVG drop shadow effect for each square. It sets the `position` to `absolute`, covers the entire area of the square, and applies a drop shadow using the filter `property`.

`.red`: This class is applied to the red squares in the checkerboard pattern. It sets the background color to red (#ff6b6b).

`.yellow`: This class is applied to the yellow squares in the checkerboard pattern. It sets the background color to yellow (#ffff00).

In the `<body>` section, we have a `<div>` element with the `class="checkerboard"` attribute, which holds the checkerboard pattern. Inside the container, we have the following JavaScript code:

We select the `.checkerboard` element using `document.querySelector()`. We create an 8 x 8 grid of squares and append them to the `.checkerboard` container. We create a new `<div>` element and add the `square` class to it. We check if the sum of the row and column indices is even or odd, and add the `red` or `yellow` class accordingly. We append the `square` to the `.checkerboard` container.

When you open this HTML file in a Web browser, you should see an 8 x 8 checkerboard pattern of red and yellow rectangles, each with an SVG drop shadow effect. The key aspects of this implementation are:

- the use of CSS `Grid` to create the 8 x 8 checkerboard pattern
- the application of the SVG drop shadow effect to each square using the `::before` pseudo-element and the `filter` property
- the use of JavaScript to dynamically generate and append the squares to the `.checkerboard` container
- the alternating red and yellow colors of the squares, determined by the row and column indices

This example demonstrates how CSS and JavaScript can be used together to create complex and visually interesting graphics, such as a checkerboard pattern with an SVG-based drop shadow effect.

Now launch the Web page `Perplex_svg_checkerboard1.html` by navigating to the directory that contains this HTML Web page and then typing the following command:

```
open perplex_svg_checkerboard1.html
```

After a few moments, you will see the image in Figure 7.16 that displays an SVG-based checkerboard.

FIGURE 7.16: An SVG-based checkerboard

AN SVG CHECKERBOARD PATTERN WITH FILTER EFFECTS

The following prompt was supplied to Perplexity in order to generate SVG-based 2D transformation effects:

"Please generate an HTML Web page that contains an 8 x 8 checkerboard pattern of red and yellow rectangles whose width is 60 and whose height is 60 that are rendered with an SVG blur filter and an SVG drop shadow, along with an explanation of the code."

Perplexity:

Here's an HTML Web page that contains an 8 x 8 checkerboard pattern of red and yellow rectangles, each with a width of 60 pixels and a height of 60 pixels, rendered with an SVG blur filter and an SVG drop shadow.

Listing 7.18 displays the contents of `perplex_svg_checkerboard_filter.html` that contains Perplexity-generated SVG code that displays an SVG-based checkerboard with an SVG filter.

LISTING 7.18: perplex_svg_checkerboard_filter.html

```
<!DOCTYPE html>
<html>
<head>
  <title>Checkerboard with SVG Blur and Drop Shadow</title>
  <style>
    body {
      margin: 0;
      padding: 0;
      display: flex;
```

```
      justify-content: center;
      align-items: center;
      height: 100vh;
      background-color: #f0f0f0;
    }

    .checkerboard {
      width: 480px;
      height: 480px;
      display: grid;
      grid-template-columns: repeat(8, 1fr);
      grid-template-rows: repeat(8, 1fr);
    }

    .square {
      width: 60px;
      height: 60px;
      position: relative;
    }

    .square:before {
      content: "";
      position: absolute;
      top: 0;
      left: 0;
      width: 100%;
      height: 100%;
      filter: url(#blur-and-shadow);
    }

    .red {
      background-color: #ff6b6b;
    }

    .yellow {
      background-color: #ffff00;
    }
  </style>
</head>
<body>
  <div class="checkerboard">
    <svg width="0" height="0">
      <defs>
        <filter id="blur-and-shadow">
          <feGaussianBlur in="SourceGraphic"
                                    stdDeviation="2" />
          <feDropShadow dx="0" dy="0" stdDeviation="5"
                    flood-color="rgba(0, 0, 0, 0.5)" />
        </filter>
      </defs>
    </svg>

    <script>
    const checkerboard = document.querySelector
                                    ('.checkerboard');
```

```
      for (let i = 0; i < 8; i++) {
        for (let j = 0; j < 8; j++) {
          const square = document.createElement('div');
          square.classList.add('square');
          if ((i + j) % 2 === 0) {
            square.classList.add('red');
          } else {
            square.classList.add('yellow');
          }
          checkerboard.appendChild(square);
        }
      }
    </script>
  </div>
</body>
</html>
```

Explanation of the Code

The HTML Web page starts with the standard `<!DOCTYPE html>` declaration, followed by the `<html>` tag. In the `<head>` section, we have a `<title>` tag that sets the page title to "Checkerboard with SVG Blur and Drop Shadow." Inside the `<style>` section, we define the following CSS:

`body`: Sets the margin and padding to 0, centers the content both horizontally and vertically using `display: flex;`, `justify-content: center;`, and `align-items: center;`, and sets the background color to a light gray (#f0f0f0).

`.checkerboard`: This class is applied to the container that holds the checkerboard pattern. It sets the width and height to 480 pixels, creates an 8 x 8 grid using `CSS Grid`, and sets the `position` to `relative`.

`.square`: This class is applied to each square in the checkerboard pattern. It sets the width and height to 60 pixels, and the `position` to `relative`.

`.square:before`: This pseudo-element creates an SVG blur and drop shadow effect for each square. It sets the `position` to `absolute`, covers the entire area of the square, and applies the blur-and-shadow filter using the `filter` property.

`.red`: This class is applied to the red squares in the checkerboard pattern. It sets the background color to red (#ff6b6b).

`.yellow`: This class is applied to the yellow squares in the checkerboard pattern. It sets the background color to yellow (#ffff00).

In the `<body>` section, we have a `<div>` element with the `class="checkerboard"` attribute, which holds the checkerboard pattern.

Inside the `.checkerboard` container, we have the following:

An `<svg>` element with a width and height of 0 pixels, which is used to define the SVG filters. Inside the `<defs>` section, we define a filter with the id `blur-and-shadow`. This filter applies a Gaussian blur with a standard deviation of 2 pixels, and a drop shadow with a standard deviation of 5 pixels and a black color with 50% opacity.

The JavaScript code is the same as the previous example, where we create an 8 x 8 grid of squares and append them to the .checkerboard container, alternating between the red and yellow classes.

When you open this HTML file in a Web browser, you should see an 8x8 checkerboard pattern of red and yellow rectangles, each with an SVG blur and drop shadow effect. The key aspects of this implementation are:

- the use of CSS Grid to create the 8 x 8 checkerboard pattern
- the application of the SVG blur and drop shadow effect to each square using the ::before pseudo-element and the filter property, which references the blur-and-shadow filter defined in the <svg> element
- the use of JavaScript to dynamically generate and append the squares to the .checkerboard container
- the alternating red and yellow colors of the squares, determined by the row and column indices

This example demonstrates how SVG filters can be used to apply complex visual effects to HTML elements, such as a combined blur and drop shadow effect, to create visually interesting and dynamic graphics within a Web page.

Now launch the Web page perplex_svg_checkerboard_filter.html by navigating to the directory that contains this HTML Web page and then typing the following command:

```
open perplex_svg_checkerboard_filter.html
```

After a few moments, you will see the image in Figure 7.17 that displays an SVG-based checkerboard pattern with an SVG filter.

FIGURE 7.17: An SVG-based checkerboard with an SVG filter

A MASTER-DETAIL HTML WEB PAGE

The following prompt was supplied to Perplexity in order to create an HTML Web page that provides master-detail functionality for a list of people (based on simulated data):

"Please generate an HTML Web page that displays a drop-down list of people based on simulated data, and when users click on one of the people in the drop-down list, the Web page displays the details of that user, which also involves simulated data."

Perplexity:

Here's an HTML Web page that displays a drop-down list of people based on simulated data, and when a user clicks on one of the people in the drop-down list, the Web page displays the details of that user, which also involves simulated data.

LISTING 7.19:   master_detail.html

```
<!DOCTYPE html>
<html>
<head>
  <title>User Details</title>
  <style>
    body {
      font-family: Arial, sans-serif;
      margin: 0;
      padding: 20px;
      background-color: #f0f0f0;
    }

    .container {
      max-width: 600px;
      margin: 0 auto;
      background-color: white;
      padding: 20px;
      box-shadow: 0 0 10px rgba(0, 0, 0, 0.1);
    }

    .dropdown {
      margin-bottom: 20px;
    }

    .user-details {
      display: none;
    }

    .user-details h2 {
      margin-top: 0;
    }

    .user-details p {
```

```
      margin: 5px 0;
    }
  </style>
</head>
<body>
  <div class="container">
    <div class="dropdown">
      <label for="user-select">Select a user:</label>
      <select id="user-select">
        <option value="">Select a user</option>
      </select>
    </div>

    <div class="user-details">
      <h2 id="user-name"></h2>
      <p>Email: <span id="user-email"></span></p>
      <p>Phone: <span id="user-phone"></span></p>
      <p>Address: <span id="user-address"></span></p>
    </div>
  </div>

  <script>
    // Simulated user data
    const users = [
      { name: 'John Doe', email: 'john.doe@example.com',
          phone: '555-1234', address: '123 Main St,
          Anytown USA' },
      { name: 'Jane Smith', email:
          'jane.smith@example.com', phone:
          '555-5678', address: '456 Oak Rd,
          Somewhere City' },
      { name: 'Bob Johnson',
          email: 'bob.johnson@example.com', phone: '555-
9012', address: '789 Elm St, Othertown' },
      { name: 'Alice Williams', email:
          'alice.williams@example.com',
          phone: '555-3456', address: '321
          Pine Ln, Somewhere Else' },
      { name: 'Tom Davis', email: 'tom.davis@example.com',
        phone: '555-7890', address: '654 Oak St,
        Anyplace' }
    ];

    // Get the user select element and the
    // user details elements
    const userSelect = document.getElementById
                                  ('user-select');
    const userDetails = document.querySelector
                                  ('.user-details');
    const userNameElement = document.getElementById
                                  ('user-name');
    const userEmailElement = document.getElementById
                                  ('user-email');
    const userPhoneElement = document.getElementById
                                  ('user-phone');
    const userAddressElement =
                document.getElementById('user-address');
```

```
    // Populate the user select options
    users.forEach(user => {
      const option = document.createElement('option');
      option.value = user.name;
      option.textContent = user.name;
      userSelect.appendChild(option);
    });

    // Add an event listener to the user select
    userSelect.addEventListener('change', () => {
      const selectedUser = users.find(user =>
                        user.name === userSelect.value);
      if (selectedUser) {
        userNameElement.textContent = selectedUser.name;
        userEmailElement.textContent = selectedUser.email;
        userPhoneElement.textContent = selectedUser.phone;
        userAddressElement.textContent =
                              selectedUser.address;
        userDetails.style.display = 'block';
      } else {
        userDetails.style.display = 'none';
      }
    });
  </script>
</body>
</html>
```

Explanation of the Code

The HTML file starts with the standard `<!DOCTYPE html>` declaration, followed by the `<html>` tag. In the `<head>` section, we have a `<title>` tag that sets the page title to "User Details." Inside the `<style>` section, we define the following CSS:

`body`: Sets the font family to Arial, sans-serif, removes the margin and padding, and sets the background color to a light gray (#f0f0f0).

`.container`: This class is applied to the main container of the page. It sets the maximum width to 600 pixels, centers the container, sets the background color to white, adds padding, and applies a subtle box shadow.

`.dropdown`: This class is applied to the dropdown container. It adds a bottom margin of 20 pixels.

`.user-details`: This class is applied to the user details section. It initially hides the user details by setting the display property to none.

`.user-details h2`: This rule sets the top margin of the username heading to 0.

`.user-details p`: This rule adds a vertical margin of 5 pixels to the user details paragraphs.

In the `<body>` section, we have a `<div>` element with the `class="container"` attribute, which holds the dropdown and user details sections.

Inside the container, we have the following HTML elements:

A <div> element with the class="dropdown" attribute, which contains a <label> and a <select> element for the user dropdown.

A <div> element with the class="user-details" attribute, which contains the user details elements (name, email, phone, and address).

In the <script> section, we have the following JavaScript code:

We define an array of simulated user data, each with a name, email, phone, and address property. We get references to the user select element and the user details elements using document.getElementById() and document.querySelector(). We populate the user select options by iterating over the users array and creating <option> elements for each user. We add an event listener to the user select element, which listens for the change event. When the user selects a different option, we find the corresponding user object in the users array and update the user details elements with the selected user's information. We also show the user details section by setting the display property to block.

When you open this HTML file in a Web browser, you should see a drop-down list with the names of the simulated users. When you select a user from the dropdown, the user details section will display the corresponding information (name, email, phone, and address). The key aspects of this implementation are:

- the use of simulated user data to populate the dropdown and user details sections
- the dynamic population of the dropdown options using JavaScript
- the event listener on the user select element, which updates the user details section based on the selected user
- the use of CSS to style the page layout and the user details section

This example demonstrates how to create a simple user interface that allows users to select from a list of people and view their details, using a combination of HTML, CSS, and JavaScript.

Now launch the Web page master_detail.html by navigating to the directory that contains this HTML Web page and then typing the following command:

```
open master_detail.html
```

After a few moments, you will see the image in Figure 7.18 that displays the output that you will see when you select one of the people in the drop-down list.

Select a User

Charlie

Charlie
Age: 35
Occupation: Teacher

FIGURE 7.18: A master-detail Web page

SUMMARY

This chapter started with a description of the strengths and weaknesses of SVG, followed by SVG use cases, SVG accessibility, and potential security issues with SVG. Then you saw examples of Perplexity generating linear gradients, radial gradients, and various SVG 2D shapes and gradients.

Next, you learned how to render quadratic Bezier curves and cubic Bezier curves, as well as how to add animation effects for Bezier curves. In addition, you saw a comparison of SVG and CSS3 as well as a comparison of SVG and PNGs.

Then you learned how to work with SVG filters, such as blur filters and turbulence filters. You also saw code samples that combine SVG and CSS3 in an HTML Web page, as well we combine SVG and JavaScript in an HTML Web page.

Finally, you saw how to create other effects that involve JavaScript and SVG, such as rendering elliptic arts, checkerboard patterns, and a master-detail HTML Web page that involves SVG.

INDEX

www.ingramcontent.com/pod-product-compliance
Lightning Source LLC
La Vergne TN
LVHW022304060326
832902LV00020B/3276